Produce Yourself

APPLY HOLLYWOOD'S PROVEN FORMULA
TO BECOME THE HERO OF YOUR LIFE

Terence Michael

100 PERCENT TERRY CLOTH

Los Angeles, CA

Copyright © 2017 by Terence Michael

All rights reserved. No part of this publication may be reproduced, distributed or transmitted in any form or by any means, including photocopying, recording, or other electronic or mechanical methods, without the prior written permission of the publisher, except in the case of brief quotations embodied in critical reviews and certain other noncommercial uses permitted by copyright law. For permission requests, write to the publisher, addressed "Attention: Permissions Coordinator," at the address below.

Disclaimer: This book contains actual events of the author's own hero's journey. It reflects his recollections of experiences over decades as truthful as his memory allows. Occasionally, dialogue has been supplemented, and events have been compressed. All persons within are actual individuals; there are no composite characters. But the names of some private people have been changed (or shrunk to an initial or two) to respect their privacy. The author and publisher assume no responsibility for any errors or omissions. No liability is assumed for damages that may result from the use of information contained within.

Terence Michael/100 Percent Terry Cloth, Inc.

c/o UTA 9336 Civic Center Drive. Beverly Hills, CA/USA 90210

Ordering Information: bookorder@terencemichael.com

Quantity sales. Special discounts are available on quantity purchases by corporations, associations, and others. For details, contact:
100 Percent Terry Cloth at the website terencemichael.com

Produce Yourself:
Apply Hollywood's Proven Formula To Become The Hero of Your Life
Terence Michael. —1st ed. 11.21.2017.

Library of Congress Control Number: 2017914453

ISBN 978-1-64136-555-0

For Siena and Alaia,

This book is not about you, but I want it to be for you. These are some of the tools I've acquired along my journey. I'm now sharing them with you, for your journey.

THANK YOU

To my dad, Sam, you have always been my hero, and perhaps the best writer I know. I've never considered myself a writer. That's why I make movies and TV. But your inspiration, support, and positive reaction were the only fuel I needed to take this journey seriously.

To Cristy, for your love and support. A writer couldn't ask for a better soulmate to allow him to think deeply while concentrating at a stand-up desk in the middle of our kitchen. Your professional knowledge and expertise about human behavior were a huge inspiration for the execution of this book.

To Jason, for helping me realize that my original book about lifehacks was just an average idea, and that, rather, I should write this book from the perspective of a film and TV producer.

To Ian, you inspired me when you told me: "Write this book. I need it!" Thank you for your enthusiasm and friendship.

To Dawn, Dave, David, Tyler, Avi, Barrett, and everyone else above, for your candid critique on the cover design of the book. You are the TV network I thought I could avoid during this process. Thanks for driving me crazy.

To Pam, Ryan, Darin, and Marina. During the posting of our TV series, I told you I was writing a book. In truth, I hadn't started yet. But your reaction prompted me to high-tail it down the hall to my office and begin writing. That was the moment I decided to accept the Call To Adventure.

And an adventure it has been.

Contents

The Manual For Your Life 1
Paths, Possessions, Luck, and Comparisons 19
Art Imitates Life: The Stages of The Hero 35
Your Ordinary World... 41
The Call To Adventure: Choices, Consequences, and Values................ 59
The Refusal: Detours, What Ifs, Present Value, and Prevention 83
Meeting The Mentor: Increasing Your Average 101
Meeting The Mentor: Power of No, Purpose 115
Commercial Break: Timing, Cycles, Deep Work, Turning Off.............. 133
Crossing The Threshold: Value, Connection, Identity 145
Tests: Risk and Struggle.. 167
Tests: Quitting, Sacrifice, Announcement, Options............................... 179
Allies: Friends, Tools, and Support.. 197
Enemies: Process, Function, Input 209
Approach To The Inmost Cave: Identity, Muses 233
Approach To The Inmost Cave: Fake-It 245
The Ordeal: Networking, Permission 257
The Ordeal: Momentum, Informality, Collaboration........................... 267
The Ordeal: Evaluation 281
The Ordeal: Patterns, Ego, Ideas, The Subconscious 287
The Reward: Input vs. Output.. 301
The Road Back: Purpose, Proximity Potential 311
The Road Back: The Now 329
The Resurrection: Authenticity, Happiness 343
Return With The Elixir: Willpower, Creation Play, Ask, Time 359

*"A hero ventures forth
from the world of common day
into a region of supernatural wonder.*

*Fabulous forces are there encountered
and a decisive victory is won."*

- Joseph Campbell

CHAPTER 1

The Manual For Your Life

"You're supposed to be the leading lady in your own life, for God's sake!"

- Kate Winslet in *Holiday*

FOR THE LAST 20 YEARS, I have been developing and producing stories in Hollywood. I've now produced over 20 feature films and over 20 television shows and specials.

That's a bunch of 20s. They say hindsight is 20/20, so keep that in mind. The bulk of this book's insight, let's say 80 percent, is due to that. The other 20 percent is due to my desire to improve and optimize effectiveness in habits, systems, and processes; and how one's approach to these impacts one's inner hero's path.

It's this facet of my own life's journey that I want to share. Not in order for you to learn how to produce movies or write TV shows, but rather to show how a character becomes a hero in cinema. By following universal, proven stages, you can make your own life as amazing, full, and satisfying as that of any hero you've admired.

You can produce yourself.

The steps a hero takes in story evolution when broken down to core themes are all the same. They're what we take in real life. No difference. Your life is a TV show. Your life is a movie. And you are the hero. If you think you've been miscast, or given the wrong script, these heroic stages will help you correct that. You're the producer of your own life. You are the boss.

This methodical flow of the heroic transformation is applicable and down-scalable from the large to the small. It covers your entire life's path from childhood to adulthood; momentous milestones like career changes, new relationships, babies; and includes components as diverse as diet, finances, and workflow.

Over the years friends and family have repeatedly barraged me for advice. After dispensing advice, I'm frequently told, "You should write a book." This might be that book. I'm not a guru living atop a mountaintop. I'm not an omniscient philosopher standing atop the Parthenon. I'm no Buddha and make no pretense to be. I'm not that different from you. I am, however, learning, discovering, hacking, and finding new ways to harness our inner tools — those available to all of us. But every day is a challenge.

Whether I'm producing a movie, developing a TV series, renovating a house, hosting a podcast, running a mortgage company, investing in real estate, writing, or just skateboarding at the beach, I get close to a dozen calls a day wanting to "schedule a call," "run something by me," "or get my thoughts," wanting advice.

You might think I was:

- a certified financial planner. I'm not.

I studied business, finance, and accounting in college. From age 12, I've been an entrepreneur most of my life. I love math and think its principles can apply to many areas of life; especially the power of regular, small, incremental steps that can compound into significant results. Accountability and analysis of a repeatable, daily process are important and revealing. Good habits start young. Today is always the best day to plan.

- a relationship expert. I'm not.

I'm far from it. I've had more relationships than I can count on both hands and am now in an 11+ year committed relationship with an amazing girlfriend, who happens to be a professional therapist. Some of that rubs off. It's sort of contact-absorption. It influences my observations about human behavior.

- a contractor. I'm not.

I held a subcontractor's license briefly for a painting company I started in college, but that's the extent of licensure. I've renovated almost a dozen properties, personally and by hand, learning the impact of design, branding, and perception. Anything can be accomplished (unless you're talking rocket science; it's not rocket science). Everything is accessible, learnable and adaptable. Plus working with your hands and seeing immediate, tangible results can be therapeutic. And creation rather than consumption feeds both your inner hero and your wallet. People have resources to accomplish whatever they can dream. It doesn't have to be a mere pipe dream.

- a realtor. I'm not.

I do have a California brokers license (CA BRE 01715653) and mortgage originators license (NMLS 1585250) and have a small business brokering mortgages (terencemichael.com/broker), mostly for freelancers and people to whom the banks normally say "No." Every obstacle is an opportunity, and I help my clients find their own journey to financial freedom and wealth, which for many is accelerated and multiplied by real estate. I've lived through the boom and bust from 2000-2008 and saw what everyone was doing right — and wrong. A herd mentality in real estate is dangerous. This is applicable to other areas of life as well.

- a computer consultant. I'm not.

I learned to code when young, pre dot-com crash, and have built websites for entertainment companies, movie sites, and still geek out over computers. Today we are in an age of the side-hustle and monetizing muses remotely. The sharing/gig/outsource economy has broken down traditional barriers and removed significant obstacles such that anyone can be a digital nomad and build multiple streams of income. You don't need to know how to code, but the basic programming of IFTTT (If This Then That), WYSIWYG (What You See Is What You Get), and simple flow-charting have shown me that anyone can program their own process or system. In short, they can have a more effective approach.

- an angel investor. I'm not.

I belong to a dozen investing syndicates and exchanges wherein I invest in new businesses, start-ups, and ideas. This has taught me the power of long-term framing and the dangers of short-term thinking — always a recipe for disaster when investing (I still struggle with this today as it's so tempting to buy the hot water cooler stock). I've also learned that most people don't know their true identity or are living the one others expect. This leads to a pursuit of faulty business ideas, sometimes creating an additional job for themselves rather than freedom. Faulty thinking leads to faulty living.

- a marketing guru. I'm not.

But I've developed and produced so many films and TV shows that I've gained access to the creative ways in which marketing works — and doesn't. There are rules, but some are broken every day. Nothing really matters if you don't think about the marketing first. You need to reverse engineer the process when putting yourself or your ideas out there. How will you reach and find your scene? I've had to launch each movie or TV show as its own business, trying to find its audience (the secret is in narrow-casting, speaking directly to the tribe of a given product or service).

Then there's this:

Why, when I just spoke to a camera operator on a specific camera set-up about which lenses to use, does this same person ask me the next day if interest rates will go up and if he should buy mutual funds or ETFs?

When an ex-girlfriend asked me for advice on buying real estate, it suddenly dovetailed into what she could do to find an extra hour in her busy day.

I have a producer friend who was discussing character arcs with me on a recent Academy Award winning movie when he randomly asked me if it was better to drive his own car daily to the office or use Uber. In answer, we figured out in two minutes that he could save hundreds of dollars a month and gain an extra half hour every day by taking Uber. This doesn't include the benefit of meditating or getting into a deeper, focused state by the time he arrived at the office if he didn't drive.

I keep having these encounters, and from people whom I care about, so I enjoy the process. When it becomes a distraction, I say "No." I ask these questions as well. I'm curious. There is so much I don't know.

I only have observations from life. These observations have helped me develop believable heroes on screen.

But why should heroes only be in the movies? Why can't you be the hero of your own life?

Aside from my thoughts springing from having lived it (again, that 20/20 hindsight), the classic journey of the hero is so ingrained in my subconscious that it must impinge on my observations and advice I give others.

I see the movie in everyone. I see it in their overall story — where they are, who they are, and how they got there. I see it when someone is down, having a stressful day, perhaps arguing about work or debt. I see it when someone is lost, floating between identity and circumstance. I see it when a tough decision need be made or when the unrequited dream is out of grasp. All of these are stages of a story, just unfinished and missing critical scenes for simple advancement.

Film and TV have a finite timeline, so we producers have to boil down the repetitive habits (good or bad) and define that character trait in simple, digestible scenes. If someone is spinning their wheels or repeating the same mistakes, producers must correct quickly.

I sometimes observe a common detrimental behavior. I can only assume if this is a prevailing pattern, it's inhibiting them, preventing them from advancing through requisite stages of their own hero. So this person's movie is incomplete. It's stuck on 'pause,' wearing down the person and everyone who's watching their story attempt to unfold.

So I've become a reluctant, inadvertent observer. A pseudo "life coach," you might say, even though I prefer not to be called that. I dislike that term and its often-associated negative connotations. There seem to be so many lately; there's probably a coach bubble about to pop.

Produce Yourself

Of course, there are some very good ones. Few can hold a candle to the greats like Jim Rohn, Wayne Dyer, or Tony Robbins. They are the epitome of a true coach for your life. But similar to crazy therapists who give good therapists a bad rap, or bad contractors who make legitimate ones seem shady, there are self-improvement hucksters who give good coaches poor credibility. Sometimes only one bad apple spoils the lot.

I don't want to pretend I know anything that I don't. And there's a lot I admittedly don't know. So I'm not a life coach. I'm not a motivational speaker. I haven't studied or trained or received any relevant degrees. True life coaches need to have legitimate, scientific training, and certification to transcend gimmicky coping mechanisms that only aid short term. Many who call themselves life coaches offer a Band-Aid, not a long-term solution.

I did coincidentally create and produce a TV show called "Life Coach" that aired for one season on Hulu, based on the distaste I have for counterfeit coaches. It was about a guy up to his ears in problems who decides to reinvent himself as a life coach and solve everyone else's problems to distract him from his own.

This stemmed from a phone call from a colleague and friend of mine asking me for career advice. He's a highly gifted and accomplished filmmaker who was at a temporary low point in his life. As happens with many in Hollywood, there was a period where he had no films on his plate. He was pitching TV ideas to various networks with no sale and going to auditions with no acting gigs on the horizon. He said to me: "I'm not sure I can afford cereal next week." He was in his mid-40s; had no girlfriend, was in debt, had no job, and would soon have to leave the Westside apartment he'd lived in for 20+ years.

Seeing the comedy in almost everything, but also wanting to help, I said to him, "Let's sell a TV show called 'Life Coach.' It's all about you. You would star in it, play yourself a la Larry David style, and eventually get out of your on-screen funk and make money by advertising as a Life Coach helping others." Bam. Idea born. Casting, development, financing, production. TV Series. Done. That really is my extent of experience with life coaches.

Through that process of the TV series, even though the show was fictional and died after one season, my colleague was able to follow his own fictional script in real life. He eventually produced his life in a way that conquered the temporary hurdles in front of him.

Again, I acknowledge there are amazing coaches out there. Should I ever meet one in person, I'd probably want to be one. I'm very interested in finding and hacking peak performance in all areas of life, and feel the key to most of that is from a device we already have: our inner hero.

It's often easier for one to analyze another person's situation or shortcomings. We can maintain emotional detachment and don't have accompanying baggage and distractions. We can laser in on the problem with objectivity. When I was semi-life-coaching my colleague, he was probably life-coaching me at the same time. Perspective helps peel away noise and distraction.

This is why I feel therapy (this includes training and mentoring) is probably effective about 80 percent of the time. People need someone who knows how to listen. We need a third party professional who isn't distracted by our past regrets and future anxieties. People need to verbalize their feelings so that their inner hero can hear the pleas and requests of the external hero. Reading a story is one thing. Telling/writing it is another — an exercise that I can attest is both therapeutic and life affirming.

That's one reason I'm writing this book: to give you some pause, perspective, and perhaps lessons that may be applicable to you, as they have been to me. But I'm also journaling my own odyssey for the benefits the writing process engenders.

Produce Yourself

The idea of helping someone else based on my own experience has always come naturally. I'm not too proud to list my failures or too egocentric to share lessons learned from triumphs. This book contains both. I often find that dispensing advice helps solidify and steady my own compass. Writing this book is as much to help my process as it is to (hopefully) help yours.

I don't know your whole story or the dozens of burdens you carry. I don't even know who you are. "You," as I will write throughout this book is a composite of everyone I have ever met, worked with, lived with, loved, lost, and encountered along my life-hike. So although I hope you think I'm writing specifically to YOU, YOU is an amalgamation of the collective "you," aggregated from years of examination and thought.

Maybe you're swapping balances from one credit card offer to another, and I know a better way for you because I've been there myself.

Or you left your job because you didn't get a raise. Yet you haven't sat down to do the math that shows you don't really need that raise at all.

Maybe you spend 20 minutes standing in front of your closet deciding what to wear. I can improve on that process for you, saving you an aggregate of months of life for better time expenditure — speculation and prospect for meaningful things.

You complain there aren't enough hours in the day, when, in truth, there are too many. Your idle hours attract anxiety, restlessness, unhappiness, and excessive consumption.

You're busy. But you're also confusing productivity with effectiveness. Were you truly effective, you would accomplish your task in less time — impactful time that works for, not against you. You need never be busy if you're effective.

There's an order in which you can accomplish tasks that will seem to slow time for you, equating to perhaps 36 hours a day instead of 24. You can utilize your brain power more effectively by following what Psycho physiologist Peretz Lavie calls "ultradian cycles."

Although we all have the same hours in a day, I'm sometimes able to do two to three times more than others. I write this without pride, in an attempt to illustrate what is possible. I work smarter, less hard, and make every task a multiplier with a whiplash of ripple outputs. It didn't come naturally. I had to dive deep and study certain techniques to form new habits.

From operations management in business school to economical storytelling in film and TV, it's been an educational process that has altered my perspective and given me clarity on a host of negatives: redundancy, overabundance, stagnation, interference, deviation, mediocrity, uncertainty, equivocation, misinterpretation, angst, and exasperation.

Life is short and there's a lot I want to accomplish. I want to do it stress-free in a state of happiness, which only comes from choice and presence.

There's a conscious mentality required — and acquired — that I want to share. I have been doing this probably since before "life coach" was a two-word partnership. Part of it is learning to say "No" a lot. Those "No"s will summate to a big "Yes" when opportunity strikes.

Part of it is living authentically in your own narrative, not someone else's. Part of it is understanding life is nothing but a set of sensory experiences that you can control by focusing on internal factors rather than external ones.

I'm a hybrid of sorts, and I suspect you are, too. But maybe you're suppressing aspects of who you really are, denying your internal hero the journey it needs in favor of the external hero who might be wrongly focused on societal acceptance.

Produce Yourself

I'm curious to the point I investigate areas of behavior and immerse myself until I have a clear understanding. I want this book to be that deep dive for you, or at least the diving board to launch you into new pools of opportunity. We all have what I like to call "proximity potential." But many of us don't exploit it.

I like to know not just how things work, but why they work. And, sometimes important, why they don't. I've asked myself this question my whole life, ranging from toys and toasters to camera equipment and complicated mortgage-backed securities; and more recently from motivation to the brain's ability to fine-tune process and performance.

In particular, I've been fascinated by mathematics; not money per se, but the calculations behind accelerating inputs and multiplying outputs. This concept has helped me apply the principles of compound interest to varied parts of life beyond finance. I like to plant seeds, then harvest trees.

I'm able to take the time right now to write this book due to gardens tended long ago. But I'm still cultivating them for my future self. Always be a gardener of your life. There's no better investment than the one you make in yourself, and the one you make today. Future You will thank Past You. Give You that amazing gift.

There's a Chinese proverb that says: "The best time to plant a tree was 20 years ago. The second best time is now." Everything that you are today, and everything you do, how you do it, why you do it, when you do it, is the result of the tree you planted 10 years ago. You are the tree's fruit, bearing the result of the seeds of the past.

So the best thing you can do today is to tend the tree for tomorrow. Your future is nothing but the sum game of your current habits, choices, and plans. The ultimate test for yourself is what you can do today for your future.

I myself fall victim to this. I think, where would I be if I had started this two years ago? Where would I be with that had I started a month ago? I'll never be able to do what he is doing because he started 20 years ago.

Those depressing reflections are a never-ending continuum. If every day I nurture new seeds of plants, those seeds will blossom in 1 week, 1 month, and 5 years from now. Growing at their own pace, those seeds of my decisions and habits today will become the trees I desire tomorrow.

At age 8, I read a children's book called "The Great Brain" by John Fitzgerald. It affected me deeply. It was about a kid who learned how to monetize everyday occurrences. Now, as I look back at the book, I see that the protagonist was a con artist, tricking his little brother out of parts of his allowance and using semantics to win bets, etc.

But the book made me realize there was a different way to view chores, allowance, games, and everything else that occupied my childhood world. I was exposed to an alternate way to have more fun doing what I liked, outsourcing what I didn't, and how to make money when there was demand (apologies to my sister, whom I charged 10 cents to enter my room whenever she wanted to play with me).

Allow me to give more context, as it dictates much of what this book is about.

Let's take taxes, for example; that's one subject no one can avoid. Everyone always talks about taxes; how much is being taken out of their paychecks; write-offs; should they form a corporation or get paid as a freelancer; etc. Even politicians (have you ever heard anyone run for any office who didn't talk about taxes?). And how sobering is it that, on average, we Americans work until mid-May of every year just to pay our taxes, keeping what we make mid-May to December. We work 4.5 months just for the government. But you don't have to. I can shorten that.

I've read the entire tax code — the whole damn thing. And I continue to read the updates every few years or so to keep current. My accountant

Produce Yourself

was charging me $850 a year (eventually $3,000 with my various corporations) to prepare my taxes. Why do we all need accountants? After reading the tax code, doing my own taxes was easy. I now fundamentally understand the lens through which the government views the tax process and have benefited many times over because I have that knowledge. Don't just do something because that's the way it's done. Society likes its members to ritualize a process so they don't ask questions. And people fall in line like sheep, accepting inefficiency as law. But it's not. Silicon Valley has proven that through disruption. Challenge breeds opportunity. There's a lot we can learn from that.

Everyone has to cut their hair. If they have hair, they pay to get their hair cut. This is simply how "it's done." Obviously, if you have a complicated cut or complicated hair, I get it. You have a hairdresser. But for 99 percent of guys, it's a big scam. Ask yourself: Why have I not learned how to cut my own hair? Time after time, I sit in the chair, look in the mirror and see exactly what they do.

When I was in college I would drive off campus to my hairdresser in Beverly Hills and pay $50 for a haircut. I realized that, with my needing a haircut basically every 4 weeks (typical for a guy with short hair), even without inflation, I was spending $650 a year. In 10 years, that's $6,500. I don't need to do the math for you. I went to the library and checked out a book on hairstyling. I read it and then cut my hair the next month. I've been doing it ever since for decades.

Next time you get your hair cut, assuming you get the same one you've been getting forever, watch what the stylist does. Record it on your iPhone if you have to. It's not rocket science. Again, challenge breeds opportunity. And opportunity can make you wealthy.

Do you know what this $50 a month in haircut savings may add up to? That $50 a month with a conservative 8 percent return (the stock market has on average returned that, doing zero trading), is now worth $48,236, twenty-five years later. Almost $50,000. That is how much more money I now effectively have just because of haircuts.

Or let me put it to you more simply without getting your hair in a bunch: Do you think you could find $100 a month extra that you don't need to spend? Maybe you can cut back on something frivolous or just develop the habit of saving. That's just $25 a week. I suspect you can do that. Put that $100 every month into a simple index equity fund accessible to everyone on the planet (go right now to www.vanguard.com and buy the "Vanguard Total Stock Market Index Fund"). Do that for 20 years straight. At that same historical 8 percent interest that the fund will earn on average, you now have $60,000 in 20 years. Think what this could be if you could sock away more than $100/month.

Most of you already know this concept. It's not groundbreaking. But surprisingly few employ it.

Finance is just one obvious measure of its power. This math fundamental can be applied to anything: ideas, progress, habits, relationships, performance. Compounding small incremental daily moments adds up. You can have anything if you chip away at it. Tiny steps. Just do it, daily. It will be huge one day. It's math; there's no arguing with it. I will repeat this concept throughout the book to the point you may become completely annoyed. Sorry.

I ask "Why." Why does something have to be done a certain way? Why does everyone approach a habit this way or that? Why is everyone frustrated that they have to do x or complain every afternoon about y? We only need observe something a few times to realize there's a problem. We can't be in denial about it. All problems have solutions. I'm a solutions guy. I hate dwelling on a problem; I want to identify it and clarify it. But that's the extent of belaboring. I prefer to improve something that isn't working.

In Hollywood, when we have tight deadlines and are spending gobs of money a day with a 45-person crew and have several million dollars worth of equipment on set, problems pop up every 6 minutes. That's not scientific, but something I've observed as a producer. That's 10 times in just one hour. So, as a producer, if I don't solve those problems quickly, they will compound and become much larger issues which could derail the entire production.

I've learned from experience, trial, and error, to identify problems as quickly as possible and implement solutions that solve it conclusively so I can advance to the problem that's almost sure to arrive 6 minutes later.

I love manuals. They demonstrate exactly how something functions. And by taking the initial time to properly learn, I can then improve and hack my way through that device's initial purpose; know how to maintain it, make it work smarter and more effectively; and eliminate or automate what may later become headaches for others.

I would never be so presumptuous to write a manual for someone else's life. I'm not even close to being in the right universe for such an undertaking. But I hope this book — my manual, as it were — helps you produce the manual for your life.

With TV shows and film, I'm in the back room making sausage. It's messy and unglamorous. It's where I put together pieces and junk no one wants to deal with, holding them up with temporary tape, fake sets, makeup, and lights, cheated angles and music that doesn't play in real life. I'm the chef in the clunky back kitchen while the consumer sits out front at a nice table with a red carpet and low lighting.

I'm still just the kid opening the telephone and questioning how it works. I saw the film "E.T. the Extra Terrestrial" as a very young kid and wanted to know how that movie was made. I wanted to be Henry Thomas. I wanted my own Alien to hide in the closet and share with my friends, and ride in the night on my BMX bike. And for the first time, I paid attention to a film that said: "Produced by Steven Spielberg."

Why do we all fall in love with the hero, want to be the hero, or otherwise relate to the hero? Any good movie or TV show has such a hero. You relate to, sympathize with, journey with through obstacles, and become connected to as she grows and transforms from her Ordinary World to her new Special World. It's a formula that has stood the test of time. It works. It's sort of a manual.

The main reason we fall in love with on-screen heroes is that we see ourselves in them; either who we are now, or who we want to be. While sitting in the comfort of our own home, we witness the hero doing what we wish we could do. We want that expedition. We want that wish fulfillment. We crave, in the moment, to be that hero who has, against odds, circumvented the ordinary for the spectacular.

There are clear traits (albeit often disguised depending on the genre) that a hero has. There are reasons you like a character or don't.

That may be obvious to you. Some movies make it painfully obvious, using the same tropes with redundancy.

A likable father is a 30-year veteran of the police force and is retiring this week to spend time with his family (likable), but oops — just this week he's got a crazy young trainee before he retires (obstacle). Or a cheating provider husband has just dumped his sweet wife (likable), so she has to hit the pavement looking for a job for the first time in 10 years (obstacle). Can the veteran police officer help the unpredictable trainee and learn something about millennials in the process, thus connecting more with his daughter upon retirement (hero)? Can the divorcee turn a job search into self-reflection and dream scenario to utilize the skills she's always had for something better (hero)? In both cases — in ALL cases of the standard tropes we use — the obstacles become the catalyst and blessing in disguise to launch the hero into their new self. A transformation was in the kindling all along but needed a fire to ignite it.

Produce Yourself

When it comes to Reality TV, for example (don't confuse "Reality TV" with reality), I immerse myself in different worlds based on the premise of the show I'm developing. In so doing, I must find a way to make that character believable and likable. I have to look at entities — society, business, group, family, couple, or single person — and see where they are, who they are, why they are; and then write/create/develop so that, as a producer, I can get them where they need to be. I pave that road for them so that they will become a sympathetic and passionate enough character for the viewer to care about. You want to see them succeed — but only if they're relatable, with real flaws and obstacles, just like us. They need to be as authentic as possible, yet follow the path of the hero. They need to be accessible, but still possess the drive to acquire the tools to develop proper habits and modulate into their future selves.

As a producer, one of my functions is to shape heroes in film and TV. I give them a believable yet compelling adventure to go on that is never easy or necessarily expected, but they get there.

Everyone's life is a movie. Everyone is currently in their own story, creating new pathways all the time with new endeavors and pursuits, large and small.

I want to help you, regardless where you are in your own life and how far down any path you've traveled, by detailing my observations alongside my own journey. I'm sure I could equally learn from yours.

It is merely the fact that I have utilized these heroic stages for two decades as the building blocks for my productions, that gives me any kind of credibility to be dispensing advice. That, and, of course, the power of 20/20 hindsight.

So, without further ado, I want you to become the person you want to be.

Terence Michael

I want you to be the hero of your own movie.

I want you to be the hero of your own life.

-

CHAPTER 2

Paths · Possessions Luck · Comparisons

"All we have to decide is what to do with the time that is given to us."

- Sir Ian McKellen in *Lord of the Rings: The Fellowship of the Rings*

THERE ARE MANY WAYS to approach and tackle life's grand path. Like snowflakes, no two people are alike in dealing with the same daily intrusions of life's pilgrimage. We each have different tools for the adventure — those from our environment, education, health, upbringing, opportunity, economics. We often juggle multiple directives at once, which is why life can seem overwhelming, even suffocating at times.

It's a wonder some people even get out of bed or decide to don clothes for the day. But they/we do it. It's part of the agreement we have with society, one that maintains: "I won't show up naked, I won't have bad breath, and I'll smile when we make eye contact." In exchange: "World, you'll let me participate."

No matter what our path or who we are, this pretty much describes everyone. We have the courage to perform the bare minimum we need to play the human game with a community. The fundamentals become natural. It's part of our physiology.

On the surface, we all have similar choices. We stand at an intersection and decide on a direction. But, depending which pathway we choose to adventure and accept, it invariably becomes successful or burdensome; sometimes it's both.

Chance and luck are huge parts of life. Whether you believe in fate or outright randomness doesn't really matter. You have the life you have. Surely informed and solidified by a series of choices (some of which may have been made for you), but made nevertheless. When those choices turn out to be beneficial, we think we made the right choice. Sometimes that's true.

Equally, when choosing to adventure down a path that becomes a dead-end, we beat ourselves up for having made a poor choice. But this may be just as much chance as choice. Don't beat yourself up. Rather, view it as an opportunity, a gift that may have something to teach.

Perhaps Mark Zuckerberg and Steve Jobs never should have finished college because of their passion for tinkering with computers. Or was it just fate that such individuals never graduated? Maybe they succeeded at Facebook and Apple despite quitting college. Perhaps their narrative might have paralleled the paths of Google founders Sergey Brin and Larry Page, who upon completion at Stanford, created the world's most powerful search engine (and even that was just the tip of the iceberg). But maybe they would have done this anyway had they not finished college. And also, perhaps in addition to their ferocious skill and tenacity, they were in the right place at the right time.

Plus, they didn't stop pursuing their ideas or dreams because someone else had already done it. They asked if the system could be improved.

Produce Yourself

There were a dozen search engines before Google. Brin and Page could easily have stalled from the competition. But they wanted to know how the search engines worked and if it had to be done that way. Why couldn't it be better? And it is. Thank you.

Ditto for Zuckerberg. Friendster and especially MySpace were already there. MySpace was huge. Remember "Meet Tom"? Why did Zuckerberg think he could compete with something already so big, with so much money and doing largely the same thing? He asked, "Why?" He asked if it could be improved.

And then there's Steve Jobs, who tried to make a smaller "friendly" computer when there were already more powerful and bigger computers everywhere. But he questioned the status quo. He knew there was a smarter, better, faster, and more effective way, just as people like Brin, Page, and Zuckerberg would later discover.

Luck may have played a role, but was not a major factor in the success of these innovators. Luck is finding an unclaimed $20 bill on the floor. You did nothing more than bend down to fetch it. Zuckerberg, Jobs, Brin, and Page — they had a chance — an opportunity. And these guys seized on that chance. A convenient event presented itself, which was fortunate. But they then grasped that gift of chance and worked tirelessly against all odds to maximize it. They made sacrifices, took risks, and abandoned the comfort of typical collegiate life. It was a choice they made. It was a path they took advantage of. That is different than luck. Luck is passive and requires no decision or consequential action.

I want to be lucky. I hope you're lucky. I'll never say 'No' to luck. No one should. But let's not diminish others' achievements when luck isn't a major factor in their success.

Most of the time we say: "Well, she was very lucky," when the fact is that she optimized a chance, worked smart, resourced solutions, and turned that chance into an opportunity. And, even then, she simply has an opportunity. It's what she does with that opportunity, digging into her own courage and resourcefulness, that makes the difference from simply being lucky. That 'she' might well be Sara Blakely, who turned the idea of Spanx from $5k into more than $1 billion.

Some of us are often in the right place at the right time, but we don't recognize it. We're too complacent to act on it, or we haven't yet developed the habits to know how to perform.

Looking back, there are times when I should have, could have, would have; had I prepared myself to be ready for an opportunity. But that's what separates me from the guy who did take the chance and monetized that opportunity. I did nothing. He did something. He prepared himself and developed the habits to do it, which is why he did it. And he deserves the spoils for recognizing that fortuity and making an active decision about it.

I hate when I hear a friend say: "OMG, that was my idea! I literally thought of that non-static dryer sheet and was gonna make millions." First, it irks me because it wasn't his idea. It was probably the idea of 300 people. Ideas are free and everyone has them. And second, why didn't he act on it?

There's a potential path, with a signpost, when you have an idea. If you don't pursue an idea, then it's not necessarily your idea.

Every idea shouldn't necessarily be acted on. That could be unhealthy and irresponsible. But don't claim ownership simply because you thought of something. We all think of something. Thinking is passive. Acting is active.

It's comfortable to keep the status quo. Sir Isaac Newton's 1st law of motion describing inertia applies here (a body at rest tends to stay at rest). It's safe. It's easy. You can be a couch if you want to. Everyone loves couches. They're dependable and available. You also see them on the side of the road when people are done using them.

Produce Yourself

Sadly, most of us stay on the path that was produced for, not by us. We start to believe what others expect from us. Be it an online dating profile or small talk at a party, we repeat the same story of who we are and what we do. We don't want to disappoint, so we robotically respond with the spiel.

Eventually, this narrative perpetuates itself, where others now define and forecast who we are based on it. There are expectations and assumptions that this is the definition of us. So they want updates. And maybe we don't want to disenchant the audience, so we stay on the prescribed path, produced by them, reasoning this is who we are. It's in the cards. It's how everyone knows us.

But if you aren't enthusiastic about who you are or what you do, you can't make the story particularly interesting, whether you or someone else is writing it. A movie is never better than its derivative script. If the script isn't interesting, the movie never stands a chance. Lights, coloring, and music can only do so much for a poorly written script.

You can be anyone you want to be. You, not someone else, are in charge of your own narrative and brand. And honestly, others care about their own brand, not yours. Don't mistake someone's pleasantries or small talk for accolades and worship. The only person you should impress is you.

You have to live with you. Look in the mirror and tell that person who you are. Tell that person your story. Take note which areas you're bored with and which you gloss over. Your story might be in need of change.

You can jump paths or pave a new path if you don't like the one you're traveling. Perhaps you're following a path's markers rather than planting them. We are simply the sum of what we do, where we work, where we live, whom we are with, what we discuss and what we pursue. Why not make it incredible?

Show me a successful person, and I'll show you where she's jumped paths or switched trajectory multiple times, correcting, pivoting, learning from failure to stay on course, or charted a new one.

The most evolved, emotionally intelligent, accomplished people are only on their coveted path because of the numerous ones they took before. They fell, slid, rolled, and got hammered countless times, reaching dead-ends, encountering dirt, rocks, and danger. What separates them from someone meandering on the same circular path every day is that they got up and created or located a new one. They produced their own path.

Don't be the horse following the carrot dangling from a string on a stick. Shake your head, change focus and direction. There's probably a whole field of carrots elsewhere if you take the time to look. Just beware the stick.

When you've taken enough detours and dark paths to recognize the one with light, you know you're on the right path. If you can't see it, then you haven't wagered enough risk and exposure. You haven't stretched beyond your comfort zone, which may be the biggest risk of all.

There are:

- societal paths (attend college, get married, buy a house, have kids)
- outlier paths (quit school, become a professional athlete, become a concert musician)
- iconoclast paths (those of ex-pats, solo-preneurs, artists, hyphenates)
- crowd-follower paths (those with trendy jobs, trendy consumption)
- ladder-climber paths (corporate, political, industrial)
- disrupter paths (of travel, innovation, philosophy)
- safe paths (of medical, legal, accounting)
- reinvention paths (e.g.: divorce, new state, new identity, new life)

- paths that meander (those of the passive observer; drugs; oversleeping; over-schooled; waiting for life to give you what you "deserve")

And each of these paths has numerous or smaller pathways within them, all of which crisscross, merge and disjoin along the excursion.

Like a story, life's approach and style can take on many forms and function. You can trail-blaze or follow the beaten path. Within those paths, there are too many styles and strategies to list. How any one person checks their life goals off their list will likely never exactly coincide with anyone else's. It might seem that way on the surface, but beneath the veneer of your co-worker or best friend who appears to be on a similar path, you'll find a system for building wealth, relationship repair, or spiritual growth different from yours. That's what makes theirs unique.

We often compare ourselves to others, justifying and complaining that they have it so easy. They don't have kids. They don't have two mortgages. They don't have grad school debt. They don't have toxic co-workers. They don't have employees. They don't have health issues. They don't have crazy parents.

Or the opposite: Wow, look at them, they are so in love. Their life is perfect. They drive the perfect car and wear the perfect makeup. They are single and can do whatever they want, whenever they want. They must make a lot of money. 'The grass is always greener' is more than an idiom. It's a human default (and fault).

You can compare yourself to others, but you can't compare your path to theirs. Everyone has their set of choices they've made and are living with. You may covet certain ones, but not realize the sacrifices made or burdens carried in exchange.

The next time you're jealous of someone's house and wish you were they so you could have that house, ask yourself if you really want to be them, 100 percent them, with every single characteristic they possess. The only way you can truly compare yourself to someone else and covet their narrative is to completely swap places with them.

You can't curate a specific aspect of someone and then compare yourself to them. That's a faulty equation that isn't weighted properly. Rather, you have to ask yourself: am I willing to give up everything I am — my family, my career, my memories, my kids, my accomplishments, my talents, my personality, my friends — and swap 100 percent across the board with another person?

Do you also covet their attitude, emotions, experiences, relationships, stress, health, loneliness, and whatever other many attributes and experiences that make up that person? Those brought them to where they are today. Who knows where they'll be tomorrow? If you really want to compare yourself to, or be jealous of, another person, ask yourself if you can do that.

I've never encountered anyone willing to swap full identity without a cherry picker.

It's disproportionate to compare someone else's sizzle reel to your blooper reel. And that's the trouble with comparing yourself to someone, especially someone famous or someone packaged by the media and presented to you for their services or products.

We paralyze ourselves and stunt our internal growth when we compare ourselves to others. We see the bloopers in ourselves because we are the raw footage without any editing. We are experiencing in first person every minute detail we encounter. Looking at others, we simply see the edited, colored, mixed, and polished sizzle that we admire. It's been highly produced.

That's why actors and musicians have become celebrities in our culture. We've seen them on the big screen or the big stage, but only after hours and years of turmoil, research, headaches, breakdowns, rewrites, rehearsals, and on and on. We see the final produced presentation. We see the glossy trailer with the 100-person orchestra. We read about them in an article in its final edited form. We see them in an interview that's been highly pre-edited with lawyers and publicists. We see them on the red carpet after 7 hours of hair and makeup with expensive jewelry and clothes (all borrowed, by the way).

If you want to level the playing field, compare someone's bloopers to yours. If you don't have enough bloopers, you aren't pushing yourself enough.

You need the outtakes of life to find the scenes that work.

I like to think of life like a big mixing board of levers.

You know when you see the stereotypical music studio where someone is recording a song, and you see the music producer in a room with that massive panel of knobs? That.

If that represents our life, it's easy to look over into someone else's and see they have row #17 and column #68 moved all the way up to 10. Wow — their life must be so amazing. I'm only at 6 or 7.

But if you look closer, to compensate for that person being at 10 in those two areas, they've had to turn other levers way down to accommodate. Do you want a ton of bass in that song? Well, you're going to have to not only turn up the bass, you'll have to also turn down the treble. But where the bass is good for her, treble may be better for you. And if you were to dig deeper, you might discover that the person with all that bass actually envies your treble.

Over-simplified and general, but hopefully a reminder to not covet or waste too much precious time on this planet thinking about the Joneses and what they have. They don't care what you have. They only care what you think they have. Don't play that backward game with an external scorecard.

I often think about the complete waste of resources, time and money (not to mention the carbon footprint) created by the possessions people acquire to impress others. The irony is that no one is impressed.

Really. No one cares what you have. When someone says: "Wow" because they see how you're dressed or what you're driving or what's in your home, or what your work title is, they are thinking: "I wish I had that." They don't care that you have it. They think, "How come I don't have it?" And then they eventually acquire it, and the game continues, back and forth. But for what? Show? Is it a contest?

What do you win if it is a contest? Wasteful debt. Trips to charity or the Goodwill. Storage fees and afternoons organizing a yard sale. Gas fees and sweat from hauling stuff around in your car. All too often, that's what you get. I've been there.

The moment you stop caring what other people think of your material things, your balance sheet, or your looks, is the moment you will be on a path to a more fulfilled, happier You.

Warren Buffett, one of the world's wealthiest men, lives in a humble house he bought in 1958. He said, "If you buy things you do not need, soon you will have to sell things you need."

The irony is that people who care about what other people think, end up showing their true colors by way of silent failures. They drift away, no longer posting or advertising all their fantastic gratifying and happy moments because they've allowed an external game of look-what-I-have kill their internal game of accomplishment.

Tom Shadyac, extremely successful director of numerous Jim Carrey blockbusters ("Ace Ventura: Pet Detective," "Liar Liar," "Bruce Almighty") sold most of his possessions. He had mansions in Beverly Hills, but now lives in a trailer near the beach and rides his bike for transportation. He found all these material possessions weighed him down, adding to his inbox, responsibilities, and stress.

Ditto for author, podcaster, and multi-successful serial entrepreneur James Altucher. He is famous for shedding his life of everything, giving everything away except for enough clothes to fit in one bag. He now lives in long-term Airbnb stays. He has a family, kids, a full life. But now, due to his strict forfeiture of stuff that was controlling his life, he has freed his life with time to do what he loves. He doesn't think about inanimate objects that need fixing, upgrading, or replacing. But he eats the wonderful healthy foods he wants, exercises, spends time with his kids, grows his podcast and writing businesses, and has time for experience rather than debt. And he has a strict policy: if he buys something new, he has to throw something out. Cool belt at the store? Great, but he must discard the one he currently owns first.

Possessions possess you. They become a tyrant and start to control your life. It's okay to have space in your house. Let that be a metaphor for space in your mind for thinking.

You love art museums; you love looking at interior design photos. Might it be because they killed the clutter? You don't need something for everything. You can be resourceful. Minimal resources require creativity. Creativity generates opportunity. Opportunity helps you choose to be happy.

Just because you eat a mango once every 4 months doesn't mean you need a special mango peeler. Just because last Friday night you and your kids made ice cream and then had popcorn in front of the TV doesn't mean you need an ice cream maker and a faux theater popcorn machine. You might use those a few more times the rest of the year, if that. And soon you're having a yard sale.

Having less and getting rid of stuff will help you be more present, live intentionally, and teach you to be content with what you have.

By removing all of the non-essential ego enhancers (things, stuff) from their lives, both Shadyac and Altucher have opened up acres of space in their surroundings for creativity, innovation, optimization, and clarity.

Their lifestyle may be too extreme for you (or me, for that matter). But there's a valuable lesson here for our internal hero to take along the journey, as it will free up time for improvement and idea generation.

No one on their deathbed has ever been remembered to have said they wished they acquired more stuff. No one. If anything, they have regrets for acquiring too much stuff and not focusing on what's important: the intangibles.

Your identity and the pathways you take should be authentically you, 100 percent. That's what people will covet. In the meantime, other people will just keep buying stuff to fill the void so that you can be impressed by their possessions. If they can't have the identity and life they want, they'll just buy things to distract it, which is nothing more than buying an ephemeral identity. Had they just changed paths or improved the one they were on, they could have filled their new story with substance and experience rather than clutter.

Because I have a mortgage business, I've seen the situations of hundreds of individuals and families on paper (credit reports, assets, tax returns, and debt). Although I keep everyone's private information completely confidential, I can divulge this: Hollywood movies and TV shows aren't the only places with minimally built foundations, fake sets, and heavy makeup. I see more smoke-and-mirrors in my clients' files sometimes than I do in sci-fi movies.

This is why I love math. Math reveals the path. And the path reveals the truth.

Produce Yourself

A cliché in Hollywood is that you can throw a stone and hit a producer who has a house mortgaged to the hilt. It's true. Because the stereotypical image of a movie producer precedes reality, many come to town thinking they need the mansion, the fancy cars, and designer clothes. There's nothing intrinsically wrong if that fulfills and inspires you.

In "Seinfeld," Jerry and George finally locate Kramer after he left NYC for dreams of making it in Hollywood. They ask him how it's going and he replies: "I'm doing what I do. You know I've always done what I do. The way I've always done it. The way I'll always do it."

Kramer is of course deflecting, hiding the truth. He was probably hoping to impress his friends with stories of Hollywood and all he achieved on his quest.

But after his best friends ask what the hell he's talking about, Kramer knows they can see through him. In a rare moment of vulnerability, he rhetorically asks:

> "What do you want me to say, that things haven't worked out the way that I've planned? That I'm struggling, barely able to keep my head above water? That L.A.'s a cold place even in the middle of summer? That it's a lonely place even when you're stuck in traffic in the middle of the Hollywood freeway? That I'm no better than the screenwriter driving a cab, the starlet turning tricks, the producer in a house he can't afford? Is that what you want me to say?

Underneath the Hollywood façade, I see the rickety scaffolding barely holding that house of cards together — not only from my own experience as a movie producer but also as the broker who helps other producers consolidate their debt and get loans. What one sometimes assumes is another person's wealth is on average probably 3 to 4 times inflated what is actually on paper, hidden in the numbers.

I make no judgment about this if it fulfills you. But if it's causing problems, I point it out in the spirit of wishing to help.

The wizard behind the curtain is often more diminutive, fragile, and insecure than you think. That's why there's a fancy curtain hiding debt and interest charges on the wizard's credit card. L. Frank Baum, the author of 'The Wizard of Oz,' would probably be astounded at how closely modern Hollywood mimics the imaginary land of his creation.

Unfortunately, many producers — my friends and colleagues — felt they needed the big fancy house and sports cars in order to complete their identity. 2009, unfortunately, taught a lot of them a hard lesson when the housing market burst. Not that it was entirely their fault. Misfortune is also often due to bad timing and forces beyond control. Chance and luck are huge parts of life, but they cut both ways. As Dolly Parton observed, "The way I see it, if you want the rainbow, you gotta be willing to put up with the rain." But how we react and take accountability for uncontrollable events is what separates a dejected downfall from a resilient ascendancy. Dorothy learned this, getting more than her fair share of rain when crossing over the rainbow into Oz.

Regardless the situation, you just can't compare yourself to others, period. Simply coveting his car or her house or their business is like looking through glasses with Swiss cheese for lenses. You're not seeing where the hardship and challenges are. You're not seeing what they've given up. Or in the case of those producers, you're not seeing the porous maze of weak finances trying to shoulder the weight of marble and stone.

As humans, we have an amazing ability to adapt. Situations are rarely ideal, and we justify. We soon forget how much we initially hated the situation we're in, yet find acceptance with it over time. New and foreign environments tend to become comfortable over time. We're resilient that way. But on the other hand, that same resiliency is what we have stored up in excess, waiting to be exercised with experiences — heading out on adventures and testing our limits.

Produce Yourself

Although there's no necessarily one right way, there's usually a general path that seems to work, as you go to school, grow up, fall in love, discover your passions, develop your habits, and taste life. The key is dissection and recognition if this path works for you. And if not, why not? What's holding you back from fixing it, improving it or joining a new one?

We often get in our own way, distorting or hiding the map that we need in order to progress. And we may not even be aware. With the level of stimuli and distraction in our modern society, it's easy to skim the surface, never diving deep into who we are and who our absolute self desires to be. The authentic being will gravitate toward its inevitable destiny, but we have to keep the path clear in order for it to optimally do so.

Don't get in the way of yourself.

CHAPTER 3

Art Imitates Life: The Stages of The Hero

"Great men are not born great, they grow great."

- Marlon Brando in *The Godfather*

AMERICAN SCHOLAR JOSEPH CAMPBELL identified a narrative pattern in mythological story and psychological evolution that has evolved into what many of us know as "The Hero's Journey." This concept was originally called the "monomyth" in his groundbreaking book, "The Hero With a Thousand Faces," wherein he discovers a template for all stories. He is like a god in the world of writers, philosophers, and creatives everywhere who are grateful for his analysis and observations of the classical journey of a hero.

The parallels in almost all story architecture from the history of time seem to be more than mere coincidence. We have a natural, perhaps genetic proclivity toward a certain path, a particular sequence of events that is at once gratifying and essential.

Because there is a predisposition to sympathize with and applaud real people who go through a certain order of events, decisions, and actions, we instinctually require this as the barometer in story (whether fiction or not). And, perhaps without realizing it, we challenge this format every time we see or hear a story. Our test of a story manifests itself in the form of impatience or distraction if it departs too much from the Hero's Journey.

We know when a story is bad. We lose patience when someone can't tell a story properly (a personal deficiency of mine, being a producer). We check our watch or fidget to walk out of a movie when it's "not going anywhere." We find relief in our phone if a TV show isn't engaging. In most cases, this happens when the stages of our hero are incomplete, or not fully realized.

There are hundreds of tropes and devices that hang tangentially off this structure to make every story unique. Similar to the mathematical behavior of Chaos Theory, and, more specifically, the Butterfly Effect, changing one character's line of dialogue, one piece of music, or one prop in one scene can alter the impact of the film. Thus, no two films are entirely alike.

In general, the stages of "The Hero's Journey" delineated by Campbell's writings are data-driven proof that story — all story — has common DNA. And this includes the story of "man" in real life — those little scenes that make up our days, and the larger story of our life. As writer Annie Dillard observed, "How we spend our days is, of course, how we spend our life."

I have to give a big shout-out to Christopher Vogler. If you're a writer in Hollywood, you've heard of him. As it was before my time, I can't confirm if this story is entirely true or partial myth. But this is how I've come to understand it over the years: Vogler took what Campbell had written about classic storytelling and turned it into a famous memo back in the 1980s while he was developing projects at Disney. It became a watershed moment for development executives, producers, and creatives all over Hollywood when it made the rounds. Suddenly, for the first time, there was a "guide" to help the writer stay on course and shape story.

In his memo, Vogler outlined how Campbell's identification of steps a hero takes in mythology (like Ulysses in Homer's "The Odyssey") is intrinsically applicable to those a lead character takes in modern day film and television. This memo eventually led to Vogler's best-selling book, "The Writer's Journey," in which he shortened Campbell's original 17 steps into 12 applicable for cinema. This book has provided major insight into the psyche and development of characters in story, helping readers understand, if nothing else, the basic foundation and framework into which a lead character should evolve and progress. Otherwise, the end result is inadequate and unfulfilling.

Of course, many writers have been aware of Campbell's original hypothesis. Vogler didn't write his memo and book until the 1980s. But a little-known writer/director/producer by the name of George Lucas had an equally small 1977 film called "Star Wars" (since retitled "Star Wars IV: A New Hope"). And it's well known that one of George's mentors was Joseph Campbell. Lucas has said in interviews that Star Wars is his version of the classic Hero's Journey as discovered and defined by Campbell. The rest is history.

To Campbell, the whole reason movies like Star Wars are so popular and successful in the first place is because the Hero's Journey is so relevant and relatable to the human journey — all humans, all journeys. He looked at all kinds of religions, myths, eastern cultures, the Bible, Chinese proverbs, and even the character of Dante in Dante Alighieri's 'Inferno.' He realized that the Hero's Journey is a rite of passage for all humans. It stands to reason that journey in movies would engage, enlighten and entertain us. Humans seek this triad in their diversions.

Terence Michael

I don't know if this pattern is something that was passed on from caveman to caveman while sitting around the campfire talking about the day's hunt. Or if wise philosophers sat around and had a primitive hack-a-thon to teach people to record and share stories. Maybe we all are just living in "The Matrix" and, if the story doesn't follow the programmed protocol, we get error codes in response to the deviation.

But all stories, fiction or real-life, with negligible exception, basically follow a methodical pattern. When it doesn't, whether we pinpoint the derailment or not, our response is to reject the story. It doesn't speak to us.

The phenomenon is consistent and quite incredible.

This is not to say that story has been one big corporate or Shakespearean scam all this time, and we've just ignorantly accepted a mass-produced output of the same story over and over again. Story comes from us, not the other way around. Art imitates and recapitulates life. Writers write what they know. Producers produce what seems entertaining to them. And audiences digest and recommend movies or shows that speak to them.

Writer, producer, viewer. It makes no difference. The common thread of enjoyability runs from intuitive design. And this is where the Hero's Journey comes from.

I owe much to Campbell and Vogler. To Campbell for his original insight, and to Vogler for his application of that insight to modern-day cinema. Were it not for them, I probably would not be able to articulate with eloquence the steps I adapt and apply for you to become the hero of your own life. It's a great skeleton, a recipe almost, for the path I want you to take to improve components of your life: daily systems, processes, habits, and approach to anything and everything.

If you were watching a movie of yourself, starring you, and it lasted for a week (assume the editor was lazy), how would you, the hero of the movie, evolve and transform from where you are today to where you are one week from now? What approaches and processes did you use? What monumental shifts in mindset and habits will you see your hero experience?

This is the most important movie you'll ever watch. And you get to produce it. When you know the steps, it's easier to answer these rhetorical questions.

Here are the official stages of The Hero's Journey as they apply to you:

1. Your Ordinary World

2. Your Call to Adventure

3. Your Refusal of The Call

4. Meeting Your Mentor

5. Crossing the Threshold

6. Your Tests, Allies, and Enemies

7. Your Approach To The Inmost cave

8. Your Ordeal

9. Your Reward

10. Your Road Back

11. Your Resurrection

12. Your Return with the Elixir

As you advance through this book, I will adjust these stages slightly, adapt them to real life, and insert some other important sub-stages that I encountered along my own journey. Also, I'll digress from time to time to interject various things I learned myself from each stage.

It may not be a perfect fit, but I believe you'll be able to draw some comparisons that are applicable and beneficial. Regardless the path in life you are taking, you'll see how your life is a movie or TV show in progress. Others may have even told you that.

You may as well be the hero.

With previews out of the way, let's now watch your movie.

-

CHAPTER 4

Your Ordinary World
(Stage 1)

"Just keep swimming. Just keep swimming. Just keep swimming, swimming, swimming. What do we do? We swim."

- Dory in *Finding Nemo*

THE BEGINNING OF ANY HERO'S STORY begins in her Ordinary World. This includes her physical environment, such as an office, car, home, or boat. But it's also the mental, spiritual, health or emotional state in which she lives, whether inadvertently, reluctantly, or by choice. The Ordinary World can be any simple singularity or a convoluted mix of layers of interlaced issues.

Regardless the scenario, the identity of our hero and her predicament are revealed here in the very 1st stage. TV show, movie, play, musical or book — it starts with this element; if not visually, at least thematically. Something is amiss; something isn't right; something isn't working.

There's a vacancy in the realization of the person's potential and desire. The mechanism and approach our hero employs clearly aren't optimal. She needs a renewal, whether several smaller modifications or one large one.

Sometimes, the hero is oblivious to what is to come. She might feel safe, complacent, seemingly complete. Or she might feel stressed from instability, dissatisfaction, or other polar forces, but accepts it as normal. It's possible she has no idea she'll soon embark on a journey. More likely, she knows she should. However, there are many reasons/excuses for remaining immobile.

She might be a reluctant hero. Taking that first step is everything. But it's scary, especially when the Ordinary World is accommodating and adequate. That's fine for many. They settle and accept a fate of mediocrity. It's okay for others to feel this way, but it's not okay for the hero. A hero becomes aware of, and attentive to, her subpar current reality.

Conversely, our hero could be passionately motivated, excited, energized and optimistic. That, too, could be her nature. She doesn't have to be at the bottom of the barrel or in the gutter. She doesn't have to be Mel Gibson in a mobile home with a gun ready to kill himself ("Lethal Weapon"). She could be Robert Downey, Jr. ("Ironman") who seems to have it all — success, intellect, innovation. Yet, does Ironman have it all? He has no family or sustainable human connection beyond his technological creations.

In "The Matrix," Keanu Reeves works in a cubicle, lonely, living the quiet life of a hermit, communicating with no one but his computer. This is his Ordinary.

In "American Beauty," Kevin Spacey lives in a Rockwellian world, so perfect he's accused of being "weird" by his family when he has thoughts outside of conversational boundaries. He is dead inside, trapped, soulless. Sadly ordinary. Yet he finds comfort in the impeccable life he's created.

Produce Yourself

In "Wonder Woman," how can Gal Gadot's Amazonian world be described as ordinary? But to her, it is a mundane and predictable world. She wants more. She wants to be a warrior but her mother won't allow it.

In "Baby Driver," Baby's world also seems far from ordinary. But for him, driving the getaway car for bank robberies is his normality. That's the repetitive process that he longs to leave. But he's trapped by his own shortcomings and devices, forcing him to follow a false purpose that keeps him from his true identity.

And in "Rain Man," Tom Cruise is an opportunistic hustler, seemingly happy selling cars and being obsessed with money. But he's empty, materialistic, and unaware who he really is. He just doesn't know it yet.

You may be amazing and extraordinary, but you're stuck in an Ordinary World that may limit you. These factors conspire to make your world challenging: debt, obligations, health, stress, isolation, family, distraction, traffic, children, environment, addiction.

This is your state, your mindset. It is holding you back. That is what is "ordinary," because to be "extraordinary" is to recognize your current reality and take the first step to exit the monotonous loop of ineffectual habits.

Jim Carrey eventually recognized this in "The Truman Show." So did Evan Rachel Wood in HBO's "Westworld" series. Both these heroes are living a loop of their Ordinary World. Comfortable, predictable, bucolic.

Conversely, Bill Murray's loop in "Groundhog Day" is the opposite. He can't seem to get it right. All three heroes had been living every day, accepting their fate as a programmed loop. They just followed instructions and accepted that this is what their life was to be. There wasn't a thought about how it could get better — until there was.

You will later return to this Ordinary World 9 stages later. You don't have to leave your physical surroundings or environment as you know it. We often see this in films because this outer journey cinematically parallels the hero's inner journey. But the inner journey is what we focus on in this book. Logistical changes in environment can be exciting, but they should follow, not lead, inner change. Otherwise, you'll replace the scenery but still travel with the same baggage. And that will weigh you down.

A change of scenery is only provisional progress in disguise. If you're moving to another state or breaking off a relationship because you're unhappy, you're not going to find happiness in the physical change. That comes from within. That's the choice you make on your inner journey. The rest will complement and support that journey, but again, it needs to follow and be subordinate to your inner one.

The hero advances from stage to stage by looking at herself in the mirror, eliminating noise and distraction to truly see and hear who she is, and takes the next step to whom she wants to be.

Maybe your journey is leaving your current ineffectual habits for ones that are spectacular and effective. Everything is about execution. Maybe that is the journey in store for you — getting a system upgrade. You, 2.0.

It doesn't seem particularly sexy or adventurous, but cultivating new habits, if that's your journey, will improve almost anything you are pursuing. We all have friends at whom we shake our heads. We can't believe how they allocate their spending, budget their daily hours, or stay at an unfulfilling job they aren't happy with. They complain about their relationship with their sister, or their neighbor, or their cubicle-mate. We can't believe we're meeting them for dinner, knowing they'll show up 20 minutes late and manage to never leave their share of the bill.

Maybe your journey is getting out of a funk, laziness, or boredom. There is so much to do in life; where do you start?

Produce Yourself

If the proverbial deathbed is as important as some people aver (I'm not sure it is, but let's go with it for now), then you don't want to be staring at the hospital ceiling asking:

- Why didn't I learn to be an architect?
- Why didn't I fly to Spain and spend one year learning the culture?
- Why didn't I smile more, laugh more, and give more?
- Why didn't I see if I could have had my own successful knitting boutique?
- Why didn't I create an app?
- Why didn't I tell my brother I loved him?
- Why didn't I adopt a kid?
- Why didn't I rebuild my dream car?
- Why didn't I volunteer just one weekend to a charity?
- Why didn't I sell my poems online?
- Why didn't I try stand-up?
- Why didn't I give a wedding planner business a shot?
- Why didn't I sell my hand-made scarves?
- Why didn't I try to invest in an apartment building?
- Why didn't I take cooking classes?
- Why didn't I join a band, learn to sing, or play guitar?
- Why didn't I gather all my best friends from high school together to take one big memorable camping trip together?
- Why didn't I ever visit the Grand Canyon?
- Why didn't I make more videos?
- Why didn't I tell that guy I was always attracted to him?
- Why didn't I write a book
- Why didn't I take more risks?
- Why didn't I learn more about this?
- Why?

For my larger life's Hero's Journey, my Ordinary World started in high school. It continues today.

For my medium ones, there are the journeys I go on when I contemplate life, where I'm at, my bucket list, and what I want to add to my plate for inspiration and creation.

For smaller journeys, there are things like improving my methods and performance for accomplishing tasks. Everything from email to exercise, driving to eating, sleeping to communicating, investing to learning, sharing to charity, walking the dog to making breakfast, running an errand to meditating, digesting news to preparing taxes, and so on.

In my senior year of high school, we had teachers and counselors who encouraged everyone to decide what they wanted to be when they grew up. That perennial, juvenescent question that typically found answers of astronaut or fireman would mature into a soul-searching exercise.

We even had to take a test that was supposed to give us options based on how we answered the multiple-choice survey. This was the year where your picture in the school yearbook would list your university acceptance and elected major. So, ready or not, a choice had to be made.

For me, it was a glaring choice, despite it being too early for such a choice. But even knowing exactly what your path is, even in hindsight, doesn't mean that the path you chose was or was not a mistake. For what you knew and who you were at that point in time, that was the choice you made.

I was always going to be a "businessman." It felt like that was my Ordinary World. I didn't know if that meant I would sell insurance, become an accountant, or market fruit juicers (none of those appeals to me, by the way). I didn't know. I just liked the idea of being in command of some kind of organization, one that I would set up and make my own money, and hence my own destiny, based on my own impetus.

Produce Yourself

I had started a couple of small ventures in high school for fun, and they were successful within my little school's economy. I covered my costs, made a small amount of money, and had fun doing it. When I realized the entire senior class needed to own a T-shirt with the name of everyone in the graduating class, one they'd cherish forever, a mini-business was born. I typed it on my little computer, printed it out, sent it to a T-shirt wholesaler, and walked around campus convincing everyone they needed to have one.

The rush and freedom I felt from being able to create my own money vs. delivering pizzas was inspiring. I learned early on the value of creating something once and then having that creation bear fruit many times over.

Most students had an hourly job where they only earned if they worked that hour. They were employees. I wanted to be an employer — which I guessed at the time meant I needed to be a businessman.

I'd like to say I've never worked for anyone but myself, but that's not really true. During this period, I thought it would be fun to deliver pizza because I would just be spending time in my car, which at 16 was the best place in the world to be. And I grew up in a neighborhood that I assumed would tip handsomely.

But on my first night of work, I learned not only how much wear and tear I was going to put on my car, potentially negating any short term cash; I also learned that sometimes the more affluent you are, the less you're inclined to part with your money.

The larger lesson, however, was that as I watched the clock tick down and I drove as fast as I safely could with hot cheese sliding around on the backseat, no matter how hard I worked, I was dependent on the main store's ability to sell pizza in the first place.

This one evening, after delivering a few pizzas, I returned to the store where I had to go in back and fold pre-cut cardboard into pizza boxes.

It was terrible. I kept thinking how much per hour I had been making delivering pizzas, and how that average was now getting battered while I assembled pizza boxes in a fluorescent bathed storage room.

I asked the night manager there, who I later learned was the franchise owner of this particular pizza shop, how much money he was making. He smirked and said, "Less than you." I was immediately sorry I asked.

I told him I wanted to run my own business one day. Maybe thinking it would roll over my head, he started spouting off numbers about how much he had to pay to get this store, the lease, the marketing, overhead, payroll, cost of the vegetables, the raw dough, how he was in debt because of it but hoped it would someday pay off.

Here was a businessman who took the initiative and risk to open his own store, yet for all intents and purposes was a servant to his own devices. Dressed in red and blue, he appeared to be just another employee in a strip mall.

I immediately quit. Not only was the fantastical idea of earning cash tips quashed by my folding skills, the tone and attitude of this owner were somber. This is not how I wanted to spend my evenings, especially when (nerd spoiler alert) I wanted to get home and do my homework.

I learned two lessons from this night of work, lessons which in hindsight were worth way more than the $18 I made in tips.

Lesson 1: Be careful in wanting to work for yourself. There will be times where you simply have the title and optics of boss, but you are nothing more than a slave to your own creation.

It's fun to think of logos, websites, business cards, and tell people you have your own business. But think about the mechanics of how that business will function and whether you are truly creating a smart business, or simply creating yet another job as an employee for yourself

— one that actually takes two to three times more of your time. And, knowing in the beginning you will be a victim of your business, make sure it's something you love to do. If you don't love the process, the product is meaningless.

The majority of retail franchise owners who own restaurants or clothing stores or sell knick-knacks are the ones who work 18 hours a day, open the store, close the store, and pay everyone else before realizing any profit for themselves. They get the prestige of owning and running their own business — something they probably chose because they hated working for anyone else. But they might just be working for their own employees, working hard so they can payroll them and keep the lights on.

Stroll down any mom-and-pop street and you'll most likely walk in and out of retail establishments where the owner herself is sweeping the floor, folding the clothes, fixing the toilet in the back room, etc. That's not all she does. But those tasks come with the territory, especially when growing a business.

Lesson 2: It's not always fun planting seeds; getting down on your knees and getting dirty to nurture the embryonic stage of an idea or business. But the fruits of that labor will outweigh that initial sacrifice 10-fold, 100-fold when it becomes passive income. Just make sure you love the input and are willing to live within that, regardless of output.

That pizza manager/owner started his store when the concept of a hot pizza delivered in less than 30 minutes was a novelty and everyone was talking about it. The guy had moved with his wife and kids from the South just to open this one store in my little town. But he saw the upscale demographics and noticed there were 4 high schools all within a mile. The last thing I knew, he owned numerous franchises. He was profiled in a write-up which I happened to read. I smiled for him and his family. His work paid off.

Terence Michael

I have friends who studied law or medicine for 12+ years because that is what they were told they would become when they grew up. It's been ingrained in children from an early age that "doctors and lawyers" are the respectable level to reach, one that would make mom and dad proud.

Willie Nelson has a famous song with these lyrics: "Mamas, don't let your babies grow up to be cowboys... Make 'em be doctors and lawyers and such..." I grew up hearing my sister blast the version of that song sung by Glen Campbell. Of course, my father is a physician, so we all loved hearing "doctors" be sung. And I don't know that my sister even knew what the song was really saying. It was just a funny, twangy song to dance around to when you're a kid.

She became a dentist.

Most of my best friends' parents viewed me as the little businessman. Someday I'd hire them, they'd say. Or someday I could manage their money. Etc. I didn't know what that would entail, but the narrative was familiar and I liked hearing the story. There was no question I would be a business major and study business in college. Yet, I didn't have any idea of what "business" meant or what the secret sauce was.

My family is in the medical field: Dad, Mom, aunts, uncles, cousins (and now all of their kids). If I have an earache, an eye infection, need anesthesia, need an x-ray, or a tooth pulled, I'm covered. So it's odd I decided to study business in the first place, judging solely from my environment. But it was the story I heard from everybody. I didn't want to disappoint them or go off script.

I just knew I wanted to enjoy myself and it came down to two buckets of study if I were going to stay in school. There were the sciences: biology, chemistry, physics; and there were the maths: algebra, geometry, calculus. I excelled at both but had zero passion for the sciences. So I allowed deductive reasoning to let math predict my future.

Produce Yourself

It doesn't matter your background or what you studied in school. You really can do anything you want, at any time. True, for highly specialized fields, it requires a lot of technical or scientific training to excel. And if you happen to love the classes and education that fulfill those requirements along the way, then you've got a head start. But the majority of people (study after study has confirmed this) get into a path they really don't love, only to continue it because that was the choice they made early on. It's also safe and comfortable once you've chosen a path — any path — rather than venture out into the unknown.

I'm pretty sure I may have become a physician had I not had the parental support of ditching my science classes. I could have sucked it up, gone to medical school, and taken the elevator to the top floor of a hospital. I know I could have done it. It was in my genes. I had over a dozen relatives already in the field.

I do respect finishing what you've started. But I don't believe anyone should spend another waking minute doing something that they aren't passionate and excited about. It's impossible to thrive without passion and purpose.

So for me, there were all kinds of mini hero paths crisscrossing, beginning and ending at different times, making choices, navigating hurdles, etc. But for the larger main hero's path, my beginning Ordinary World was as a young wannabe businessman. I felt I'd be good at it.

What is your Ordinary World now, today?

Here's an exercise for you. Step back as a giant Supreme Being and look at yourself as if you're a tiny little ant in an ant farm. Shrink your life — your neighborhood, your husband or wife, your children, your career, pursuits, hobbies... all the many physical things — down to something you can see in a little snow globe so you have the Google Earth view. Describe what you see.

Who is the ant version of you?

Jennifer:

- lives in a 2-bedroom apartment where the rent is cheap
- takes the bus to her job downtown as an account executive at the bank to save money to buy a house
- has two best friends she loves from college whom she sees every Thursday night (one of them is a bit draining)
- is dating a guy whom she wants to get serious with but he seems to be seeing other people
- has a sick brother she has to take care of but wants her other family members to help
- is looking to find her passion which would involve research and writing but isn't sure how to make money at that
- wishes she dressed differently but needs to lose 15 pounds
- probably isn't saving enough for retirement but has no idea how to save when she's out of discretionary money at the end of each month
- knows she wastes too much time bingeing TV but needs the "drug" to come down from the day
- is about to buy a dog but might have to move apartments if she does
- thinks maybe she could start a consulting business but doesn't know where to begin
- and wishes she had more time in her day even though she admits she's on Facebook a dozen times a day
- wants to reconnect with a friend she had a falling out with
- wonders if her reputation for being harsh and brash is holding her back
- knows she has more things than she needs but she loves to shop
- loves to learn but that seems like a luxury
- sometimes fantasizes about a better relationship with her parents

- and, in general, feels like she's successful, but if she were to lose her job may be only a month away from being broke.

No one sees this but you, so it shouldn't be a puff piece. This is your private diary to journal your genuine state, as it exists, today. Be ferociously forthright. Find the courage to really critique yourself, especially the sub-optimal areas that you normally cover up. This is you helping you.

You are saving for a _____. You want to one day be a _____. You wish you could do _____ if you only had _____.

Fill in the blanks and expand them into story. You are revealing to the audience who your hero is. They want to sympathize with this hero, so make her relatable, vulnerable, flaws and all.

Don't forget the things you do every day in terms of time commitment. You may not consider it a description of you, but something that you spend a substantial amount of time doing is who you currently are, like it or not.

You may not describe commuting to and from work, for example, as we all do it, and it seems inconsequential. I wouldn't include it in my current narrative (I've included it in my narrative, however; numerous times in the medium journeys I take on a per-project basis when I drive an hour across town). If that commute involves 3 hours of driving a day due to traffic or logistics, absolutely include it. That is enormously significant. If you're awake 16 hours a day, that driving is almost 20 percent of your waking life.

If it's easier, and you don't like writing, as much as you may want to plow through the chapters in this book, stop and log the next 2 weeks of your life. Just note what you do and when you do it. You want to get a total of how long you spend doing each repetitive task. You are just the sum of those tasks — the ant rolling the pebble up the mountain. Or, if you prefer myth, like Sisyphus rolling a boulder up a mountain, only to have to return to the base of the mountain in perpetuity. His job is never done.

Every story is about the journey, not the destination, which is why I want you to journal this and take the time to complete Stage 1. That's why we watch the best movies over and over again, even though we know (many spoilers ahead) that:

- Bruce Willis is the dead person in "The Sixth Sense"
- Edward Norton and Brad Pitt are actually the same person in "Fight Club"
- Brian Cranston is going to die in "Breaking Bad"
- John Snow will come back to life in "Game of Thrones"
- The Titanic is going to sink
- Kevin Spacey is faking his limp and is actually the real Keyser Soze
- The body in the middle of the room is actually the killer in "Saw"

It's not news, but it doesn't matter. That's my point. You now know Hans Solo dies in "Star Wars: The Force Awakens." You will still watch the film even if you know that. You will binge all six seasons of "House of Cards" even though you know Kevin Spacey and then Robin Wright both become the POTUS.

The journey is what matters. Dorothy from "The Wizard of Oz" would concur. Everything she learned came from that yellow brick road, not from seeing the faux wizard behind the curtain. Ditto for Charlize Theron in "Mad Max: Fury Road." Her trip to find water was doomed in the end. But the journey taught her it wasn't about the water; it was about redemption, something she could have only learned from the journey itself.

Unfortunately, it's the journey that most people want to skip. There is often no reward without putting in the work, but here's my advice: Put in the work. It doesn't have to be labor intensive. Little by little, take baby steps and accumulate the sum of the minimal or sporadic inputs. 1 + 1 = 2. 2 + 1 = 3. 3 + 1 = 4. And so on.

Any big journey is simply made up of numerous smaller pathways. I don't think I could walk 10 miles tomorrow morning. That's too far. But I could walk to the end of the block. Easy. Well, 10 of those blocks and that's a mile. Then ten of those and that's 10 miles. So if I could only walk one block a day and 10 blocks was a mile, I could walk 10 miles in 100 days. That's 1/3rd of a year or 4 months. So if that's my big obstacle, my big goal, my big dream and I could achieve it with tiny steps every day, and I'd have it in under 4 months, why wouldn't I start walking? One block a day is nothing.

Can you improve something by just 1 percent a day? Whatever you do, whatever you love, whatever you want to learn, fix, or get closer to; can you improve that by only 1 percent? It's so small it's almost immeasurable. And that's the point. Even without compounding that would equal 365 percent at the end of the year. Who wouldn't love to be 365 percent (or 3.65x) better at anything they do every day, by year's end?

The main difference between that "great idea" you had and the one some other guy had who is making millions, is that the other person didn't just DREAM. She DID. There are a lot of dreamers in this world, like the ones who post daily affirmations in your social media feeds. And there are doers in this world. We all need people who actually perform the function and crank those wheels of industry. But it's the DREAMERS who also DO who make all the difference. Few do both.

That's where I want you to reside — in the universe between dreaming and doing, such that you're accomplishing both.

Musician Ted Nugent once said: "You're born at point A and you die at point B. In between, kick maximum ass." I don't even know if I like Ted Nugent very much. But I would take advice from him, as he has a perspective and attitude that has worked for him. If nothing else, he lives with authenticity.

People usually need direction, even if their ego tells them otherwise. And they need to receive that direction in progressive steps. And they need to hold themselves accountable for doing the work and taking the steps. Otherwise, the advice in this book or any book is equivalent to scrolling through your social media account for inspirational quotes like a lifeless zombie. You're obtaining the information, but you're not doing anything with it. You nod your head. Good point, but you continue to sit there scrolling down to the next pithy quote, letting the prior one evaporate. Waste of time.

If you read a book about saving 15 percent of your paycheck, the hours and weeks invested in that book will probably motivate you to implement a plan for saving 15 percent of your paycheck, which could make you a millionaire fast. But reading that same quick quote on Facebook: "Save 15 percent of your paycheck" only gets a nod of recognition and maybe a thumbs up. There's no real call to action. There's no substantial take away that you ever really implement into your daily routine because without the book's guidance, it's just tacit acknowledgment.

This is the type of character for which we Hollywood producers create story for the undeveloped, unrealized hero in Act I — the listless readers who read the information but aren't digesting and processing it. They are consumers, not creators. They focus on output, not input. That is, until we make them stand up and get off the couch and experience the world in color. We produce them.

The irony is that someone can spend every morning for 20 years complaining how it's difficult to get out of bed, jump in the car and fight the traffic to work, all the while worried about being late to an office meeting. But you could take just 30 minutes to sit down, write some numbers, write a plan, and make that go away in one day. What has been ineffectual, in this example, is 5,000 days of torturous mornings without someone taking the time to fix it.

But if one produces his morning so it's an incredible gift to himself, he can own his day. It just takes developing and implementing better habits. There's no reason you can't look forward to the parts of your day that are frequent drags by mixing them and making them spectacular. Whether mornings or afternoons, there are clear habits and patterns that will turn those sluggish times into effective, energetic ones.

We are a species who shoots for the stars. We send people to the moon. Your going to Starbucks every morning, fighting the traffic, and waiting for your assistant to give you your daily schedule is a loop of Ordinary that with tiny daily 1 percent changes can compound into Special. Nothing that the hero does in these twelve stages has to create huge shifts to have a monumental impact. The tiny, regular, systematic habits will win the day. Always. And the days will win the weeks, which will win the months, which will win the years. And that's what your life is made of.

Think about how much time we spend:

- planning a wedding
- mapping out a road trip
- redecorating an apartment
- organizing a surprise birthday party
- searching for the perfect movie to watch
- deciding what classes to take in school
- putting together an outfit at the mall
- maintaining our car properly
- building an exercise routine
- making a grocery list for a dinner gathering

How much time have you spent working on a manual for your life?

How much time have you spent sitting down and saying to yourself, "I'm always chasing the day and never have enough time, I should stop what I'm doing, write a plan that works, and then adopt that plan"? Very few people know how to analyze themselves and then write a system to fix what isn't working. Some emulate the proverbial ostrich with its head below ground.

I love doing, analyzing, and improving. I've been doing it my whole life. Hollywood ended up being the perfect sanctuary for me to create, shape, and mold characters. In other words, be a producer.

I get to produce someone to be anyone. Why should that only be fictional?

Why can't you do that — for yourself? You can.

You can produce You.

-

CHAPTER 5

The Call To Adventure: Choices · Consequences Values
(Stage 2)

"We are who we choose to be."

— Willem Dafoe in *Spider-Man*

THE NEXT STAGE IN YOUR HERO'S MOVIE is to recognize that there's a Call To Adventure. We've already learned about your predicament and situation in your Ordinary World. Now we need to discover the impetus for improvement, whether you desire it or it's thrust upon you. And we need to see how, or if, you'll react to this compelling invitation to journey.

Maybe the hero senses her current situation could be better. Not that it's terrible, but she's aware it could be optimized. That in itself is a call to adventure — the evolvement to upgrade. Maybe she wants to diminish distraction or minimize unfulfilling activities. Maybe there are toxic people from whom she wants to separate. Or maybe she seeks laser clarity and awareness on a new project she's having difficulty with. Any of these can be calls for her to question her current situation and explore reasons she's not where she dreams of being.

Or, the hero might have the ideal situation going for her, but suddenly a family member falls ill or unexpected tragedy strikes. Some incendiary agitation or event is thrust upon her. Life happens and it could turn her into despair, throwing a new Call to Adventure at her to reframe what's meaningful in her life.

- In "The Hunger Games," Jennifer Lawrence's Call to Adventure is volunteering to join a deadly game so she can spare her sister's life (reluctant call).
- In "Fight Club," Edward Norton's IKEA-filled apartment blows up (involuntary call).
- In "The Wizard of Oz," a huge tornado sweeps through Kansas (passionate call after song: "Somewhere Over the Rainbow").
- In "The Matrix" or "Back To The Future," Keanu Reeves and Michael J. Fox literally receive a phone call requesting they accept the adventure (surprise calls).
- In "The Natural," Robert Redford leaves his farm for big city baseball (intrinsic call).
- In "Shawshank Redemption" Tim Robbins is sentenced to prison (situational call).
- In "Good Will Hunting," Matt Damon can avoid prison by accepting therapy sessions with Robin Williams (compromising call).

The call isn't always self-generated. Usually, in fact, it isn't (ironic, given we are describing a courageous and gutsy character). The resolute action on the hero's part is merely recognizing and contemplating the call — realizing there's an opportunity to leave her Ordinary World for one with greener pastures, but it doesn't mean she'll easily accept, or accept at all.

These calls are all around us. The hero simply observes and distinguishes this call from other distractions as an invitation to leave the unremarkable and perfunctory current world.

- Baby in "Baby Driver" gets the call from waitress Lily James when she dreams of hitting the road and never looking back. Baby hates the predicament he's in driving getaway cars for Kevin Spacey. This Call To Adventure gives him pause.

- Jennifer Grey witnesses "Dirty Dancing" through a cabin's window — literally a window into a new world for her. But should she leave her family's traditional summer vacation for this? Is this appropriate?

- Whereas Kevin Spacey's "window" in "American Beauty" is fantasizing about his daughter's friend at a school event, which is the catalyst wake-up call that his mundane and "perfect" life actually sucks. But should he accept this call? What does it even mean?

- The students in "Dead Poet's Society" aren't aware of their Ordinary World until teacher Robin Williams inspires them to live authentically and "seize the day." Only then do they realize how rigid their existence is. Robin Williams challenges their Ordinary World — that's their Call to Adventure.

We can't change things beyond our control, but we can choose how to react to those things. I'm not saying: "Don't feel" when misfortune knocks. Do feel. But become a lightning rod rather than a mop in a bucket, and illuminate the darkness so you can make the right choices.

The hero in the movie reacts heroically because that's how she is written. She is written to fall into the pool at the wedding and have her career sideswiped by a competitor. That makes her human, accessible and sympathetic. She has more failures than wins. This is heroic and describes the majority of female driven romantic comedies, like "Bridesmaids" or "Trainwreck." How she next reacts and responds to the call is what separates her from a supporting, non-heroic character. It doesn't necessarily happen right away, but it does require a response. Eventually.

The call is for you, the hero, to be proactive and be accountable for your current Ordinary World, reactions and subsequent steps. Don't blame anything on anyone else or any situation. Stuff happens. Cards are dealt. Pick yourself up, grab your tools (you have them: but they might be hiding beneath the distraction and clutter of your life), and move forward.

I occasionally have employees who love to blame their deficiencies on external factors, rather than develop a positive and effective routine. I get why they do it. It's comfortable and safe to justify an unfavorable situation and blame it on extraneous occurrences. It deflects attention from themselves. I'm sure you've heard it, too. It's become a sort of social currency (even welcomed comedy) to complain at the office water cooler. People find community in commiseration. It's cool to criticize the office politics, infrastructure, co-workers, or the project you're working on.

Here are some complaints:

- "Well, I wouldn't have been late to this creative meeting but for the horrendous traffic!"

Here's how I interpret that: "I don't respect my career and co-workers enough to properly budget my time and allow for the fact there will always be traffic. I haven't learned to prioritize — which happens the day before in scheduling my evening (I was out drinking), which prompts my sleep schedule (I was binge-watching), which prompts my morning rituals (I was on Facebook) — so I can find clarity and win the day. So I was forced to jump in the car in defense mode (everyone drives like a moron), accomplishing the bare minimum of functions (putting socks on in the car), with no time to spare and arrive at the office 15 minutes late. And not only do I arrive late, I arrive unprepared because my tardiness became the focus of my morning. I had no room for thought, whimsy, contemplation — qualities I need to contribute to a creative meeting."

I acknowledge my translation may be a bit harsh. But it's not the traffic's fault. It's the one dozen steps in the flow of the employee's priorities that resulted in his being late. And, just to put the nail in this employee's pink-slip, his being 15 minutes late to a project meeting with, say, 6 other people equates to 1.5 person-hours lost.

This concept is similar to the sports buff who yells at the kicker during the last 5 seconds of a football game who misses the one extra point that would have won the game for the team. It's all the kicker's fault. He is to blame for the loss of the game. What about the 4 quarters of play that preceded with 10 other teammates contributing? Did none of that equally necessitate the extra point? Apparently, mistakes are forgiven in the 1st quarter but not the 4th.

- "I'm shouldering all the work because so-and-so doesn't know how to communicate."

Everyone communicates. That's what they do, even in silence. Communication isn't the issue; it's a scapegoat. The issue is clarity. And clarity is a two-way street. If you don't ask the right questions or articulate the information in a digestible fashion, you won't get the right answers. If you don't foster an environment to take criticism or hear ideas, you may as well work with a robot rather than with a human being.

Seek clarity by giving others the proper tools to generously communicate with you. A baby has no clarity so it cries. And so will your colleagues if you ineffectively articulate what you want or need from them.

And equally, foster a culture where employees (or substitute friends and family here as needed) can speak freely and honestly. When someone can't be honest, their critical, impactful work is dulled by censoring. If they have to constantly mince words and lawyer their comments, the benefit of collaboration in the first place is lost.

- "I'm working 18 hours a day and need a vacation. I work too hard."

A vacation is the last thing you need if you work 18 hours a day. A vacation won't provide you with the habits to learn to be more effective and accomplish 18 hours of work in 6 hours. You're highly ineffectual if you are working too many hours.

If anything, you should double-down and do the opposite. You should be working more hours to figure out how to work smart and cut the fat. Great things that get accomplished don't necessarily happen because people work longer hours. Rather, they happen because the people involved work effectually. That can be 15 minutes or 4 hours. But people mistakenly conflate the number of hours worked with quality of output. It's a false equation with diminishing returns.

Blame yourself for mismanagement of your resources. What you need is to put pen to paper, journal and map out how you spend those 18 hour days. If you didn't do this in the last chapter for your bio, do it now.

There is plenty of time in everyone's day. But successful people know how to use their time wisely and make it impactful. They delete. They say "No." They prioritize. They work less, because "working" less means having more time to process and strategize the more significant multipliers for whatever they're doing.

Allocating time to clear your mind and lead the issue rather than follow it will save you from 18 hours of nonsensical work that likely doesn't even need doing. Just 1 hour of deep planning on complex and impactful issues will usually kill 4 to 5 times that in lighter, superficial tasks. Many of those become irrelevant.

If you're working 18 hours a day I suspect you're wasting time on email, social media, gossip, and administrative distraction disguised as productivity. Those things simply devalue your time and worth.

- "I'm so mad at my boss for promoting so-and-so when I've been here forever and work twice as many hours. She's an idiot."

Most likely your boss hires the person who makes her job easier. You, working longer and more, don't make her life easier. If you're an hourly employee, it, in fact, costs her more. 80 percent of being a boss is hiring. So if you're not being promoted, getting a raise or given the opportunity to advance to the next level, you are the problem, not your boss.

Take responsibility and be better than the next guy, or leave. Prove to your boss that you are deserving. Take the Call To Adventure where you're appreciated, recognized, or able to change your attitude and benefit your boss.

It's basically all YOUR responsibility. It's yours to win, and yours to lose. You have a set of choices you can make. You can do what you want; live where you want; get married and have children or not; work for yourself or someone else; have more time for outdoors or climb the corporate ladder; exercise or watch TV; eat healthily or eat fast food; buy an expensive suit or don't wear a suit. Whatever you want, it's up to you. And if you tolerate anything long enough, that is what you want. That is what you chose for your Ordinary World.

Don't smoke and then blame your later lung cancer on something other than cigarettes. Don't eat junk food daily and then complain that it takes too long to lose weight in the gym (you control what's on the end of your fork. That's all it comes down to). Don't seclude yourself at home and complain you don't have good friends. These are all choices you make and they have consequences that create other consequences. Don't forget the Law of Unintended Consequences. Sometimes it bites.

And the opposite is true. Saving, eating healthy, budgeting your time, all are simple and quick upfront activities with lasting consequences on the back end. Seeds become trees. Trees bear fruit. Fruit becomes a compounding multiplication of seeds that in turn makes an entire orchard. We reap what we sow.

Recognize opportunity. Make choices. And take the Call To Adventure rather than complain and outsource your accountability to someone else. People preclude themselves from the Call To Adventure when they shield themselves from responsibility.

You are responsible for those decisions and can do whatever you want, whenever you want, and in whatever amount you want. But be accountable for those decisions. Don't blame the traffic, the credit card company, the landlord, the co-worker, the ex-boyfriend, or the line at the post office or DMV.

You weren't born yesterday, and for every problem, there is not only a solution, there are elegant hacks and ways to improve anything repetitious. You know this. Stop to access the tools, most of which are already at your disposal, waiting for you.

Step back and think about that "thing" you do 14 times a day and seem to hem-and-haw every time you do it. Yet you automatically repeat the process because it makes you feel productive, when in fact you're wasting time and energy. Take the call. Fix it. Improve it so you don't do it 14 times daily.

If you do anything 14 times a day, pretend it's a puzzle. Stop. Sit down and say okay, how can I do this 13 times a day (baby steps), and then 12 the next day, and so on. I assure you, you have the answer right under

Produce Yourself

your nose. You just haven't taken responsibility. You have the ultimate power to fix it.

You're the CEO of You, Inc. Treat your flaws, inefficiencies, and shortcomings as challenges. You, Inc. has just been hired to solve those problems. What plans do you propose? You do that at work. Why not do it for yourself? The benefits are exponential when you solve yourself.

You are an ever-adapting organism who can learn and accelerate better habits. You are the variable that overrides and solves fixed, repetitive problems.

But sometimes the problem doesn't need fixing. Sometimes you need to let the problem exist. Take it as a sign, a Call to Adventure, and go find your inspiration.

Here's an exercise for you:

- If you never had another bill in your life starting today...
- If all of your debt, student loans, and obligations mysteriously went away this very moment...
- If circumstance and logistics need not be a consideration...
- If money was just falling on you left and right and you could do anything to occupy your time, what would you do?

One rule is that you have to have a career — you must pick something — but you're doing it free. There is no payment, fee, or compensation of any kind, and you don't need it because money is insignificant in this exercise. But you have to do something. Contemplate it — what would it be?

- Would you want to be an interior designer because you love to shop, love people, love colors, fabrics, furniture, design?

- Would you be a sports commentator because you love watching and analyzing sports?
- Would you write, photograph, sing, paint, build, travel, manage, haul, fix, consult, teach, sew, train, speak, sell?
- What is your purpose?

That — that purpose — is what you need to be doing, or else doing everything to get in line for, and within the vicinity of, that purpose. If there are issues and problems to solve within that purpose, tackle them. But if the obstacles you're bumping into are outside your purpose, let them be the impetus to possibly change zip codes.

I'm loosely paraphrasing here, but Warren Buffett has an exercise where he says to list the top 25 things you want to do in life — everything that you ever hope to accomplish. (Spoiler alert — if you want to do this exercise, don't read beyond this paragraph until you've done it).

Then, he says prioritize the top 5 of those 25 and put them on a new piece of paper. Make a new list.

Now, the original list of 25 things you want to do in life: discard it. And for the rest of your life, just look at only those top 5. That's it. Spend the rest of your life doing everything it takes to accomplish those 5 and never look back at the other 20.

I assure you your purpose is somewhere in those top 5, if not a hybrid of some of those top 5.

And those other 20? Good stuff there? Don't look back. This is why so many people are distracted, spread thin, and can't focus and excel at their purpose(s). They are pursuing too many random things. Stick with your 5.

Produce Yourself

If, for some miraculous reason, you accomplish and excel at those 5, I'm sure an inspiration or side-hustle may surface from the other 20 you tossed. Buffett doesn't mention this. But I'm giving you some leeway.

There are dozens of ways to make money, and make great money at any pursuit, as obscure or odd as it may seem. But you must first dream it. You have to contemplate what it is that you truly want. This is why I remove money from this equation in discovering aspirations. The money will follow. It always does. Your passion will become contagious; your process will then be authentic. And the myriad ways to monetize will find you when you create a good or service that you genuinely care about.

Others will see that. There's a scarcity of goods and services where it's obvious the owner loves what they do. That makes those few purpose-followers unique and successful.

I learned in business classes that in order to problem solve, you simplify the parameters to a basic model, then analyze that over-simplified model for perspective. I like doing this for most predicaments, business or otherwise, where you shrink your heavy burdens and problems down to something silly, like the ant exercise in the last chapter. Proper perspective is crucial.

I read about a guy who has been at the Xerox plant for 30 years assembling parts. I hear about the accountant sitting in a dingy office in an old building for 40 years filing returns. Day in, day out. If those people were ants, that might seem normal.

It has been estimated that around 70 percent of workers in the USA are unhappy at their jobs. I find this regrettable, if not sad. Perhaps the people above are not unhappy. But what if they are?

Life offers so much. Why are we getting up and moving dirt from this side to that, like an ant? For some of us, it's all we know. Only — we do know better. But we don't recognize the Call To Adventure.

I was fortunate. I admit that. I have super-supportive parents who wanted me to pursue whatever my heart desired. We don't all get that kind of support. We are all products of environment. We aren't all dealt the same hand. We have to make the best with what tools and support system we've been given. But it's not the hand you're dealt. It's how you play the cards.

It would take me almost 5 years to recognize the Call to Adventure. This is why I emphasize these points.

Maybe I was the ant.

So often it's not until we're adults and looking for the next chapter of our lives that we recognize that we're either on the wrong path or need to find the courage to carve a new one. Sometimes while walking a new one, we realize that path is wrong too. It's a discovery process — trial and error, backtracking and re-routing.

Developing story is no different. Ask any writer and she'll tell you the process is one of going down a path, backing up, scrapping, reshaping, editing, throwing out entirely, starting over, changing mid-way, rewriting an ending, removing a character, introducing another, changing the tone, the feel, the vibe. The choose-your-own-adventure options are endless.

And so are yours in real life. I don't care if you're 82 and thought it would have been fun to study law and become a private practice attorney. You can do it. You must.

The end game is never what's important. It's the journey. Reading the book, seeing the movie, is what's enjoyable. The ending is just that: the ending. You won't watch a terrible TV show just because you want to get to the ending you heard is amazing. That experience is terrible. But you can watch a fantastic episode of TV despite its bad ending. You'll still talk about and love that series, even if you hated how "The Sopranos" or "Seinfeld" or "Game of Thrones" ended.

Remember, your ending may be irrelevant. It's mainly the journey that matters.

If your rich, fulfilling life ends at age 40, isn't that better than living to 100 unhappy and slumped in a lazy-boy? You should never reach the end because your goals keep evolving and growing. There are lookout points along the way — rest stops, picnic areas, bathroom breaks.

But when you find that enjoyable path to hike, you don't need to reach the final destination. You want to keep hiking. Don't pressure yourself that you've not arrived. If it's that frustrating for you that you need to see your final destination right now, then you're perhaps not hearing the Call To Adventure that tells you to advance from your Ordinary World.

The adventure is everything and if you're not enjoying it, pay attention to the warnings and signs around you. Don't think, "Oh, I'll be happy once I get there. It's gonna suck for the next 10 years, but then it'll be fantastic." It doesn't work that way.

If you don't love studying and being a student for at least 12 years after high school (and continuing education forever thereafter), you should never become a physician. The journey of being a doctor is never ending, and it's constant studying for the rest of your life. That is the course — and a very enjoyable one if you love to study and learn abundantly every day. But there's no end game. You are never done.

If people would stop putting pressure on the result or end-game (the one they never reach anyway) they'd be happier and make choices that better suit them.

Take relationships or marriage, for example. Don't worry if you're going to marry a specific person or not, or if you're even going to get married. The pressure and unnecessary societal weight are what keeps relationships from growing, evolving, or existing in the first place.

Many break-ups are lazy. Many unexplored relationships sit idle. Many relationships never transpire because we disproportionately weight a false set of parameters like "forever," "always," "never," and "marriage."

I wager there's someone in your past whom you memory-rotate every now and then, wondering whatever became of him or her. What would it be like if you were still together? Things don't seem so bad now that you've had distance, growth, and perspective. Not to imply you don't love your current relationship, but rather that you have regrets over prematurely ending something, or ending it in a suboptimal manner.

We all do this when we're coming of age. We're learning, experimenting, and exploring. It's actually one of the best assets of youth: that one can access the power of the present more and be playful. But due to inexperience and ignorance, we also discontinue friendships and relationships impulsively and carelessly because of the thought of being around "that behavior" for the rest of our lives.

I've had over 30 relationships. Some amazing ones. Some learning experiences. Some very short ones that were intensely 24/7 for only 2 weeks. Had I surrendered to societal pressures that every time I was "with" someone, it was an audition for "forever," certain ones might have lasted longer. This is not necessarily a good thing.

Aside from primal chemistry, the only consequential barometer in evaluating relationships should be one's values. Do your values align? If they do, other stuff doesn't matter. When people constantly argue and declare incompatibility, it's usually because their values aren't in sync, and unfortunately, they may never be.

I don't know that values are something that change much over time. It may take time to discover what your true values are, but you basically have them from when you were a kid.

Produce Yourself

That's my take. I may be wrong. We obviously evolve as new inputs are introduced to our environment. We improve our reactions, attitude, and mindset as we grow and experience new stimuli and events. But our core compass is usually fairly fixed. So we learn to adapt and suppress our differences as much as possible, but only until they reach a tipping point of noncompliance. At that point, values are too out of sync.

What are your values? Have you ever stopped to think about them?

Here's another exercise. It's another tool your inner hero can use on the journey when finding your allies, making decisions, and seeking collaborative opportunities.

Ask yourself: What am I unwilling to compromise on? What is your "religion," as in, what is your "way of life"? Those are your values.

Here are 10 of my fundamental values to help your list along. Most of these are expanded on throughout the book. This isn't my complete list, but ones possibly accessible and recognizable to most people.

1. Honesty. I need to be able to speak my mind without worrying about consequences. When I start censoring, my focus is tainted by future reactions. I want to be honest and want honest people in my life. There's a responsibility that comes with honesty: to be clear, accurate, and generous. Honesty requires articulation and thought. It's tough, especially with employees, to find those who are honest. I don't want "yes men" to simply make me happy. That concerns me and I won't hire them. They don't benefit me and vice-versa.

2. Selflessness. I've had to cut people out of my life, some who were fun to be around, made me laugh, and showed me a good time. I sometimes miss them. But I can't foster a one-way street when it becomes clear the other person is a vacuum, always needing, consuming and taking from me. You'll read later in this book the importance I place on providing value to your tribe and surrounding yourself with people who increase

your average. Selfish people do the opposite of that. Those people should simply clone themselves and have a beautiful life with their 4 replicates.

3. Punctuality. This falls somewhat in the Selflessness category. Emergencies and unexpected events will always happen. But chronic tardiness to any activity, whether it be work or pleasure, discounts the value of the other person's time. The aggregate of minutes and hours you wait for someone, when you've already sacrificed and properly planned to accommodate the agreed-upon time, compounds into months and years. It's not okay for someone to consistently show up 15 minutes late. Their ill-preparation should not become your loss in schedule, efficiency, time or focus. Be early. Get in the zone. Imagine how much more effective and competent meetings would be if all parties brought their groomed A-game. This is what I like about movies in a physical theater. They have a set start time whether you're there or not. Funny how some respect a film's start time more than a meeting with a person. Time is the most valuable asset anyone has. You will never get it back and cannot generate more.

4. Big Picture Outlook. I can't collaborate or work with people who only see two feet in front of them, constantly adjust and make quick decisions based on what's at hand. Short-term thinking produces short-term results, which don't last. Long-term thinkers win at life and understand the benefit of doing things once, right, smart so that short-term problems don't surface in the first place, or at least as often.

5. Gratitude. I refuse to be around people who complain for complaint's sake — meaning the people who default to this behavior as a resting, normal state. "Seinfeld" is my favorite sitcom ever. In the context of comedy, it's masterful. But in actuality, I couldn't spend five minutes with the four main protagonists because they do nothing but complain. Complaining is easy. It's basic, lazy, and takes no skill or effort to just spew problems into the universe. But it takes thought, presence of mind, and proactive habits to address problems with solutions. It takes a mind

tempered with gratitude to appreciate the complexities and colors of life. And it takes sympathy of a grievance to solve the problem, even if that means saying "No" or amputating a person from your life. Gratitude helps form a habit of sourcing solutions before the problem or complaint has time to surface. This leads to...

6. Silence. People love to gossip. It makes them feel better to diminish someone else. It's cheap, fast food that goes down easy. We all like to catch up and hear what someone's doing. But I can't surround myself with people who make a habit of putting someone down for no other reason than to get a reaction or fill space with small talk. I value comedy. I value levity. I also value silence. It is one of the lost tools that heroes tend to find on their journey. It's powerful and has so many benefits. But the complete opposite of meditating and listening to your inner hero is inimical gossip and hearsay. There's a reason the hero in film is often quiet, while the sidekick does all the talking.

7. Movement. Immobility is depressing. I can't align with people who don't move, seek adventure, take advantage of their time, play, work, create, explore, exercise, experiment, dream and do. The body and the mind need movement every day. This is one of my most fundamental values. Friends and ex-girlfriends who didn't move didn't last long. And it's not that they didn't fit my values; it's that I didn't fit theirs. I don't want to smoke pot, sit on the couch, and watch 12 hours of "The Kardashians." That's great if you do. I totally get it. But we will argue over tiny things that have more to do with this value than whatever those "things" are.

8. Boredom. This is related to movement. I have no one in my life who says to me: "I'm bored." I have the opposite, because we share the same values. I have friends and family who tell me they're excited, they're concerned, they're frustrated, or they're feeling energetic. They are lively and full of vigor and feeling, good or bad. Whether consciously or not, we have aligned with each other, as our values are similar. I may write this a dozen more times in this this book: life is simply too short. I'm not sure

how anyone in my community can ever be bored. There is too much to discover and explore in this world. It would take me 7 lifetimes to find boredom after exhausting my purpose, passions, and muses.

9. Health. I can't be around people who don't exercise, either their mind or their body. I can't be around people who hate themselves, sometimes manifested by their diets and habits (sleep, exercise, creation). I realize we all are blessed or cursed with certain genes we can't change. This value has nothing to do with appearance, weight or addiction. It has everything to do with attitude in loving yourself and caring for your own existence because you cherish life and want to be alive to enjoy it as long as possible.

10. Accountability. I have little patience for people who blame others and don't take responsibility. This value is described in detail throughout the book, as it's a value of almost every hero in cinema. It's relevant and personal at every stage the hero encounters.

For me, a sub-value of this is finances. People love to blame the market, the economy, a lost job, student debt, and bills. But no one's finances are as a result of any of those. Their finances, good or bad, are a result of agreements to make a purchase and subsequently have a bill due because of that purchase.

It's easy to blame credit cards. But what are credit cards? They're simply an ambassador of your bills. You purchased, received, and enjoyed the new bean bag office chair and agreed to pay $300 for it. But now, 30 days later there's a bill for that $300. You choose not to pay it because you don't understand basic math. If you make minimum payments, that $300 will now take almost 4 years to pay off at the average credit card rate of 14.5 percent. Credit card companies love people like you.

A person gains weight when they consume more calories than they burn. When they don't budget their rate of caloric burn properly, they gain weight. Finances are no different. By spending what you don't have (eating too much), you gain debt (fat).

I likely sound pompous in describing my values. But that's the point. You will, too. These are the uncompromisable, the aspects of your integrity and existence that you can't relinquish. However, almost no one sits down to list them. Know your values and align with like-valued people. All of the small stuff will work itself out. But values are stubborn.

I live my life in my current relationship (11+ years now) as chapters at a time, just like the stages of the hero. I don't know what the next chapter will hold. I'm enjoying the book, living mindfully, and turning the page and the story is awesome. I'm enjoying the movie. I love this girl; I'm crazy about her. But will we be together 10 years from now? Next year? I don't know. And for that reason, I'm happy. I get to cherish each day as a new gift without expectations.

Time gives us wisdom. And wisdom gives us perspective. My perspective is that there isn't any "one" person for us. And that romantic notion is what hurts us.

There may be 20 people in the world you'd be compatible and in love with. But you have to remove the pressure of "forever" to find those people. I wouldn't be enjoying such a multi-chaptered book with my girlfriend had I not removed this pressure. The delicious irony is now I just want to be with her forever.

One of the biggest flaws in thinking is that we have to be where we are because of the choices we made in the past. You absolutely are where you are because of your past choices. But today is today, and today you can equally make whatever choices you want to emerge and expand. You, today, are the result of your past choices. But you, tomorrow, are equally the result of your choices today. How's that for existentialism?

Today is your do-over. Actually, every day of the hero during the entire journey is a do-over. The hero doesn't accept the notion that a past decision need dictate their present decision.

In economics, there's a theory called sunk costs. It stuck more than any other theories I learned in business school, not as it relates to business, but in helping my hero make better decisions.

The theory basically states that if a cost has already been incurred, it can't be recovered. It was made in the past, so it's gone. Therefore, regardless the corresponding benefit of the product or service as a result of that cost, the decisions that one must make in the present can't include that cost as a factor.

I'll further explain it by the exact same story my economics teacher explained it to our Econ 101 class my freshman year in college.

You paid $200 for the tickets to the upcoming U2 concert this weekend. You love U2 and are super excited to go. It's completely sold out.

A day before the concert, five of your best high school friends are coming into town to see you. They want to go down to the beach and catch up.

What do you do? They can't go to the sold out concert with you. And you just paid $200, which is a ton of money for a starving college student. Do you go to the concert and then meet up with them the next day? Or do you throw away $200 and hang out with your friends? There's a correct answer, but it's not necessarily what you think.

The answer is actually reframing the question to simply: "Would you rather go to a U2 concert or hang with your friends at the beach?" Because the $200 is a sunk cost. The second you completed the transaction and purchased the ticket, that $200 became a sunk cost. It's gone. So whatever you do in the future — the very next second, minutes, weeks — shouldn't factor in the $200. It has to be removed from the equation.

A day before the concert. You have to make a decision. You can still do anything and everything you want to. You're not losing $200 by even lying in your bed and deciding to say 'No' to all of the above and taking a nap. You spent the $200 in the past. It's gone no matter what.

Now, in the present, you need to make a decision as to what will bring you the most enjoyment and satisfaction, period. Today, right now, you decide on a concert or the beach. That's the proper question to ask.

As pedantic as this may seem, it has enabled me to make decisions on my journey I wouldn't have otherwise. It's contributed to my attempt to live in the now, be present, and focus on today rather than yesterday. If I think a concert isn't worth $200, then I won't spend it. If I do, then I'll spend it. But come the day of the concert, and come any day of my life, I have to ask myself, what activity is going to give me the most benefit, the most value, and the most satisfaction?

I can't grudgingly go into a situation because I feel I need "my money's worth." That's a recipe for unhappiness because it's never about the money. It's about the emotional attachment you put on the money and think you now deserve because you've spent it.

Allow the future version of you to benefit by making the decisions and taking the actions that you can take today for Future You. Future You is just an infant and counting on you to properly plan and invest to take care of her. Past You doesn't exist, regardless of what she paid, trained for, or spent 20 years chasing. She's gone.

My larger life's Call to Adventure hit me like an electric shock during my senior year in high school.

I was nervously sitting in my childhood bedroom with a girl during a high school party. It was the end of the school year and everyone would soon be taking off to various colleges.

I had only gone on one date with this girl and I thought I liked her. I was trying to impress her so I told her to check out a video I made the prior weekend.

Flashback to a montage of the last couple of summers and you would see that for no other purpose than silly fun, I was running around with a video camera making shorts with my friends — music videos, spoofs, silly soap operas, SNL-type sketches, fake weather broadcasts. I was the one kid with the camera so it was always fun for everyone to drink at my parent's house and be silly in front of the camera. If only YouTube existed back then.

But again, this was pure, 100 percent fun. No one took these seriously. I certainly didn't. It was just a novelty to be able to film something and see it instantly on your TV. It was more about the gimmick, less about the content.

While sitting on my bed with this girl as she laughed at the little short we had made, I was hoping to steal a kiss from her. She could not have been more glued to the TV. I was hoping she'd find our little catch-a-drug-dealer short funny. So it ended and she turned to me and said, "So, you're gonna be a film director, right?"

I wish the camera had been on me when she asked that question. I was actually annoyed and insulted. Without processing or thinking that she was actually complimenting me, I indignantly retorted, "I'm going to be studying business."

Suffice it to say, I didn't get that kiss. It got a little uncomfortable. We sat like awkward teenagers drinking, and then she eventually left the room going back downstairs to the party in progress.

Produce Yourself

But this bothered me. She made me think.

My Ordinary World had been challenged. I received a Call to Adventure from this girl, who wasn't even significant in my life. I was so confident and secure with who I was and what I was going to become when I grew up, that receiving this paralyzing question was a bit frightening. I asked myself, "Could I become some film person?" I didn't know titles or roles. All I knew was that business people were revered and looked up to. Wasn't a film person one with a hat and megaphone working out in the cold somewhere? I think the stereotypical cartoon was all I could conjure, having no reference. I discounted the night's experience as a stupid moment between teenagers.

But in the weeks that followed, I couldn't stop worrying if I was suddenly making some awful mistake. Should I be a film major instead of business? They didn't even have a film major at the school I would soon attend.

People loved my little videos. I had so much fun making them. Was that something people did? I had math class in high school. I didn't have film class. How could this be a tangible vocation? It seems ridiculous now to think that I didn't put 2 and 2 together. I loved my video camera. I loved writing sketches. I loved having all my friends be actors in them. But it was pure silly fun. There were no retakes and no one ever did a bad job.

I was stuck on an image of who I should be based on the narrative I heard from others. I didn't know how to access emotions and an awareness of my purpose. But the call came in for me to adventure in an unexpected form.

My image of my identity was challenged, and I thought I had to defend it. Without knowing it at the time, I had a brand that I liked.

In my group of friends, I was always the leader. I was active, I took risks, and I was always in charge of school or weekend activities. Wasn't that what a businessman did? I wanted to be in a band, I started one. I wanted to make money, I started a tutoring business. I wanted our school to have a newspaper, I started one. It was always like this for me. I created my own destiny.

So to have a girl whom I met at a party assume I was going to be a film director meant nothing to me. I rejected that Call to Adventure. I never spoke to her again. But she's never disappeared from memory (interestingly, she attended a university with possibly the best film program in the world).

I was heading to business school where important people went to study.

CHAPTER 6

The Refusal: Detours · What Ifs Present Value Prevention
(Stage 3)

"Our lives are defined by opportunities, even the ones we miss."

- Brad Pitt in *The Curious Case of Benjamin Button*

ONCE OUR HERO HAS RECEIVED THE CALL, there is often a moment, however brief, of resistance. Sometimes this appears in the form of self-doubt, fear, or feelings of inadequacy. Other times, it's a friend who expresses doubt or confusion as to the logic of such an undertaking. The hero may second-guess herself.

Your community of trusted friends often wants to protect you but does so with its own set of priorities, motivations, and challenges. And, similar to other areas of life where "No" is typically a safe default, recommendations from your core tribe may be tainted with protective bias.

The risk inherent in a "Yes" carries more responsibility than the resignation of a "No." "No" keeps things even keel and smooth sailing. "Yes" makes waves, disrupts the tide, and rocks the boat. A "Yes" has consequences that may affect the person who voices it. That person might suddenly become culpable and have to support his reasoning.

It's important to acknowledge this when getting the Call to Adventure. Is this something that works for you, or is it maybe something that doesn't work for someone else?

Your loyal crowd is not necessarily filled with selfish or dishonest people. And, while it may not be even conscious, friends and family, at a minimum, have a predilection to protect their clan. They are predisposed to keep you safe from the dangers of the wild. However, protection from danger may also mean preclusion from adventure.

In "A Few Good Men," Jack Nicholson's infamous outburst: "You can't handle the truth," stems from his dogmatic instinct to protect.

In "The King's Speech," Colin Firth is hesitant to embark on an unheard of and unorthodox method to correct his stuttering. Even his closest advisors question the approach. There's inherent risk in the adventure.

In "The Social Network," Andrew Garfield makes Jesse Eisenberg examine whether forming Facebook is prudent, given a format wherein girls are compared to barnyard animals. Garfield's intentions are noble and an extension of his own moral compass, but not necessarily the best advice for the founder of Facebook. Still, there's a moment when Jesse Eisenberg is reluctant and questions the journey.

Condemning someone's attempt at a new system is common. It's expected. It's habitual. We are accustomed to memes and late-night jokes, all engendered from observation of someone doing something different, stretching the boundaries and challenging the norm.

But, assuming you are now a fully evolved adult, you have the freedom of choice to decide. Intellectually you know this. But in practice it's difficult. You can listen to your co-worker, you can listen to the doubt residing inside you, and you can refuse this Call to Adventure. It's your decision to make.

Regardless the reason for resistance, this stage is usually swiftly overcome in cinema, but rarely in real life. An audience won't put up with a hero who spends too much time avoiding or discounting opportunity. With a running time of 90-130 minutes, the hero is intended to get into the meatier, more visual aspects of the journey as soon as possible.

This Refusal stage is sometimes just a story device to display the balance of thought or highlight risk. Producers need the audience to connect with the hero, so she's written to have the same doubts and concerns that anyone might.

The hero's accessibility and empathy are paramount right out the gate. If a story fails to draw the audience to the hero's plight, it doesn't matter how entertaining or engaging it is. It will have failed at enlightenment (all story must have all three "e"s to be fulfilling to an audience). Enlightenment is the engine driving the entire journey. The hero seeks understanding and awareness to eventually improve her situation.

In "Million Dollar Baby," boxer Hilary Swank refuses nothing. She wants to box and wants the best trainer she can find, period. But we come to learn she can skip this stage of Refusal because she's not the hero. The hero is Clint Eastwood (can you blame him? He directed the movie). He is the one stuck in Refusal when he continually turns her offer down to train her. His policy is that he doesn't train girls, so he refuses the call.

In reality, the Refusal stage can stump and kill the hero. The journey ends right here during stage 3, leaving 9 more critical stages left unexplored.

I think every high school, for example, has those few individuals who never really left. They graduated but hung on as long as they could, finding local jobs at pizza joints or department stores, while the rest of their herd left for greener pastures. These individuals may have been the heroes of days past, spiking touchdowns, winning talent contests, and gaining popularity and affection. But in the global journey of their life, the entire post high school experience has been one Refusal (stage) to evolve and find their inner hero. They've sacrificed personal growth and transformation for short-term approval and decoration.

To me, it would be personal hell to remain in Refusal for eternity. I particularly like this anonymous definition of Hell: "On your last day on earth, the person you became will meet the person you could have become."

We all have one or two of these "lost souls" in our social network somewhere, reminiscing about the good old days and eating out of a bucket filled with should-have-could-have-would-have. These are the same individuals who like to justify just about every misfortune in their lives, outsourcing blame of their current state to third parties or events.

But in general, it's natural and human for all of us to go through and experience this stage as part of the 12 stages. If you've generated a litany of reasons why you can't accept the call, then you're similar to most heroes.

Sometimes the Refusal becomes the heroic call itself when the original call is involuntary.

For example, in "The Shawshank Redemption," Tim Robbins's involuntary Call to Adventure is being sentenced to prison. This is the journey he has to take, both visually and internally, mentally preparing for a completely new world. So in his case, it's his refusal to accept this fate that in turn becomes his personal Call to Adventure. His original one would be navigating and surviving prison, which he does quite well. He is aware of that call and becomes the tax guy for the warden to improve his accommodations. But his Refusal of this call is what saves him and makes him a hero by generating a new Call to Adventure — to start tunneling out of prison, one spoonful of concrete at a time.

However, in real life, the Refusal is typically complacency instead of risk. There's genuine risk in doing something new or different, especially when it's foreign to your experience or knowledge. But complacency is a powerful lure. It's how our evolutionary instinct for survival maintains safety from predators.

It's how we're programmed. Our operating system tells us not to go outside that door, not to reach into that cabinet, not to touch the fire on the stove — all for our safety and protection. We behave this way for survival of our species.

In other cases, one which happened in my personal case, the Refusal can become a new alternate Call to Adventure that detours the hero before getting her back on track. It's possible the larger call will happen, but the current Refusal supplants the main call with a smaller, temporary call. It becomes a tangential deviation, one that possibly will benefit her later, but it ultimately keeps her from answering the main call at the moment.

In this case, the Refusal is merely responding to a smaller parallel call that becomes important for whatever reason in the short-term. That's not to say this is the best decision for the hero. But based on everything she has to work with at the time, she takes the detour, ignoring or delaying the larger call.

This happened to me for almost 5 years. It wasn't until just 3 months before college graduation when I finally accepted my original

Call to Adventure from that girl at the party. It kept surfacing, trying to get my attention, but I repressed it in favor of a familiar, more comfortable narrative.

I went to business school. This was my alternate call. It was in the cards I was dealt, and I chose to play the hand this way. To this day, I am so grateful for that experience. I access it every day in most things I do, applying the principles to many aspects of life (you're getting a large dose of it in this book). But in hindsight, I'm also aware that my chosen college studies were largely my Refusal to accept the larger call to pursue film and TV.

If my Hero's Journey had been an actual movie that I was producing, I may have edited this alternate call for time. Or I may have made it a flashback to explain character development. Perhaps it would have made a good prequel.

That girl at the house party really shook my world in assuming I was going to be a filmmaker. And, like a recurring thought that haunts you in wee hours of quiet nights, I continued to lie in my college dorm room wondering if I was on the right path.

I found myself running around campus with my video camera, continuing to make little shorts, spoofs, and music videos for my fraternity. I would even put my name on everything I did, calling it a "Terence Michael Production." The call that wouldn't go away was staring at me in the face. I was aware of it. I struggled with it but reasoned that I had already bought my ticket and stood in line for my ride, and this was it — business school.

I didn't want to disappoint my supporters, my tribe, my family, and the story in which I had a character from a very young age. My sister always said (still says) I am Michael J. Fox from "Family Ties." He's the son in the sitcom who explains everything to his liberal hippy family in economic philosophy and business fundamentals. I actually liked the comparison. Today she'd probably update that to Jason Bateman from the TV series "Ozark" — similarly obsessed with economics.

The difference between rejecting the call and detouring is vast. Whereas rejecting the unrequited opportunity for a prosaic world is unheroic, discovering other nearby possibilities isn't. It's not necessarily heroic to take the detour, but it's also not necessarily unheroic. For every hero's journey has smaller extraneous ones, side trips if you will, some of which are important to answer and follow.

My overall college experience was a Hero's Journey unto itself, and each course I took, in turn, had its own journey, and each concept I grappled and tackled had yet another. Ditto this for every friendship I earned, every girl I dated, and every roommate I lived with.

But for my larger life's journey, I was stuck in the Refusal stage, circumventing yet another path, taking a long way around. This circuitous route would benefit me later, I would realize only in hindsight. Prospectively, it may have prevented or delayed opportunity.

Even today, decades later, I sometimes bemuse myself with how my life would be different had I accepted the call right then and there. I don't dwell on it as a mistake, but rather whimsy. How might my life have been different? Not necessarily better or worse — just different.

The whole Butterfly Effect makes it too difficult to attempt to predict the "what if" scenarios. The entire TV series "Lost" is rooted somewhat in this theory. What if someone had done something different? What if they didn't get on that plane? How is the parallel universe with you in it unfolding based on a set of different decisions you made? Is Gwyneth Paltrow better off in "Sliding Doors" having passed through those doors, or not? If a butterfly flaps its wings does it generate a sequence of events different than if it had not?

The choices we make, whether right or wrong, can always be questioned multiple ways in hindsight. So many people, situations, and things in our life are sometimes just at the end of a dozen pieces of strings tied together. You moved there, so you met him, who introduced you to her, who became your business partner, which caused you to work with them, which made you realize this, that, and the other; causing you to pivot and be whatever. That "whatever" end of the string is absolutely tied to the move you made at the top of the string. There are too many variables to know what would have happened by changing any one of those.

Don't let the "what ifs" keep you up at night. There is zero benefit in dwelling on anything you can't control. I know it's not easy, but it's only a toxic time drain. Concentrate on the "what now" which will help you appreciate the Now and find the current calls. The "what now"s will allow you to analyze Present You and see what is working — and what isn't.

If you feel nothing is working, freely dispose of things that contribute: ineffectiveness, repetition, fatigue, distraction, lassitude. It will engender a new set of approaches that does work. Like the butterfly that flutters its wings, you may need to fly left, rather than right; talk to a different person today, meet with a new person tomorrow, change your route and routine. Connect. Share. Collaborate. Discuss. Build.

Why should you change something that isn't working if you can deal with it? "The good outweighs the bad," you may reason. Or "Everyone has to go through this so I should consider myself lucky. I'll someday come up with a better way to address that."

Be grateful for the larger blueprint of your existence. But simultaneously tackle the activities that could be optimized to build a stronger foundation from your blueprint.

Starting and ending your day with the same pattern of incompletion or forfeiture is resistance. You are telling yourself that you aren't worthy enough to improve. You are allowing yourself to repeat, daily, a process that could be improved. But why bother? Why spend time and energy to change something that isn't killing you?

In "Good Will Hunting" Matt Damon refuses to address who he really is by scaring off half-a-dozen therapists with his intellect and hubris. There is an amazing person brimming with potential underneath a façade of resistance, who we see when the perfect girl stands in front of him. Even knowing his current life isn't working for him — getting in fights and evading the law — he refuses to let his new therapist, Robin Williams, help him find the way; find the authentic character buried beneath layers of abnegation.

I will continue to drive home this theme throughout the book, as it's one of the tools the hero utilizes at every stage: if something isn't working, STOP.

As the adage goes, when you find yourself in a hole, stop digging. I know it's trite and obvious, and easier said than done. Often the excuse is that you don't have time to make a change or attempt a new approach.

In the middle of a defective process, you often can't stop that second, because your current state is the result of your prior actions. So when I say if something isn't working: stop, I mean discontinue the steps that lead to the result that isn't working. Correct and adopt a better process so you don't repeat it tomorrow or next week.

For example, let's say you're the type to whiz through your kitchen to barely make/eat your breakfast before you jump in your car to fight the traffic to the corporate office in the morning. So there's no time to change what isn't working about your morning set-up. The few things you do just to get out the door you've got down to a science, so there's little time to inspect and implement. You're also worried you'll be late, so it's just "do" in the short-term, don't "think." You can't stop that morning system you employ. It's already too late because you've initiated the program long before you woke up. You justify that there's always tomorrow.

You think you're being efficient in a system you've developed to quickly blaze through accomplishing the bare necessities you need before hopping in the car. And given the circumstances, you are indeed efficient. But while you might be turning up the efficiency dial for your morning kitchen ritual, you're turning down a dozen other dials of effectiveness, exponentially negating the overall results where they matter. You want effectiveness, not necessarily efficiency.

Sticking with this example, if your morning is rushed, you probably aren't grabbing the healthiest food to eat, or aren't preparing it in a healthy way. You're having to chug down or heat up and take processed foods with you in the car (or worse, you're driving through fast food joints) — high in sodium, fat, sugar, with little nutritional value.

How much in aggregate is this, day after day, adding to the time you need to spend with a personal trainer to shed the extra pounds you've incrementally gained from this habit?

How much more money are you spending to counteract this approach with trendy detox diets, fad exercise equipment, or buying larger size clothes?

How much time is lost when you have a sugar or simple carb crash 3 hours later and need twice the time to find and return to your deeper work flow and concentration, but are stuck with a spinning pinwheel of death over your head?

If your morning is this rushed, are you flossing your teeth daily (like you should)? What does this in aggregate cost you at the dentist?

Are you stretching? Do you go from lying down to sitting? What in accumulated time and money is this costing you in terms of later posture issues, nerve numbness, stiff joints, and dozens of visits and perhaps thousands of dollars to the physical therapist? I've been there.

How much are you spending on excessive massages or other services to reduce and counter these results of being sedentary and stiff because of improper planning?

Is the expensive vacation you think you desperately need required to counteract a constant ineffectual routine that compounds itself, burying you in stress and obligation? Is that vacation just bringing you back up to zero when you've been operating in the negative for so long? A vacation should be a catapult to multiply your positive, not a tractor to pull you out of an unnecessary negative.

What are these short-term habits costing you in terms of relationship when you have to be short, curt, and even selfishly aggressive just so you can make it out the door to avoid tardiness?

How leveraged is the rest of your day, if you haven't meditated or at least pre-processed your priorities, or taken the time to strategize your day? A plan of action will affect your next day, giving you the extra time you lack. You don't want to join the playing field of work in defense mode, having to tackle and deflect everything that comes your way. Military strategy 101 dictates you will lose not only the battle but also the war.

What is this costing in terms of the value of your time, time for offensive play, commanding your own approach for the day, giving you the quality time you need to do what's effectual and cogent? When you're in defense mode, you can't determine what's important because you're treading water or sinking and ricocheting off every notification and distraction that reaches you. Rather than being able to devise and tackle your own outbox, you're stuck as a slave to the inbox of others.

We tend to float through life with the misconception that we just need to get through today. Tomorrow will be better. Well, tomorrow may be better if you invest in yourself today.

There's a simple concept in business called Net Present Value (NPV). Applied to life, it resides in the same concentric circles as compounding your growth and benefits, planting seeds for the future, and thinking long-term rather than short-term. NPV mathematically makes a comparison between something today vs. tomorrow or yesterday, removing the guesswork in decisions. It helps the hero by almost making the decision for her, with numbers that are relevant today.

For example, what if I lost a $100 bet with you and offered you two choices to collect? I will give you $100 today or, if you allow me to wait an entire year, I'll pay you $115. Which do you choose? Well, as attractive as $100 is today and everything you can buy and do with it, unless you can grow that $100 at least 15 percent a year (most people can't obtain anywhere near that kind of growth), the $115 in a year is the best choice. Not only will I pay you the $100 I owe, I'm simultaneously paying off a 15 percent investment for you. By delaying present-day gratification for a later date, favoring long-term strategy over short-term, you earn an extra 15 percent.

And the converse is true, where it may be less obvious. Let's say you're a marketing specialist and a business offers you $18,000 upfront to overhaul their marketing techniques. It'll take you 6 months to complete it. But a competing company needing the exact same services says if you'll do the job for them, they can match that $18,000 fee, plus give you a $300 gift card to a department store if you can wait to get paid until the job is complete in 6 months — a typical scenario in freelance.

Which deal do you take? The one with the extra $300 seems to be the best choice. But it's not. $300 extra sounds nice, but since it takes 6 months to get there from an $18,000 delay, that's a 3.3 percent annual

Produce Yourself

interest rate, which on average you can make more from investing. In fact, on average, you are losing 4.7 percent of your money by taking the $18,300 deal since historical averages with simple stock market investing have been 8 percent.

And, adding injury to insult, it's a gift card, forcing you to acquire more possessions. Potentially items you don't even need, but because it's "free" money, you spend and acquire depreciable oddities you don't even want. But they'll collect dust, need fixing, need storage, need selling, possibly costing you more in time than the money you spent. Congratulations. You just gave yourself a series of obligations.

This is just a long way of saying that you can apply the concept of investing growth to many things you do today. Sometimes small activities or functions you perform in the present may seem insignificant or trivial, but have a multiplier effect for the future.

This would appear to go against the concept of living mindfully in the Now and not worrying about the future. But it's just the opposite. It's a mindset shift of your hero, to absolutely think in present day terms, but wherein your Now is filled with gratitude and generosity for Future You. Live in the Now, but take small fractions of Now and store them as treasure for Future You's eventual Now.

It's like when you buy a gift for a loved one. It's usually fun to shop for them, thinking what they might like and how they'll react when they see the thought you put into a gift. Buying a gift for someone is often more for you, the donor, rather than the recipient, as you like the way you feel when you've found the perfect gift.

This is exactly the shift in thinking the hero acquires when creating "gifts" for herself. She still lives and enjoys the Now, but she knows Future She will have a more fulfilling Present She because of Past She. There's a ramp up to systematically building this. By doing so, every single day she receives "gifts" in the present due to past actions.

I currently invest in slip-and-fall complaints, generating between 11-13 percent returns on cash. A typical example is that Andrew slips and falls on a banana peel in a grocery store. He contacts a law firm to sue the grocery chain for negligence, etc. The law firm, who specializes in these cases, is able to calculate that, on average, they will be able to settle with the grocery chain for about $10,000. No one wants to go to court, but the chain will settle by keeping it quiet and not admitting fault. But this will probably take 6 months of negotiations, depositions, back and forth maneuvering, etc. Andrew wants his money now, today. He doesn't want to wait until tomorrow.

That's where I come in. I say to Andrew, tell you what. I'll give you $5,000 right now in exchange for the rights to your case. I'll take the risk that your case may never settle, and in fact, you might even lose, so I'm out $5,000.

For Andrew's own journey, this may be the best decision for him, taking $5,000 today for various needs and pursuits. So he agrees to it.

I give him the $5,000 cash and take the rights to his case, hopefully, worth the $10,000 per the law firm's estimates. I have now invested in the future value of this case settling. And, playing the averages of the law firm's track record to settle for $10,000 in 6 months, this would make me a nice, rather quick profit. Once you subtract expenses, the law firm's cut, the investment company's cut, and the averages of not all of these panning out, I arrive at my roughly 11-13 percent. And I don't invest in just Andrew's case. I invest in hundreds of these, creating a portfolio effect.

Every day Present Me is receiving a gift from the actions of Past Me. I live in the present, but benefit from my glimpse into the future

It's a phenomenal investment technique, taking advantage of NPV and Present Me giving gifts to Future Me. And today I am Future Me, thanking Past Me for these gifts.

Produce Yourself

The other benefit of this mindset is that whenever you take action today, much less effort in time and skill is required tomorrow.

It's like prevention. It's not sexy, it's not fun, and most people ignore prevention only to inherit disaster (or high costs) later, whether the arena is finances, health, relationships or career. "An ounce of prevention is worth a pound of cure," as Ben Franklin once wrote.

For example, do you check your tire air pressure once a month and make sure the tires are inflated properly, to the recommended pressure suggested by your car manufacturer (on the inside of the driver's side door jam. It's printed right there by law. Do NOT look at the actual tire, that's irrelevant)?

I know: you want to race through the gas station, so checking your tires is the last thing you have time for, as easy as it is (takes only minutes). But as part of your Refusal, you are substituting a false sense of time management for ill preparation, which would have eliminated the need for time management at the gas station in the first place if Past You was gifting Present You.

Is avoiding this two-minute tire check worth the 3 hours you're stuck at the auto shop when you prematurely need a new set of tires? And how long do you spend sourcing that tire shop to find the best price? Or what about the Uber you have to take from the shop to work, or hitching a ride from a friend, now infringing on their time? What about the $1,100 it will cost for the new tires, installation, balancing, rotating, and alignment?

Ditto this for changing your oil and oil filter.

I dislike getting too intricate to make a point, but I almost never see people check their tire pressure, so the analogy seems apropos. Everyone intuitively knows and has heard that it's important to check and maintain the right pressure. It prevents your tires from wearing unevenly, which sometimes shaves 10,000 miles off of a perfectly good set of tires.

Terence Michael

I challenge myself when I gas my car. I put the fuel dispensing pump handle on lock and race around all 4 tires to check the psi. I additionally check the tire tread by doing the penny test, taught to me by my Dad, who is the grandmaster of prevention. If you see space between the top of Lincoln's head and the edge of a penny when you place the penny upside down between the treads on a tire, then you need new tires. It means you have less than 1/16th of an inch of tread left. President Lincoln was the 16th President, so it's easy to remember. But if the top of Lincoln's head disappears, you're good to go.

And what about you? Are you not the most important vessel you own?

Prevention is everything, and the cost and time it takes is a fraction of the cost by ignoring it, whether your car or your own habits. By refusing this simple call, you are spending more money and wasting more time in the long run.

Shouldering your backpack and hiking up that mountain isn't as fun as sitting down at base camp with the warm fire and marshmallows. What's up there? Will I encounter a beast? I can't even see the top. Will my friends join me? Will I be lonely?

This hesitation is what your Hero's Journey calls for at this stage, but again, let's recognize it and take action to eventually counter it. You don't want anyone walking out of your movie because you're sitting comfortably at base camp. The audience wants to see you take those steps. They vicariously live through you. They want to take those steps with you. But, as the hero, you need to instigate the journey.

We're happy to have reluctant heroes — heroes who refuse, and heroes who don't know they're the hero yet. But they must have impulse and inclination to at least find out if they can be heroic and then plan to be the hero of their own life.

Produce Yourself

The Hero's Journey is all about acquiring and optimizing your skills for peak performance. This is about movement, action, and effectiveness.

Again, I resided in this space for almost 5 years. But I never sat idle. Even within my lengthy stay in the Refusal stage, I trained and readied my hero for the battles ahead.

If you've thought about it; if you've dreamt it; if you have wondered "what if..."; consider moving in that direction toward answers, despite small incremental moves — that important 1 percent a day.

I don't agree with other entrepreneurial advisors who say quit your job at all costs, go pursue your dream. That may be inspiring, but it's terrible advice. You have to take baby steps. You must mitigate your exposure and risk. BUT you have to take those steps.

Your first car, your first date, marriage, babies, houses, careers, loss, and change — all milestones of life that interweave joy with anxiety. It's exasperating and sometimes exhausting to face these landmarks. But once you initiate that first step, even if you're still technically refusing the journey, your options will become more viable and your steps will become easier, forming a pattern of progress.

I'm in the same boat. I'm still in my own movie as well. I'm deep into my own journey(s) going through the stages for various aspects of my daily life. And for some of the ongoing narratives, I'm at this stage, refusing to answer the call. We all have our own issues and justifications. We love to rationalize why story lines should stay the way they are. And we all have our own burdens that feel unique to us.

But trust the Hero's Journey. Trust our own DNA's acknowledgment of a satisfying character arc and story. Take notice of that call. It's there for a reason. Your inner hero is trying to break out and show you what you're capable of.

That phone keeps ringing with new calls all the time. And that's a good thing. It means you're open to change, to improvement, to upgrading, to optimization. You want to advance so every waking hour is meaningful and fulfilling.

Refuse. But take the steps. Even 1 percent a day. You will get there.

-

CHAPTER 7

Meeting The Mentor: Increasing Your Average
(Stage 4 - Part 1)

"It is not our abilities that show what we truly are. It is our choices."

- Richard Harris in *Harry Potter and the Chamber of Secrets*

WHETHER IT'S YODA FOR LUKE, Alfred for Bruce, Mr. Miyagi for Ralph Macchio, your boss, your sister, or even yourself, there is always a being or force that helps you get past a hesitation, arming you with the tools to proceed on your journey.

This doesn't have to be a singular person or source. Mentors come in the form of different influencers and allies. There's often one initial force that inspires the hero. But then there are additional advisors who continue to attack doubt and fear, keeping the hero on track.

In "The Wizard of Oz," Dorothy's mentor appears in the form of the Good Witch of the North, who gives her direction and a pair of fancy red shoes. But were it not for The Scarecrow, The Tin Man, and The Lion — dubious mentors on the surface, but faithful friends with counsel — she wouldn't have completed her yellow-bricked journey.

This is an important stage for the hero. Heroics doesn't mean you just run out the door and start flying — that's a limited-dimension cartoon. Even superheroes have their learning curve and a need for mentorship. Luke Skywalker had no idea how to use the lightsaber until he spent excruciating time with Obi Wan and Yoda. Wonder Woman was useless until she was trained properly by Robin Wright. And in "The Dark Night," Christian Bale was a weakling before studying under Liam Neeson.

Heroes gain their title because of self-imposed assessment of their situation, and choices they enact to improve them. This is why there's a hero in all of us. We all have the capability to find the best version of ourselves. We can be ambitious and methodical, yet still remain vulnerable and ask for help. This is a crucial part of being a hero — knowing when to seek guidance, gain knowledge, learn a skill, research information, or admit defeat to regroup and reaffirm direction.

A huge misconception is that a hero is born that way. Or she's so "heroic" that she doesn't need help. But it's just the opposite. A genuine hero, both in cinema and real life, is able to recognize and admit her weaknesses and vulnerabilities, ask for help, seek knowledge, acquire training and skills, and highlight flaws and shortcomings.

This might be the single most important characteristic of highly successful people in almost all industry. If you dig into the biographies of everyone from Arnold Schwarzenegger to Tony Robbins, from Steve Jobs to Tom Ford, from Henry Ford to JFK, from Bill Gates to the founders of DryBar or SoulCycle or anyone in between, you'll find habits of

Produce Yourself

highlighting deficiencies and measured approaches to gaining the know-how to overcome them.

This is why we love to read about success stories. They are all Hero's Journeys. They all show the ordinary person, just like you and me, tinkering in their garage, dreaming of entering a special world. Like you and me, they have certain insecurities and inadequacies. But they overcome them with help from a Mentor — whatever form, person, or thing that takes.

If you look back at your heroes in literature, film or television, you'll find that there's someone on their side, someone they encountered, someone who offered advice, someone who inspired them to overcome the reluctance to change and advance.

There's the buddy, the best friend, the lover, the roommate, the co-worker, or even the stranger in a cafe who helped motivate our hero. On the surface, the mentorship could be comic relief, but underneath the jokes, there's a persuasive argument presented, giving her pause and perspective.

The hero will ultimately make the decision. But it's the mentor who becomes her consciousness by proxy.

Even in the classic Tom Cruise movie "Risky Business," it took the best friend to repeat: "... sometimes, you just gotta say, what the fuck?" And that's what helped Tom's character choose his risky business. Of course, he had pitfalls (Dad's Porsche 928 sliding into the harbor) and got sidetracked (romance with Rebecca De Mornay), but had it not been for his unassuming mentor, played by Booger from "Revenge of The Nerds," he may not have taken the first step.

Not that he's one of my heroes, but Mao Tse-tung said, and he knew whereof he spoke: "The journey of a thousand miles begins with a single step."

Booger didn't really mentor Tom Cruise. But Booger was the manifestation of his thoughts. Tom already wanted to throw caution to the wind and take the risk. But he needed the vote of confidence from his friend. He needed to hear someone else voice what he had already been thinking.

In "Baby Driver," Baby's foster dad continues to encourage Baby to deliver pizzas or take a normal job and escape from the criminals he drives for. Baby knows this. His mentor isn't revealing any secret strategy to solve Baby's predicament; he's merely echoing Baby's own internal voice.

In movies with the teacher-student relationship, the mentor is quite literally the mentor. With films like "Lean on Me," "Dead Poets Society" or "Dangerous Minds," or dance films like "Fame," "Save The Last Dance," "Honey," and "Step Up," the teacher teaches and the student learns.

There's a Zen saying: "When the student is ready, the teacher appears."

Classic sports films like "Hoosiers" or "Remember The Titans" reveal the coach is helping the hero transform into a better person, not just a better athlete.

But sometimes, the teacher, in turn, becomes the student. Without doing deep, focused work on yourself, another person becomes the window into yourself, voicing the advice you already know, but aren't following.

In "Good Will Hunting," we see this dynamic when Robin Williams is the obvious mentor to a reluctant Matt Damon. But it's Matt's intuitive intellect that exposes Robin's vulnerabilities and sadness for losing his wife, becoming his proxy therapist and mentor. Within Robin William's Hero's Journey, Matt is simply the outsourced assessment Robin already has for himself. He knows everything Matt is telling him. That's why it bothers him. Matt nailed Robin's issue on the head.

Produce Yourself

Ditto for "The Sixth Sense." Bruce Willis thinks he's mentoring Haley Joel Osment the entire time (as does the audience), helping a scared kid cope with seeing dead people. But it's Haley Joel Osment who ends up mentoring our hero Bruce Willis, helping him talk to his wife, and expose the fact that he's already dead, and not just metaphorically. In this case, Bruce would have eventually figured out he was dead. It was only a matter of time. But his protective bias wouldn't allow that knowledge to reach him. So Haley becomes the catalyst Bruce needs to allow him to pass, complete his period of purgatory, have peace with his life and move on. The mentor becomes the mentee.

In "Rain Man," Tom Cruise's mentor ends up being his savant brother. Tom doesn't realize at the time that he's a narcissistic shallow ass, and he's just holding his brother ransom for inheritance. But what he learns from Dustin Hoffman is much more valuable than the money he seeks. It's the beginning of the transformation Tom desperately needs as a human being. And it took Dustin, a mentor in disguise all the time, to help Tom overcome the refusal stage.

The mentor is rarely an obvious choice. I make this point, as in real-life you don't need the expensive coach or accomplished expert to guide you. It can come from anyone who is either seeing the real you or giving you context and perspective for you to see the real you. Whereas during the Refusal stage, the hero has to be skeptical of potentially impartial advice from a close friend or family member, during the Mentor stage, the hero needs that someone who can be brutally honest.

Your mentor can even be the knowledge and wisdom gained from books, lectures, YouTube, Udemy, Khan Academy, or any other form of research. The research itself can be your mentor.

One of my biggest mentors today: podcasts. I love that I can listen to experts in almost any field because they either host or are guests of a podcast. And as much as I enjoy reading from experts in various fields, hearing someone I admire talk about their life and journey with all their inflections and imperfect trials and errors is so much more valuable. I can hear the human in them, which makes their journey all the more relatable to mine.

For example, after listening to over 100 podcasts, just from authors, I've been consoled that everyone goes through the same stages I'm currently facing with the pursuit of this book. They've all felt like they write complete drivel, if not crap, at times. They've all thought there were 100 other books that said the same thing. Many have written entire books, fully edited, and then thrown them away. Still others have so many book ideas in their heads they feel overwhelmed in starting them. This is no different for me. Being able to eavesdrop in on their conversations about this has been reassuring.

This is no different than any other endeavor. But because writing a book is new to me, the stages of the hero become accentuated. Whereas with a film or TV show I may know how to quickly overcome certain stages like The Refusal; with the book process being so foreign, I experience those challenges all over again.

Another form that the mentor can take is what I like to think of as sort of "Superfriends" mentor, wherein, instead of one person or podcast as mentor, there's an assemblage of people. It's kind of your very own Avengers or Justice League. Only the "crime" they are fighting is your mediocrity.

You may have heard this philosophy before — originally coined by Jim Rohn, but adopted by many motivational speakers as a widely accepted concept — that we are merely the average of the 5 people we surround ourselves with.

Our perspective, wisdom, attitude, motivation, mood, ambition, tenacity, resourcefulness, generosity, kindness, political beliefs, love — all are the sum average of the 5 people we spend the most time with.

Produce Yourself

Who you insulate your world and surround yourself with becomes a confluence of ideas and approaches you acquire and absorb.

The law of averages in mathematics states that the end result of any given situation will be the average of all outcomes. In life it's obviously less calculable and exacting in terms of influence and impact, but the metaphor is applicable. We are indeed an average of our surroundings.

The people you chose to work, befriend, and socialize with — their average aggregate experiences, systems, approaches, values, and habits become yours. We emulate, sometimes by osmosis, and tend to adopt styles of our "scene." Hopefully, this scene is created naturally, as you gravitate to like-minded people whom you find enjoyable to be around. But at the same time, understanding math, make sure you don't just have 4 stoner dudes in your life and nothing else. Your average will be severely hampered by those numbers, bringing down your progress.

This seems abundantly obvious. We may subconsciously do this already, as we are inspired by certain individuals or companies. But sometimes it only takes one colleague or business partner to bring your average down without your even realizing it.

It's kind of like your collection of credit cards and your credit score. It only takes one card that carries a high balance to offset your credit score, negating all the good work you've done on the other ones.

If the hero inside you isn't seeking better solutions, isn't provoked to upgrade, isn't receiving true discourse from your tribe, you need to rethink your scene and the averages that comprise it.

For example, don't expect the boutique jeans store you own to last more than 6 months if the brain trust you assembled to run it is 3 of your closest friends who have little fashion, marketing, or sales experience. Even if you add one incredible fashion guru and average him in with those 3, your average is still depressed.

You need to be challenged and inspired, yet cautioned about whatever you're considering from your team. If you aren't getting that kind of feedback and reflection, your endeavor may not be as important as you thought, because you're more interested in the comfort of your friends or mediocre associates than spending the time to find the right chamber of intellect and skills to help you get there. It's just math.

I've also been there, thinking how fun it would be to build something with friends. It would be. But it's more often the exception, and unfortunately often the most expensive employee on your payroll.

Many directors in Hollywood feel like frauds. I know this because they've told me in so many words (and I direct many of my own TV shows, so I know what they mean). Many of them have revealed in interviews or when receiving awards that they owe it all to fill-in-the-blank actor. That's because as a director 90 percent of your job is done during the casting process. That's the big effective hack as a director: cast properly and you're nearly done directing.

Casting is one of the toughest things to do — finding the right people for the right roles that, when interacting with each other, help sell your characters and world. Casting often takes months, sometimes even years to get the right mix of actors. So much comes into play with nuance, timing, tone, skill, vibe, chemistry, look, age.

IF casting is done just right, the director has already leveraged 90 percent of what she needs to do. Turn on the cameras because brilliance will happen when she has the right cast. The average of her project is already starting off high. It's easy to fall prey to a name star or someone who has become available who will get the project financed. But if it's not the right person, she's got an uphill battle as a director because her average has just been lowered.

Even when you've done the best job possible casting your movie or show, you sometimes have to make the tough choices of recasting.

Chemistry tests, rehearsals, camera tests — all remain stages a director continues to navigate, making sure casting is right.

Robert Zemeckis (the director) and Steven Speilberg (the producer) started out with Eric Stoltz ("Masked") in the lead role for "Back To The Future." They even filmed for several weeks and it wasn't until watching dailies (rough footage of takes from a specific day) that they realized something was amiss. The movie was ultimately a comedy. Eric Stoltz (I love him professionally and personally) isn't the "funny guy" that the movie needed. All other actors were firing on all cylinders, but with the film being the average of the 5, the sum wasn't large enough to achieve the right result. Sadly, Eric Stoltz was let go and the film was completely reshot with Michael J. Fox.

The mentor that the film itself needed to get past the Refusal stage and eventually cross the threshold was a total number that could only be reached with the higher average of Michael J. Fox. For this mixture of ingredients, he was the spice that was missing.

Contractors, electricians, plumbers, carpenters — what separates them from an amateur? What makes one better than, and more hirable than, another? The smart ones surround themselves with the best associates, apprentices, and laborers. They find the best tools. They hire the best management, bookkeeping, and customer service. Their sum becomes the average of all of these elements combined. Anyone can unclog a toilet or install a light switch. But the ones who get hired over again and can charge more? Those are the ones who have focused attention, inadvertently or not, on their average.

I learned firsthand after 2 years in college the importance of those you surround yourself with.

A friend from high school, J, was doing everything he could to get into Pepperdine University, where I was now ending my second year studying business.

J hadn't gotten accepted his freshman year when I did. So he was now attempting to transfer in after earning some college credits elsewhere. It was something we always talked and dreamed about. I had some fraternity brothers who were working in the admissions office and I was trying to get intel on his application. I wrote an essay about his character and qualifications and why I thought he'd make a good Wave (UCLA has Bruins, USC has Trojans; Pepperdine has Waves).

When J didn't get accepted, he decided to move to San Diego and go to SDSU, a state school with similar business classes, but easier to get into. At the time, I was really pissed off. In my youthful ignorance, I wanted to blame the school rather than J's credentials. So with the skyrocketing tuition and a few other justifications, I decided to quit Pepperdine and join my friend. I could just transfer over all of my credits and get the same education down there.

I thought the adventure of our getting an apartment together sounded pretty awesome at age 20. So we moved to San Diego, got our first apartment (outside of dorms I had never lived away from my parents), waxed our surfboards and bused tables at a fancy fish house. Within weeks, my world changed. Drastically.

I don't mean for this to sound elitist; it's just the facts. As the average of my surroundings, I was quickly getting brain drain. The environment I was in was one of laziness, numbness, and short-term comfort — like the salty air, it permeated. For many, this was paradise. I get why they liked it.

But the people I encountered mostly just wanted to party and fulfill absolute minimum requirements (pay their rent, get a diploma). And as much as I loved surfing and making decent cash at a fancy restaurant, I just felt the inspiration and ambition I had gained in Malibu was quickly dissipating. There was a clear disparity in motivation and aspiration of people in my vicinity. Night and day, from my perspective.

Produce Yourself

In hindsight, I definitely could have corrected this then and there. This had little to do with San Diego as a location. I simply needed to change my surroundings and whom I associated with. I needed to alter my average. But I didn't.

Was I supposed to ditch my friend? Much of the scene I was experiencing was attractive to him for numerous reasons. I had just moved with everything I owned. We had an awesome two-bedroom apartment, our own cars, and were making friends, etc. We were too young to go to bars so we trekked into Tijuana on weekends and met other people our age. But the hangover was setting in.

I hate to profile, but sometimes stereotypes are there for a reason. I was hanging with unemployed surfers. I was hanging with a night restaurant crew. I was hanging with part-time students in overcrowded classrooms who showed up in beach chairs and towels and sat on the floor.

I quickly developed nostalgia for the 2 years I'd had back at Pepperdine. There was a certain quality of the student body that just reeked "I'll-be-doing-something-great-some-day." And whether that happened for everyone or not, that vigor was everywhere. I know a lot of it had to do with the university being private. The cost alone filtered out non-serious students, as it was simply too expensive to take casually and coast. But regardless, the facts and logistics, as well as my own impetuosity, I just couldn't bear my world in San Diego anymore.

Would I look like a failure, returning to Pepperdine now having missed a whole semester? What would I tell my roommate? And I think we were only 1 month into a 1-year apartment lease.

It was a great lesson for later in life, knowing when to confront your fears even if that means hurting someone you love. And to show how amazing J was/is, as soon as I said we needed to talk, he said he already knew it was coming. He could tell this wasn't the climate for me. He loved it and was indeed making the most of it. But he was also pursuing goals in a different direction; he went into the Coast Guard and later became a cop.

He had been in Malibu many weekends visiting me, meeting my friends and dorm mates, and hanging out on campus. He saw the difference, too. I apologized and said we'd obviously be friends forever, but I had to do this. As painful as the thought of moving out from my best friend, and the apartment was, I had to get back.

He completely understood and couldn't have been more gracious. I still don't think I've ever told him how much it meant to me that day for the way he reacted and how supportive he was. I need to do that.

To this day, when I enter into a phase where I think something isn't working, I get PTSD flashbacks to standing in the kitchen with J in San Diego and telling him I needed to head back to Malibu. It could be a show I'm doing, an agent I'm with, or even a process I've been practicing. When something isn't working, I know I need to confront it.

Whether you believe that things happen for a reason, or setbacks become lessons, or failures become motivators, makes no difference. It's your reaction and response to a mistake or detour that becomes critical. You must adapt.

I had to pivot from the average of my environment, people, social conversations and attitudes that made up my average. I don't blame J. But J gravitated toward people and places that probably didn't help my average. I needed ambition, stimulus, and innovation. But the totality of who I was becoming based on my geographical resources and absorption was changing too fast into someone I didn't want to be. So as difficult as it was, I ultimately had no other choice but to change the factors that made up my sum.

In math, you change the input if you want a different result. I quite frankly needed to surround myself with other people. J will always be my friend. But at that point in my life, smack in the middle of my college years, I had to remove his circle of influence from mine.

I probably helped his average too. I probably weighed him down and pulled him too far away from where he was going, so he in turn needed to surround himself with the best people for him. He too is merely the average of his surroundings, people, and environment.

By now you know the "average of 5" is an analogy for life

- Your health? It's the sum of the 5 main exercises you perform, the 5 main foods you always eat, the 5 habits of sleep you employ.
- Your wealth? It's the sum of the 5 investing habits you have or the 5 debt habits you have.
- Your relationship? It's the sum of the 5 repeatable experiences you share daily.
- And don't forget the exercise Warren Buffett recommended in the last chapter about setting 5 goals and writing them down on a piece of paper.

This average that I was experiencing in decline was the opposite of a mentor for me. It made me realize the "mentor" I already had back at Pepperdine was the sum of my classmates, professors, suitemates, and fraternity brothers. So moving to San Diego didn't gain me a mentor; it lost me the one I didn't realize I already had.

Moving back to Malibu was a course correction. Now a semester behind, I was flooded with an average overload. And I loved every minute of it. In my larger journey, I was still in my Refusal stage. But in my smaller scholastic one, I was entering an accelerated phase of appreciation, gratitude, and opportunity.

CHAPTER 8

Meeting The Mentor: Power of No · Purpose
(Stage 4 - Part 2)

"I don't want to survive. I want to live."

- Chiwetel Ejiofor in *12 Years a Slave*

THERE'S A SAYING that you don't appreciate what you have until it's gone. We learn this at an early age when a toy is taken away, the ice cream cone falls on the ground, or the sleepover must come to an end.

As we grow up, we learn to appreciate. We learn the powerful benefits of gratitude. But missing something or someone never goes away. However, the initial rush of excitement does wane.

Economists call this the law of diminishing returns. Put the best-tasting pizza you could ever imagine in front of you, and eat it. The first bite will give you 10 points of satisfaction (arbitrary measurement). You absolutely love this pizza. It's the best you've ever had. You take a second bite. That second bite, although delivering the same mix of ingredients in the same amount, gives you 9.9 points of satisfaction.

It's still incredible. But that second bite just isn't the same as the very first one, because the second one now carries with it memories and expectations of reaching the same 10-point level you had in the 1st bite. And so on. By the time you get to the last bite, you might have 9.1 points of satisfaction. Again, it's still amazing. You probably want another slice. But each subsequent bite will have a return of satisfaction that is some increment less, however infinitesimal, than the prior one.

In retrospect, this happened to me during my first 2 years of college. I was having the best time of my life. But toward the end of year two, my intake of the beautiful big blue ocean didn't register the same marvel. I stopped appreciating the opportunity to be able to study, learn, and grow — all with an ocean view.

I took my habitat for granted and became relatively refractory to the professors and courses that were offered — any one of which I could enroll in, Pepperdine being a liberal arts college. So many groups, clubs, and events in which to participate. But other than my fraternity, I really hadn't branched out.

I was a typical freshman, wanting to make friends quickly, do well in my classes, and survive what seemed a place of smarter, taller and tanner people.

I suspect this is why students drink so much in college: suddenly everyone is thrust into a situation of unknowns, with lots of strangers, and drinking is the security blanket that helps lower inhibitions. Alcohol helped us feel less insecure and more courageous.

It had only been a short time that I was absent — just one summer and a semester. Yet I felt like Rip Van Winkle as if I had woken from a lengthy sleep. Previously I had connected all of the dots. But now, some of the dots seemed disconnected. It was a bit disconcerting like I was an outsider with limited updates on everyone's Now.

Friends had new roommates, new girlfriends, new classes, and some were out of the country for an international semester of study. The experience of leaving the Malibu ecosystem and then returning was surreal, but it also gave me unexpected insight.

I was able to appreciate the value of resources that were available to me. I was exposed to opportunities I had neglected. I wasn't the center of the universe. Life advanced without me. It's as if I had missed an episode of my favorite TV series and didn't DVR it. So I had to catch up. The ocean seemed bluer, the parties were more engaging, my friendships were more essential. Even the food in the cafeteria seemed to taste better.

Obviously, it was all mindset. It was all perspective — the power of the brain mixed with appreciation, optimism, and apology.

Rather than have the minimalist attitude of "survive college, get a degree on paper, and have a career," I wanted to absorb all that collegiate life had to offer. Like Jim Carrey in "Yes Man," I tried to metaphorically say "Yes" to everything. I let curiosity out of the cage to roam free and devour.

It's a trite philosophy to say "Yes" to opportunity. I think everyone theoretically agrees with the benefits of "Yes." But the turbocharger of the engine of "Yes" is actually the power of "No."

"No" needs to become a go-to for the advancing hero in order to empower and allow her freedom to pursue her purpose, rather than shallow activities. "No" is what enables a "Yes" to follow when opportunity presents itself.

Because you didn't say "No" enough times before, the time will come when you wish you could say "Yes," but can't, and opportunity, like a star in the daytime sky, vanishes.

This has become a societal cycle where people feel obligated to become the ambassador for others' to-do list. People complain they are too busy and can't pursue their purpose or begin those steps because they're up to their eyeballs in "stuff" they have to do. But I wager at least 25 percent of that "stuff" is that person either becoming a delegate to someone else's requests or a slave to their own.

- "We're heading to New Mexico, would you mind if we crashed with you for a few days?"
- "Could I pick your brain for a couple of hours? I'm thinking of leaving my job, but need advice"
- "Would you come over and fix my computer?"
- "Could I borrow your car while I'm in town for a couple of days?"
- "I'm looking for fun things for my kids to do this summer; can you give me a list?"
- "Could I store my boat in at your house for a week?"
- "Could you help me move this weekend? And can we borrow your truck too?"
- "Can't wait to see you at our kid's birthday party"

In the context of work, close friends, and family, there are obvious compromises and benefits to generosity and sharing. Some of the above examples I'd personally love to participate in because I enjoy the process and sharing memories. At other times, the choice between "Yes" and "No" may be nebulous and weighted by other factors.

Unselfish loved ones without an agenda want you to be honest, not burdened by a sense of obligation. Sometimes you end up lying to yourself as well as being dishonest with them.

In the long run, the "No"s will make room for the "Yes"s that accelerate and positively transform your hero.

Produce Yourself

You have to take care of yourself first. You choose you to be the priority. Once you're all good there, go cat sit, join a painting party, or drive 2 hours to see your cubicle mate's husband's band play all you want. Spend 12 hours at Disneyland when distant relatives visit and want a tour guide. Tell your co-worker you'll go to that book signing with them. But only after you have already helped YOU.

Be honest with yourself. Doing so requires saying "No" when the activity isn't your purpose, your passion, your muse; when it's an uncomfortable or stressful burden. The hike you are taking on the Hero's Journey requires shedding baggage, not adding more. Minimize so you can be available for opportunity.

When you have a big enough, important enough "Yes" burning with passion inside of you, the unmerciful "No"s will flow easily.

Opportunity is everywhere. We don't always recognize it. But we may as well have blinders on if we don't harness the power of "No." It might be uncomfortable to be forthright and not commit. But that discomfort is tiny compared to the sweaty day straining your back so your friend can save renting a truck and hiring movers. Your friend already says "No" to spending money on movers so they can say "Yes" for their money elsewhere. They are already employing the same habit that you should by saying "No" if moving boxes for the day won't be meaningful and fulfilling. It's okay to be honest. Your real friends and family require it of you.

If others viewed requests from you as constraints but endured them grudgingly without being honest, you would feel terrible. You don't want anyone agreeing to something that pulls down their average or derails a future opportunity because they feel you lobbed a time grenade at them.

A request, going in either direction, should be a gift. Not an internal monologue of burden or requirement.

Again, there are exceptions. We make compromises when we want to help and make others happy. That is different. That is our doing something for us because we like how it makes us feel.

It's better to be honest and say "No" to a camping trip than buy supplies, make arrangements, camp for a week, only to have the distaste and displeasure of the experience put you in a bad mood or ruin the experience simply because you weren't honest about hating camping (or substitute scenario). Rather than buzz kill what should be an overall fun experience, simply say "No, I'm not interested in camping." The right people will respect your different preference, as they would want you to do for them. And if they're not the right people, why would you want to be with them?

This might seem selfish. It's just the opposite. What's selfish is someone requesting something of you and not respecting what's right for you, your situation, your pursuits, your personal needs, and desires. What's selfish is someone else expecting something of you that you don't enjoy or want to do.

Someone requesting something of you is, by definition, selfish (of them). And that's okay. We can be selfish. But we must also be selfless so that we can all have more opportunity for "Yes"s in our lives.

I was able to herd the power of "Yes" in school because the "No"s gave me all the time and opportunity I needed to stimulate the "Yes"s.

I started waking up at 5:30 am to train with the swim team. I became the president of my fraternity. I started a radio show with one of my other friends and learned to DJ and produce at the local radio station. I became involved as a mentor to incoming freshman students. I formed a band. I started a house painting company and eventually sold it. I did some minor acting on the side. I took scuba and sailing classes. I then became the president of the Inter-Greek Council, sort of the president of the entire

Greek system at the school. I started taking classes in other majors like sociology, psychology, and telecommunications.

I don't know if all of those "Yes"s would have happened had I not taken the detour into San Diego, learning from my adventurous miscalculations and returning with tools of objectivity. They certainly wouldn't have happened without the number of "No" responses to party invitations, ski-trips, beach barbecues, sporting events, drunken brunches, etc.

I was really hungry for all I could consume at the college smorgasbord, but I had to prioritize. As in life, there are simply too many choices. Like Buffett's bucket list of 25 things, I had to pare priorities down to 5. I know from going to Disneyland as a kid I can't just get in line for every ride I happen upon. There is only so much time, so I have to prioritize or the day will end while I'm stuck on rides I don't care for because I didn't say "No."

Decades later, seldom does a day pass where I'm not drawing upon lessons I learned in college. Not so much the actual classes, but the lessons I learned from my mistakes, from taking risks, from making tough decisions, from pursuing opportunity.

Nowadays there's a movement supporting the logic for not attending college. I subscribe to this. I don't think college is necessary, at least right out of high school. And I especially think it may be a mistake if you don't know what you want to do.

Spending $50k a year or whatever it costs to figure out what you want to do is money that you will almost never see a return on. It's why so many millennials, even going into age 35, are 15 years later completely burdened by debt. I have 45 and even 55-year-old mortgage clients who are still paying off debt from 25 and 35 years earlier. If you add up the aggregate, including interest, some of them have spent close to $400k. I'm not exaggerating. And this doesn't account for the lost opportunity due to debt and struggle this has cost along the way.

Doctor, lawyer, engineer? Go! If you know that's what you want to do, absolutely go. Or if you know you specifically want to do anything, fantastic; college may be for you. Only you can weigh the benefits and costs. But do yourself a huge favor and map it out. Write the numbers down. See what the debt actually is and will be. It's shocking.

But for those students trying to find themselves? Work. Live. Travel. Think. Explore. And then go to college — maybe. It's 100 percent not needed to be successful, proven over and over by looking at the most successful people in any field. And I don't just mean celebrity or wealth. I mean in the true sense of success — having found your meaning, your purpose and living relatively stress-free with enough money to follow your passions along the way.

But for some, for me, it was one of the best things that happened. Of course, it took my leaving college smack in the middle to understand this. Had I not had that break, I don't know that my hero would have ever left the Refusal stage. I may have easily become a supporting player in someone else's journey (perhaps corporate America).

So although I don't think anyone needs to go to college, and should seriously consider working and living life for a year or two first, I can't imagine my current life with college removed from my foundation. I can't calculate the ancillary benefits that helped shape who I am.

I discovered that I was just one credit shy of 128 credits required to graduate. Fortunately, that one remaining credit could be an elective, which meant I would get to peruse through the fun section of the college catalog. I stumbled across one class with the title: "Entering The Film and Television Business." I don't remember all my class titles. That one I'll never forget.

Throughout college, and especially after returning from San Diego, I continued my hobby of picking up my video camera and filming my friends, my fraternity brothers, college parties. I made spoofs, documented rituals, and made fun music videos to show at events and fraternity rushes with everyone in them (another "Yes" for me due to prior "No"s).

This was a fun outlet; nothing more. My brand was that I was studying prestigious, innovative business concepts, strategies, and operations. I was going to work in an ivory tower some day for a Fortune 500 company. That was my mindset at this point in my journey. Since I was 12, this is who I was. So this was simply recess for me. But it was a great outlet. I didn't do drugs, smoke, and actually drank very little. Making little video productions was my vice.

So "Entering the Film and Television Business" was staring me in the face. I think it's the first time that I had read or at least paid attention to the phrasing of "film," "TV," and "business" in the same sentence.

I had not been exposed to or had anything remotely like Hollywood in my blood. I would watch TV or movies, but I never thought about making them.

I grew up playing the piano and the drums and singing in choir. I was aware of the arts, but for story as an art form, it was more in the form of stage or plays. Films and TV shows to me were entertainment. No one really made them — massive disassociation, I know. But as a "business" man, it just wasn't in my vernacular.

This class, as a one-unit elective, met only once a week at night with a Hollywood guy, BR. He was a bigwig, a legend, a veteran agent in Hollywood, and founder of one of the biggest agencies. He happened to live in Malibu. This was a fun thing he did to give back to the community.

I thought, all right, that sounds easy. I mean how hard can it be? Plus I figured, the operative word in the class title was "Entering" so maybe it was more about résumés, what suits to wear when interviewing, which could be applicable to me in the corporate business world as well.

The first night of this elective class, BR walks in. It's jam packed, and if I recall correctly, some students were even standing outside with the door open. So BR, Hollywood Icon, stubs out his cigarette and proceeds to tell us that he only has time and space in the class for people who are serious. If any of us aren't serious about entering the film and TV business, we had better exit now. Of course, no one leaves. We're all waiting for the punch line.

Expecting this, he then adds that no one in his class will get a grade better than a "C." WTF? Everyone is looking at each other, shifting in their chairs. Did we hear correctly? Can he do that?

I had been consistently getting mostly As and some Bs throughout college. I received one C, which I "traded," but I was pretty much an A/B student.

Fortunately, I learned early on that grades weren't everything, and in many cases meant absolutely nothing. So if I didn't get straight As, it wasn't the end of the world. My only C class in college was when Ben Stein (Bueller; Ferris Bueller, anyone?) taught a "Communication in Culture" class and I was going through hell week at the time during my freshman year as a fraternity pledge.

I was content taking a lower grade in exchange for learning from President Nixon's speechwriter. I agreed to sacrifice grades for experience. I was willing to trade them, like currency, knowing he would be awesome, and my fraternity experience would be equally so.

Could I have had straight-As? Probably. But for that, I would have wasted my tuition. In that scenario, I would say I should never have gone to college. I should have stayed home and gone online to learn business theory and simultaneously started a business so I could fail and learn from my mistakes as early as possible.

Produce Yourself

But my parents were supportive and encouraged diversity and social activities to round out my education. They had been part of the Peace Corps, traveled the world, were both highly educated and well read, yet taught me early on about false measurements like grades vs. life experiences.

Some of my classmates struggled with this concept. I get it. It's an expensive school, you want to graduate with honors and go get a high-paying job. And depending what kind of scholarship you might have, keeping minimal grades is probably critical. But for most, it's nothing but a piece of paper. No one cares. As an employer, I can tell you: No. One. Cares.

While your experience in life is the seeds of the future, you are putting too many seeds into one section of soil by only concentrating on grades, or titles, or trophies and plaques, or any superficial appraisal. Same can be said about anything from money, exercise, sleep, food, sun — all desirable things. Too much, however, will lead to a bloating of one, and not enough of the other, causing illness and stress. The balance of your life will not be level; one side will be lower than the other, and you'll notice it.

Perhaps love is the only thing that doesn't diminish anything else. You can never have too much, give too much, run out, or partition it from one person to another. No matter how many slices you take or give out, there's always more love to go around. But I digress.

This close to graduation, I didn't want to trade down a letter grade just for some pompous guy to wax about his old days in Hollywood. Not for a silly one-unit elective, anyhow. It seemed absurd to me that a professor could arbitrarily do this — limit grades to a C.

BR then proceeds into a long story about how Hollywood is ruthless, competitive, gut wrenching, yet simultaneously beautiful and rewarding. It will tear you up, spit you out, but elevate you if you succeed. It's not for the faint of heart and there are 1,000 people for every one position available in Hollywood (not counting actors; add another zero for them).

And grades mean squat. If you care about your grades here at college, you are not serious about Hollywood. You might be serious about something else, but not Hollywood. Because if you're serious about Hollywood, you don't even need college.

That's what he told us. We then learned that he barely graduated high school himself. He was an agent and had major icons as clients, from James Garner to Carol Burnett to Robert Duvall (who weren't icons, by the way, when he discovered them. He made them into icons). He and people like Robert Redford and director Robert Zemeckis rose through the industry when he and they were struggling ladder climbers. I mean this guy was quintessential "Hollywood." He had seen it all, knew it all and had mentored hundreds of people.

As romantic as he made Hollywood sound, I still feared it as a playground of drugs and parties. Again, this was my limited scope from hearing stories about overdoses and celebrity deaths in hotels. I now know today that this is more the exception than the rule.

Still, years later I would see part of this same dark side of Hollywood with friendships and business dealings with both Tom Sizemore and Robert Downey, Jr. None of this is a revelation; their temporary downfalls have been well documented and are public information.

My producing partner and I had paid Robert Downey, Jr. to write a screenplay for us at one point, one that his dad would possibly direct. This was the Robert Downey Jr. who had an Oscar nomination for playing Charlie Chaplin but was simultaneously on a downward drug-induced spiral. He was writing pages for us from jail, of all places.

We spent some time together at Sundance and later in L.A., preparing the project before he was incarcerated. There was no denying his charisma and talent. He was/is one of the best actors of our lifetime and has clearly picked himself up and changed his life-script.

Produce Yourself

Talk about someone who personally went through every stage of a hero. That's Robert. He was stuck in that tree. He had rocks thrown at him. He had complications, doubts, reluctance, mentors, but he was receiving the call for greatness and he climbed his way back and crossed the threshold. I wish I could say this about so many other actors in Hollywood who we lost too early to their own demons.

Today Robert is one of the highest paid actors in the world. We'll probably never make the script he wrote in jail. He's no longer that person and no longer in that world. He saw the essence of his future identity and left his comfortable but toxic world for a much brighter and bolder one. I can't even imagine anyone else playing Iron-Man. Kudos to Robert for completing the stages of his inner hero. He has definitely returned from the ordeal with the spoils.

Then there was Tom Sizemore. Strung out on meth and heroin, dating Hollywood's madam Heidi Fleiss. He pissed away a $5 million/picture career with films like "Heat" and "Saving Private Ryan."

I encountered him living in a garage in the valley, broke and in a rehab facility. When I wanted to turn on cameras and make a documentary about him, I had to meet him at his recovery center where he was chain-smoking and nervous about his future. I doubt he had this setback in his original script. It was a twist that caught many by surprise. But even heroes succumb to the dark side and get knocked off their pedestal.

Maintaining sharp focus and perseverance when you're at your peak is tougher sometimes than climbing out of a hole. Tom got lazy. He was weak and fell prey to his inner demons, ones we have since learned were always there.

I wanted to re-cast Tom as the hero of his own life. I wanted to show him the heroic road for taking the steps to get his life out of the gutter. My pitch to him worked and we signed a deal. I created and executive-produced a TV show called "Shooting Sizemore" on VH1.

The show was the first step in the right direction for him, admitting he had a problem, showing the world, and seeking to make amends to those he hurt. He was willing to do the work and begin anew when he started making B-movies in Canada you've probably never heard of. But it kept the lights on, enough for him to rent a little apartment in downtown L.A.

Cut to today and I suspect his journey is somewhere in the Tests, Allies and Enemies stage (Stage 6). He knows the Hero's Journey well. He's probably read thousands of screenplays. He's very aware of the stages. But, of interest, rarely has he ever played the actual hero.

He tends to gravitate to the pessimist, the villain, the stray. And he probably continues to play that role at times in real life. Those characters don't follow the Hero's Journey. They have stages, but they never complete them, or attempt to skip them.

He's had his ups and downs, and I couldn't tell you exactly where he is or what he's doing today. I wish him well, as he's a tough, ambitious guy. But he needs to find the courage to be the hero, not the villain, of his own life. I think/hope he will get there one day through the practice of gratitude, meditation, therapy, and taking those baby steps to advance through the stages.

These were just a couple of the dozens of tenebrous experiences and encounters I had in Hollywood many years later. They were the ones I had feared and forecast as an outsider growing up in a somewhat sheltered bubble. I didn't think any of this scene could be part of my destiny back when I was studying business in college.

BR flat out said that if we weren't willing to accept C grades on our transcripts then there's no way we could handle Hollywood. He said (and I paraphrase here) that our mindset was in the wrong place if we thought a grade meant anything whatsoever in Hollywood. And not being able to let go of that mentality would cost us dearly. He then asked for everyone

Produce Yourself

who wasn't okay with this to exit the room. More than half the room emptied immediately.

BR ignited something in me that I hadn't felt in awhile — fear. I suddenly felt like I didn't have a grasp of what I was doing. Do I stay? Do I go? Why am I even here, I thought. I learned quickly that I wasn't even guaranteed this class even if I stayed. He was still going to eliminate more students because he only had time to deal with 20 of us. He said anyone who remained would have to have one-on-one interviews with him at his house to prove to him that we had the guts to make it in Hollywood.

And I guess this was his first lesson to us in Entering the Film and TV Business — everything you know, everything you've learned, whatever you've done, or not done in your past — none of it matters. I don't think this is entirely true, today. However, making this point to students in college is impactful enough to really separate those looking to skate through an easy elective and those who wanted to squeeze every lime of opportunity. BR professed he was handing us opportunity. But he was only giving his map to the hard-core explorers.

It was a good metaphor for life. No matter how much you prepare, no matter how much you follow proven steps (including those of the Hero's Journey), no matter how assured you are of an outcome, life doesn't always reward you for your work. Output isn't always related to input.

Rather, life tends to reward purpose. This was BR's subtext to us. Who in the class feels this is their purpose? Who really needs this? Not want, but need? It was a bit dramatic, but his point was well taken.

He asked us remaining students if anyone in the room wanted to be an actor, and a few hands went up. He then sent a shiver down their spine.

He said (and I paraphrase again; it's been a few years): "If you can do anything other than act, please do it. If you have a skill, if you have a talent or knowledge outside of acting, I implore you to follow that. 97

percent of all actors don't make a living. They spend their entire life following their passion, which ends up being waiting tables the rest of their lives. As a side hobby, fine. But if you can do anything, if you can mow a lawn (this was literally his example), please do it. I beg you, do not become an actor. But if you tell me you can't breathe, you can't live, you will fall over and die if you don't act, then you must act."

BR wanted to separate the students with passion from those with purpose. So many people use passion as the justification for following a dream. "I have to follow my passion." But just because you want something doesn't mean it's a healthy pursuit. How many times have you been energized and excited about something (or someone) only to discover later that it was a whim or passing phase? How many things in your past were you nuts about, that today you can care less about? Those are your passions.

I was passionate about business. I loved thinking about economics and business concepts and ways to build a service or good. But was it my purpose? Is that what I really needed to do or I would be unfulfilled?

Purpose is something you would pursue and do the rest of your life if you never made a dime at it. That's your purpose. It's the core fabric of you. It's not just an interesting or exciting hobby to pursue that will fade with time. It's really who you are. There's no compromise because it's the magnet that will forever pull you.

I have friends who say they are passionate about wanting to write a screenplay. They want to see a movie poster on buses and billboards and they want to walk the red carpet at a premiere and make a lot of money. And then in the same breath, they ask me what they should write about, what would be commercial, what would sell.

That might be passion, but that is so far from purpose that, while those friends may gain some lessons from writing a screenplay, they will be disappointed because it's not their purpose. They are writing for an outcome rather than the purposeful process itself.

Produce Yourself

Success often follows purpose. Rarely does it follow passion. This may seem like semantics, but I'm defining the separation as want vs. need. If you need to do something or you will explode, that's your purpose. That process of doing what you want to do is your purpose. It's why you are here on this planet and what makes you unique.

If you want something because you think the outcome would be amazing, that's passion. You are passionate about having something, so you put in the hard work (that you dislike) to get there. Nothing wrong with hard work. It's required. But if you don't like the hard work, you are trading your predictable present self's worth for the unpredictable worth of your future self, where there is no guarantee of a successful outcome.

Your purpose is today. Your passion is tomorrow.

This is what BR was trying to tell us. He wanted those who were solely passionate about the idea of "Hollywood" to leave. You can throw a rock and hit someone passionate about the glamour and fame of Hollywood. But those who were passionate and felt it was their purpose could stay.

As he continued to define purpose, a highlights reel whizzed through my head of probably the most fun I had in my life up until now. It was my making shorts and producing sketches with my camera. No matter what class I was taking, what breakup I was going through, where I was living, what time of year it was, I was always making something with my camera. I never made money at it, and I never expected any outcome. I just loved the input. I loved the creation, the storytelling. If money were no concern, I would do it the rest of my life. I felt alive, creative, and fully in the zone when I was making content.

How did I miss this? That girl from the high-school party knew it before I did.

I decided to stay and officially take the class. I would now officially have two Cs in college.

The next 4 months with BR and his class changed my life and career direction forever. It really was just a primer for what various roles were in the business (agent, manager, producer, director, studio exec, actor). And each class he'd bring in someone who was doing it and give us the 411 on it. The Internet was only in its infancy back then, mostly academic (we turned our homework in via the Internet) so this kind of access and information wasn't readily available.

Not to take anything away from BR and the impact he had on me (and others), but this was really a basic information class. Nothing more. It was BR's attitude and perspective, however, that collided with my inner hero and gave me pause. His contemplation and wisdom revealed a simmering purpose I had all this time. I just didn't know what do with it, or what was possible until he came along.

And it was only because I was one unit shy, which happened when I left for San Diego — the gift that keeps on giving.

The next 6 months put me half a year longer in college as I took an additional semester of creative writing and behavioral classes (Pepperdine didn't have a film program at the time). I opened my eyes and finally answered that call — the call I had been refusing for close to 5 years. I never felt more hunger in my gut for something than I had for film at this time. BR became my wise Yoda who would help me learn the Force. I had found my mentor.

At the end of BR's class, I got an A. Apparently, most of us got As. I think that was our test all along: to see if we could understand that once we left college it was going to take creative approaches, stamina, and resourcefulness to make it in life. Grades are meaningless — and for accepting that truth for a full semester, we were rewarded with As.

The irony.

-

CHAPTER 9

Commercial Break: Timing · Turning Off Deep Work · Cycles

"Life moves pretty fast. If you don't stop and look around once in a while, you could miss it."

- Matthew Broderick in *Ferris Bueller's Day Off*

Don't you hate commercials when you're watching TV?

One reason binge watching has become so popular is the ability to begin the next episode just as soon as you've finished one. Another reason is the inclusion of commercials as a format is gone. Other than the occasional ad at the beginning or end, your immersion experience is not disrupted when watching any of the newer platforms such as Hulu, Netflix or Amazon.

Viewing television episodes has become more like the cinematic experience of watching movies in a theatre. This is one of the reasons there's been a decline in attendance at cinema houses. Theaters are less of a novelty. The isolation of the world can now be achieved with tablets and a pair of headphones in the comfort of your own home.

Combine this with the fact that major movie stars have now flocked to television in a manner that was once considered a downgrade. But the quality, look, tone, feel, and now experience are almost the same, if not often better, with TV.

When actress Charlize Theron was just starting her career, she had a small part in Tom Hank's directorial debut: "That Thing You Do." He signed a copy of the script for her, telling her how great she was and then gave her advice to "Please never do television." That used to be the sentiment of the movie world. Tom would probably never write that today. TV content and quality have changed dramatically to coincide with newer technology and habits.

Lower expectation also contributes to TV's insurgency. When you pay the babysitter, walk the dog, hop in the car, fight traffic, pay for parking, pay for popcorn, sit in a crowded theatre, and wait for 20 minutes of trailers and dancing soda cups to finish, you are justifiably less patient with the product. Your expectations are high and you psychologically want your investment of time, effort and expense to pay off. So the gamble is great. The opportunity cost of what else you could be doing has a high price tag if the movie sucks. Not so with TV.

With TV — like music — you can simply skip ahead or choose a different product or feel no loss of investment by turning it off. Expectations are lower so your enjoyment is commensurately higher (see the happiness formula in Chapter 24), even if, in fact, you were to watch the same movie or show on TV or in a theater.

But, as much as we enjoy the absence of commercials, they have traditionally served an important purpose for the storytellers. Audiences tend to think the broadcaster just throws in a commercial to interrupt content whenever they want.

What the audience doesn't know is producers carefully craft story and plan for every single commercial break, down to the second. As a producer, I have very specific spec sheets of delivery requirements for how long each act can be and what second I have to go out to a commercial, and what second I have to return to the script. So we write and produce material to not only cater to that but to also benefit from the breaks. We shoot a moment in a scene knowing exactly when a commercial is coming.

Even during the best movies, if you were to view a security camera of an audience in a theater, you would see clear moments when almost everyone choreographs their seat-shifting simultaneously. There could be something dramatic that has happened or has been revealed, and the audience needs a moment to — just be.

I argue (as sacrilegious as this may sound) that movies need commercials, whether they're on TV or in the theater. Don't hate them.

Audiences need breaks to process and let the impact of story resonate. When the narrative is on a train that never stops, the journey sometimes glosses over important signposts because it's moving too fast.

We need a momentary reprieve to reflect on the development of characters, especially the hero; and as that hero relates to our own inner hero.

The movies and TV shows we love the most are the ones where we see ourselves in the hero. His struggle, conflict, contemplation, pursuit, purpose, doubt, regret, dream, courage — when those are aligned with ours, we connect and empathize. We temporarily outsource our own heroic journey to the fictional hero's journey so that we can safely fantasize that we are making those decisions and gaining that wisdom but in the safety of our Ordinary World. The on-screen hero becomes our proxy.

That's really all we do when we watch entertainment. We see other Hero's Journeys and compare them to our own. Think about any recent movie you've seen that you didn't like; your journey didn't align with the hero's own journey. If it did, you would have probably loved the movie.

Think about your favorite movies or shows. There is something in the Hero's Journey that aligns with you. Even if the hero is evil or psychopathic, there's something in his inner hero that resonates with you.

TV Heroes Bryan Cranston, Jon Hamm, Jason Bateman, Liev Schrieber, and Kyle Chandler are all flawed and often evil, appearing respectively in "Breaking Bad," "Mad Men," "Ozark," "Ray Donovan," and "Bloodline." But if you love one of those shows, you relate to the lead's plight. Something inside the TV hero parallels with your inner hero's desires, struggles, obstacles, or situation.

But without the act-breaks, it's more difficult for the story of the hero to resonate. Assessment and inventory not only help keep us on track and motivated but also provide pause to remind us we're all human.

This is why we also need commercial breaks in real life. It seems counter-intuitive to a Hero of action, but it's during the breaks — the moments of silence and retrospect — when issues and conflict can often be resolved or optimized.

- Are you stuck on a finance or budget issue you can't solve? Perhaps your taxes, investments, or credit card debt?

Take a commercial break.

- Are you trying to optimize your time during the day?

- Are you trying to build better health habits?
- Are you trying to figure out how to manage your boss or an employee?

Take a commercial break.

Cool off. Walk around the block, take deep breaths, stretch, pretend you're someone else and tasked with the issue at hand. What are the steps to resolution?

- Are you having an unproductive argument with a family member that seems to go in circles?

Take a commercial break.

What are you even arguing over? Be silent for two minutes and think: if you were producing this dispute for a scene in a movie, what would the hero do next to make it productive? You're the producer; what do you want your hero to do next that shows she understands the issue and can resolve it?

Come back from the break, recap, elucidate and define what you're both bickering about, and then advance. Clarify. De-escalate. Repair. Find common ground, or agree to disagree, but keep it solely about the current issue, not the person or the past of the person.

Bringing up the past tells the other person that you can't focus on the current issue so you're bringing up past issues as ammunition to compensate. You want to go to battle, not find solutions.

Opposing forces move so quickly the real issues get buried and left behind. Knowing this scenario is an "episode," finish it. Don't let it drag on or hang overnight, only to rehash it another day during another episode. This applies to all issues, not just relationships.

Take the beneficial commercial break. You'll ironically get there faster by putting on the brakes. In Aesop's fable, it was the tortoise that won the race, not the hare.

We may lose perspective of what we're trying to accomplish when we have total engagement. Engagement is a laudable behavior. We should work hard to achieve that level of absorption when complex matters are at hand. We need to have deep focus and be diligent in our pursuits.

But superficial noise gets in the way.

So a break — commercial, intermission, call it what you will — between acts helps establish how far we've come, and what remains to be done. We come up for air after a deep dive so that our perspective isn't too myopic.

I employ this tactic often when making a decision about anything I'm pursuing. If the goal is important enough to expend time, then my taking a moment to say: "Here's what I've accomplished so far in this pursuit, and here's where I'd like to be" helps define steps and place road markers.

Attention is important, but when you're done making your laser cut, you want to straighten up, remove the welding mask and see your work as a whole — not just the laser cut. Are you accomplishing the larger pursuit? Or are you currently stuck on a tiny detail that doesn't contribute much to the final outcome? It's possible you're so caught up in a task that you're ignoring the larger Why. In other words, don't lose sight of the forest because of a tree.

If you want to take this metaphor literally, next time you watch TV and you get off the couch due to a commercial, and, halfway through the break, you can't even remember what you were watching, turn the TV off. That brief forgetfulness is a sign you're wasting time.

A great break is to talk a walk and listen to a podcast or read a book on a topic you want to learn more about. Successful icons seek education and learning as part of their downtime. On the other hand, non-heroic people by default seek entertainment and compulsory consumption.

Many of us ignore our body's signs when it's time to take a break. We want to binge our productive periods just like we do our TV shows. But when we become irritable, restless, and have difficulty focusing, signs are hitting us over the head. It's time to cut to commercial.

I admit I have moments of writer's block while writing this very book. As much as I would love to binge-write my way through it and feel a sense of accomplishment, I'm only doing the writing a disservice and wasting your time as a reader. So I can take a commercial break, or it will soon break me. One way or another, there needs to be a break.

Allow your natural cycles to dictate when to do certain work. When you need a break, it's time for light, perfunctory tasks. Do more impactful and concentration-heavy work when you're in a flow and optimized for clarity and mastery.

We have natural cycles that alternate bursts of energized concentration with relaxation throughout the day.

Psycho physiologist Peretz Lavie calls these natural cycles "ultradian cycles." The body and brain have alternating peaks of maximum energy, as well as troughs, during which they rest and get ready for the next peak.

If you can listen to, and align with your cycle, you will be in sync and become more effective. You might already be efficient, but you're wasting time if you're not effective. You can't be effective unless you're aware of your cycle and know when to concentrate and when to relax.

For most people, this is a Morning and Evening cycle. Your energy is strongest in the morning and lessens throughout the day until you go to bed. You rest during the night. The next day you are ready to perform at a maximal level.

Others have mini-cycles like 90 minutes of bursts at a time followed by 30 minutes of downtime, and so on, throughout the day. You have to listen and find yours so you can align with it.

I have an acronym I use, CAP. I attempt to structure my day so that CAP comes in order of my diurnal cycle. Morning-Afternoon-Evening = Create-Administer-Play. C-A-P.

In the morning it's all about Creativity. This is when I keep my email and notifications off. Without apology I say "No" to distractions, conference calls, meetings (in most cases), and am on offense building, making, strategizing and doing requisite deep thinking to drive my purpose and passions forward.

This period is when I come up with ideas. The world is full of possibility, and suddenly, like Bradley Cooper in "Limitless," everything is alive and crystal clear. I'm metaphorically unstoppable.

The tsunami sirens could be blaring, but it's going to have to wait for me to get through this 2-3 hour period that is worth perhaps two entire days of a typical person's distracted, fractured, and multi-tasked work. I win the day because I have a highly concentrated focus on prioritized projects and tasks which trump tangential ambient noise. I achieve flow for ideas to force-multiply my goals.

This period or zone is what author Cal Newport would call Deep Work, based on his best-selling book of the same name (I admit I haven't read his book, but upon research am aware he writes extensively on this subject).

For me, this deep work takes place early in the morning, which is why I've adjusted my body clock to wake up early and go to bed early. It gives me a longer saturation of deep work and a shorter period of shallow work. So I effectively hack my cycle by adjusting my sleep pattern.

Produce Yourself

If I know I need to write a certain day, whether it's fiction for film and TV, voiceover, or this book, I don't waste my early morning hours after a strong cup of coffee sorting through yesterday's junk mail or going on Facebook to see what my coworker ate last night. That is mindless and purely fast food. There is a time for that. For me, it's after the sun goes down and I want to unwind before meditating and stretching.

When the kitchen is bustling, TV is on, and family is cooking, I crack a beer. I can't turn on my laptop and suddenly come up with a new movie or solve a complex work problem. It's simply not going to happen, at least effectively. But I can knock some items off my daily list while all that is happening. I can catch up with others about their day and simultaneously toss out grocery coupons that clutter my mailbox.

As a film and television producer, I've worked with hundreds of writers, hunkered down in writing rooms, brainstorming. Searching for new and fresh angles is a tedious task that challenges and exercises the brain. For this reason, most writers only write for about 3-4 hours a day, max. It's true. It doesn't mean they aren't planning and plotting another 7 hours beyond that. But the actual writing is a small window when their brain is most active and effective.

Then, in the afternoon, it's the "A," for me: Administration. This involves more perfunctory tasks: financing, bills, calendars, returning emails, supervising and delegating, check-marking boxes on the list. This is when I can finally go on defense and take care of incoming requests at the same time. I can accept a little more noise into my life, as I'm doing shallow work.

Finally, I Play, the final phase that becomes my "commercial break." This is when I can meditate, have gratitude, read, stretch, learn, exercise, educate myself and re-energize. I also do light planning for the next day. My next morning will be full of more complex issues to solve (part of this is asking my subconscious for help before I sleep. See Chapter 20).

Unfortunately for most people, light work consumes and distracts their entire day. They've not learned to compartmentalize. They never find time to do the leveraged work that is really important. Sure, the calendared tasks like paying bills or doing laundry or having to run an errand are part of life. We have to perform certain functions. But when your brain is a Ferrari, take it to the racetrack, not to the grocery store parking lot.

There's a difference between important activities and urgent activities. Too many people assume all important activities are urgent, and all urgent activities are important. Big difference.

In addition, attempt to reduce or eliminate those light tasks as much as possible in the first place. Here's another acronym I applied to my email system a few years back. But it applies to almost anything outside of complex work. I call it DAD, which stands for Delete, Automate, Delegate.

Delete. We covered this in the last chapter. That's basically saying "No" whenever you can. When your priorities are straight and you have a yearning purpose that needs a "Yes," you can have the courage to remorselessly say "No" to other things.

Say "No" when you can and don't overpromise. Don't commit to things that you don't absolutely love and want to be part of your life. A lot of tasks that you repeat every day may not even need be addressed. Just delete them. Throw it out, give it away, stop doing it. Ask yourself if it's important enough to keep you from the "Yes"s that you need in your life. If not, delete.

Automate. Like bills, there are many repetitive occurrences that require the same repetitive response. Automate those. If you absolutely can't delete it, then do your best to automate it.

With artificial intelligence, online billing, payroll, smartphones, password-programs, Siri, Alexa, Google Home, Phillips Hue lighting system, Wemo plugs, Coffee Makers, dry cleaning pick-up and drop-off, cooked meals, house thermostats, pool pumps, unlocking your house and car — almost everything can be automated. Some call this "The Internet of Things." Small things add up. Small things also distract and create noise. Automate them.

The time it takes to set up the automation may be longer than the actual task, but infinitely smaller than the aggregate of that task day after day.

Delegate. If the light task at hand couldn't be deleted and couldn't be automated, delegate it. Outsource unpleasant or overly time intensive activities if they're outside your passion, purpose, inspiration, or hobby. If you don't enjoy it or find meaning in it, don't do it. Delegate it. Virtual assistants are awesome and cheap. There's also TaskRabbit and ThumbTack and Fiverr and 25 other great gig or connection-economy sites to outsource that IKEA assembly or furniture pickup.

Then, if something has passed the gauntlet of DAD and it's still on your plate, make sure you address it at the proper time.

Your brain is like a dog wanting to go for a walk. It's jumping up and down, scratching at the door, saying, "Use me!" And you make it sit idle while you fold your sweatpants? Let your brain take you to amazing places by listening to it.

When you're done with the shallow tasks and functions, return from your commercial break by meditating. You don't have to repetitively tone chant or play background Indian music. You don't have to sit in the middle of the room and cross your legs. It may be incredibly beneficial, but it's not my thing. And it doesn't have to be yours.

You can simply lift your butt out of your office chair, take your eyes off of your computer screen and STARE out the window for 10 minutes straight (on this topic, it's been recommended that a good exercise for your eyes, when you're at the computer, is to, every 20 minutes, take your eyes off the screen and stare at something at least 20 feet away for 20 seconds). Ten minutes is a long time, by the way, when meditating. But turn off your phone notifications and just stare. Let your mind wander; let it bring you back to the organics and authenticity of your thoughts. Free-flow, don't force it. Take deep, slow breaths. Smile. Do not think about work. Do not think about family. Just be. You are not wasting time. You are not procrastinating. This is a commercial break and a reset for coming back to your next act.

Some people spend a lot of money to turn themselves off from noise and stimuli (float tanks, gurus, retreats, vacations). That's really all meditation is about: turning off your ego so you can come back into reality and think clearly, deeply, and with focus. Ten minutes of meditation can erase hours, days, even weeks of baggage-induced misdirection and misguidance in your pursuits.

We become busy robots and forget to think and process. Give yourself the utility you already have: your brain's ability to solve problems. But you have to turn off the world to access this. Your mind is a finely tuned machine, but its reptilian processing will revert to survival mode when your phone buzzes and you read an email asking you for something. Turn the world off.

This is your commercial. It's also your secret weapon to advancing and optimizing your life.

In typical TV fashion, now that we're back from commercial break, let's tease what's next:

Coming Up: You will Cross The Threshold.

You finally leave your familiar world for the new one.

-

CHAPTER 10

Crossing The Threshold: Value · Connection Identity
(Stage 5)

"Do, or do not. There is no 'try'."

- Yoda in *The Empire Strikes Back*

IN STAGE 5, THE HERO IS COMMITTED TO HER GOAL and finally ready to Cross The Threshold. She has surpassed the initial hurdles and is about to enter an unfamiliar world, called the Special World.

This exit-entrance from the Ordinary World to The Special World signifies her eventual acceptance of the passage to come. She already battled reluctance, doubt, and fear. Her regular life is now in the rearview mirror. Unchartered territory awaits.

In movies, this threshold is sometimes quite literal. In "Men in Black," Will Smith steps over the elevator threshold and into the offices of MIB. He's given his suit, gadgets, and his mind is erased. He completely leaves his Ordinary World for the new Special One.

In "Dirty Dancing," Jennifer Grey also literally crosses the threshold when she steps over the bungalow's doorstep where Patrick Swayze and others are dancing seductively. From that point on, Jennifer's innocence is left behind.

And in "The Wizard of Oz," Dorothy and Toto cross a Munchkinland threshold, igniting a musical event that will map out her subsequent serpentine journey

In film, this is typically a visual and visceral experience. It is at the end of the first act (roughly 30 minutes into a movie) when the audience is catapulted into excitement and adventure. Exposition is largely over and it's time for commotion and liveliness.

Michael J. Fox gets the Delorean up to 88 miles per hour and we're transported "Back to the Future." The movie goes into overdrive. Or Roy Scheider gets into a small boat in choppy waters to hunt down "Jaws," beginning a harrowing battle for the rest of the film. Matthew McConaughey boards the rocket and blasts into space in "Interstellar."

In real life, our own Hero's Journeys tend to be more metaphorical, spiritual, emotional, or mental. They can still be active or physical, like changing jobs, moving states, remarrying, having kids, or starting a business. But they don't have to time travel, hunt a shark, or find a new planet to inhabit. They can cross into psychological or habitual terrain. In all these films, this is what the Hero's Journey is really about: the inner-journey. Everything else is usually window dressing.

In "Good Will Hunting," Matt Damon Crosses the Threshold when he finally calls Minnie Driver back after a first date. His Ordinary World cast women aside haphazardly. He was fearful of ruining perfect first-dates and idealistic visions that come with them. He camouflaged his emotions and left a trail of heartbreak. But his new anomalous world asks him, with the help of mentor Robin Williams, to be exposed and authentic. Matt crosses over, developing his opportunity to feel, love, and in return be loved. It's an emotional mindset alien to his Ordinary World.

This is analogous to Tom Cruise's inner-journey in "Rain Man." Tom is a shallow, selfish, materialistic brother to an autistic Dustin Hoffman. Tom only reaches out to Dustin in an attempt to extract an inheritance he's been cut out of. After hearing specific airline crash statistics, Dustin forces Tom to road trip with him. It is on that road trip — Crossing the Threshold — where Tom discovers a Special World cultivated by his brother's condition. The disruption, maintenance needs, and routines of his brother transform Tom into an improved version of himself he didn't know was available, providing increased value and growth to his inner hero's identity.

I was committed to becoming a movie producer. I'd never seen what a movie producer actually does. I didn't know a movie producer personally. I hadn't grown up with any inclination or awareness whatsoever. But I knew it was my destiny, my purpose, based on what BR helped me envision, and I was now leaving my comfortable business college life behind.

My inner hero was already halfway across the threshold. I was there in spirit. But I needed to have my outer hero catch up and get there, quite literally.

I sent out 200 résumés to 200 production companies. As impressive as I thought it was at the time, it was a passive, insecure exercise. My mindset mistook productivity and volume for effectiveness. It was a numbers game and I was playing the odds. I thought I was being smart by automating a form letter with rotating contacts.

This flawed approach had obvious problems, which is why I only received one phone call, which resulted in one interview, which ultimately went nowhere. For that interview, I bought a suit. I only wore it once. Big fail all around.

What were the problems?

First, I wasn't providing any value to anyone. I was simply trying to cast a line into a lake and hope a fish would bite — not very strategic or influential, especially when the lake has thousands of fishermen and only 10 fish.

Second, I had the misconception that merely performing a function was advancement; that by spending hours and "working hard" I could displace any competition seeking the same job.

Both of these positions were crippling me. I needed an upgrade in my approach.

Executives who received my résumé needed to perceive value. There's no benefit to them or their company to receive a random query from someone wanting to work in Hollywood. Fire and passion don't account for much, as that's already a given. Zeal is a minimum requirement, not an asset. If you want someone to digest your request, you need to project more than desire and persistence. There's no reward for mere craving.

People embrace the fallacy that because they want something so bad they deserve it. This is especially true of artists. They reason their sheer passion and determination will eventually win in the end.

These aren't bad qualities to have. Determination, desire, and persistence have immense benefit in helping you find purpose. But, like a dirty windshield, they can hide reality.

Produce Yourself

Most senior-level professionals in any industry specifically reject the advances of people who are persistent for persistent's sake, or ambitious for the sake of ambition. Management knows when it responds to unsolicited requests for meetings, phone calls or interviews, the response only encourages more distraction, additional inquiry, and more attempts for time.

Yet the disillusioned repeat this process and then wallow in disappointment and feelings of rejection. What some people never realize is that it's not personal. They're not rejecting you; they're rejecting your lack of effective communication. You've not demonstrated your benefit to them.

Everyone is following their own Hero's Journey. You as an outsider play into others' journeys as a supporting character or guest appearance when you request attention. You need to become an advantage for them in overcoming their own challenges. Show them you can be a Watson to their Sherlock. You don't want to be another obstacle, which is what often happens with unsolicited submissions that don't provide value.

You, as someone who wants something and they, as someone who has that something to offer, are like dancers. You have to entice them enough to step onto the floor where you'll meet in the middle, crisscrossing paths in a way that you help each other's hero become heroic. Properly executed, it can be a thing of beauty.

This applies to almost anything when two people need to work together wherein one needs something from the other.

If you're a startup and you want an angel investor; if you're a real estate agent and want a client; if you're a dance instructor and want to teach, you have to demonstrate your value. Handing someone homework isn't value.

I get many emails from people who want to be in the film or TV business. They want to pick my brain or buy me coffee. If I could just share some tips and advice on screenwriting or how to get a job in development or how to sell a show. They just have a few questions for me. It won't take long. Of course.

Much as I enjoy meeting new people and being generous and available, were I to say "Yes" to all queries, the sheer volume of unsolicited inquiries would incapacitate my progress and alter my path. I can't afford to be the outsourced inbox for others I don't know. I would in effect become their employee if I complied with every request.

I've made this mistake before and spent large chunks of my days simply responding to these, taking every request as a personal plea as if I were the only one they were contacting.

Whereas they reach out for selfish reasons, I say "No" for selfless reasons. The notion of asking for someone's time for no other benefit than to serve as free research diminishes one's value. In other words, if my time is worth so little that I can spend an hour at coffee with a stranger, how valuable can my advice be?

Unless, of course, we both agree to dance. A dance is different. Synergetic. Both people get to know each other and benefit from the union because effective needs, strengths, ideas were communicated upfront.

I personally love to mentor. I love to coach, teach, guide and give advice. But I can't do that with submissions requesting something as broad and impersonal as "How do I make movies?" That question can apply to hundreds of us in the business and has no personal connection to me. The answer is readily available on the Internet.

The problem with these requests is that they don't offer me anything — operative emphasis being on "anything," not "me."

Anything general that I could throw out as "advice" can be found anywhere and doesn't provide the questioner value. There isn't a magic pill to take, shirt to wear, or mantra to repeat to these seekers when there's nothing unique in the request or personally identifiable about the requester.

Furthermore, the thought of someone "picking" my brain isn't pleasant either. Aside from the literal visual of the idiom, I'm not sure I could offer the best advice without knowing where someone is in their own life's movie — their own journey. Worse yet, perhaps my advice would do more damage than good.

Rather, if someone does their homework, learns about me, my projects, my companies, my pursuits; and offers me advice or ways I could improve something in my business; a way I could use such and such a service to grow this or that; a way I could learn from them; then there's potentially an opportunity to dance. Someone who needs something from me is offering me something I could in turn use. It's a tango. And it takes two.

By offering value to someone you want to meet — a referral, tip, advice, connection with someone, information, knowledge — it becomes a win-win.

This was the trouble with my misguided and undeveloped action of sending out 200 résumés. I was playing the odds that someone somewhere was just dying to hire a kid straight out of college. Long odds indeed.

What I have since learned, that would have been much smarter and more helpful than just adding inches to someone's desk junk, is this: research every company and person I contacted to see how I could benefit them and add value. In an interview (if I am so fortunate to book one), they can potentially give me value by showing me who I am.

I had seen the movies their companies produced. I could learn about projects they had in development; books they had recently optioned;

read articles and interviews of troubles they had in the business; or ways they wanted to improve. And that would have shown not only did I have initiative, but I cared and was capable of resourcefulness.

That would provide them benefit if that's the kind of person their company needed. I would let them see what kind of person I was. I would give them the proper tools to understand me.

In a blind letter of introduction, I have the reader's attention for maybe 10 seconds. I need to make those 10 seconds effective.

I would have been better off focusing on 20 companies, not 200. I would have been better off making very personal proposals of value-adds.

Everyone needs to achieve certain goals. If you need something from someone, ask yourself how you can help them toward one of their goals. Think about that, and then contact them. You'll have a decent shot at not only a reply, but potentially a future ally, friend, or co-worker.

Do you want to work for GoPro? What are they doing wrong? What do you wish they would change? Why do you think their stock has sunk almost 90 percent?

You want to design the next children's toy but are not sure where to begin? Contacting Mattel, Hasbro, or Disney may make sense, but I imagine you're joining a pile of submissions from around the world. Perhaps you could find a sympathetic ear, however, by contacting the companies and sharing some free ideas for a current product line. What could improve it? What's an accessory that would complement an existing toy? What's something unique you've noticed by studying their history? What's your take on why a certain toy may have failed? Suddenly, you're not take-take-take but give-give-give. Free analysis. You'll probably get a response. That's when it's time to dance.

Produce Yourself

We all need value and benefit. Whenever you provide that, without asking for anything in return, you'll get your return. Thinking selflessly will benefit you in the long run. This applies to many areas of life.

Whether it's out of pure generosity and love, or you have an ulterior motive, providing value for someone else is like planting a seed in their garden. While you continue to cultivate your own sprouting plants and trees for future fruit, the value you give another person becomes a seed that may propagate. Think of it as another diversified investment. But at the same time, do it because you care. Do it because you want to help someone.

Four years ago I helped a friend of a friend get his first house. Although I'm not a realtor, because I have a broker's license, I can do any real estate transaction. He didn't have a realtor and I happened to intimately know the area where he wanted to buy.

So I helped him figure out his finances; I pre-approved him for a mortgage loan; I helped him find his house. I was happy to do all of this. I love real estate. I love finance. I was also happy to help out a friend.

In the end, he bought the house through a realtor he met at a party and chose a mortgage company that the realtor recommended. I was out of the loop and completely cut out financially.

Candidly, I was a little bummed. But I was also happy for him. The house and transactions were about him, not me.

Cut to recent times. This friend called me, thanking me for helping him find that house, his first one, 4 years ago. He now had amassed over $675,000 equity in the house.

I'm currently refinancing his mortgage, refinancing another income property that his wife owns, and will be writing the mortgage for their new home — 3 loans all at once from the same client.

He told me he never forgot the time I spent educating and helping him get going 4 years before and insisted on bringing me all his business. I don't want to get too detailed about how the mortgage world works, but let's just say closing three new mortgages for the same person in the same week is a good week. And aside from having a great friend, I have a client for life who is now an ambassador for my services.

The most valuable advertising in the world is referral. It's too expensive for anyone to buy. They have to earn it. Providing value will do that, creating megaphones for your brand or pursuit while you sleep.

I have a colleague who is a graphic designer. He now works remotely on the East coast and is constantly busy. I have sent him numerous clients over the years because he does fantastic work. Plus, when I've had projects with smaller budgets, he's always been accommodating. That accommodation is his advertising. I'm quite sure he has 50 other clients he's done this for, which is why he need not spend a penny on advertising.

Whereas our economy used to be driven by industrialization — scaling up businesses to be more productive, making products cheaper and faster, and selling to as many people as possible — almost the converse is true today.

Today we are in a connection economy. Value is perceived when you gain a connection you wouldn't otherwise have had. And you don't need to be connected to the whole world. Just your audience, just your tribe. And that's where the value lies. There's immense value in agency.

If you're an entrepreneur with a product, service, or idea, you would be willing to pay to immediately reach that niche audience that finds value in it. If you can find just those 500 or 1000 people — not the whole world — who find the value you offer, you will have a successful business.

Perhaps you can be that agency. Maybe you can connect someone with someone, providing value to both for the introduction. Now your résumé isn't just raising the paperweight on someone's desk. Now you are someone who adds value.

The people who help or support you in significant ways are the ones who love you or feel loved by you. And they'll particularly feel loved if you've connected them, hooked them up, presented them opportunity, given them advice, helped them get a job, genuinely cared about their well being, fought for their side, listened to their narrative and understood their brand.

This ties in with following your purpose first and the money second. The return on your good deeds will eventually come in unexpected form or when you least expect it. And it's also just a great way to live your life — do what you love, do favors for others, help others, advise others, teach others without expecting anything in return.

If the "return" is important to you, it will come anyway. But living your life without that concern is a more pristine and healthy way to approach your endeavors, in business and personal relationships.

But it requires work and habit. You need to do your groundwork and learn about the people or companies you are trying to collaborate with — employee or partner, customer or vendor, friend or family. Learn who they are and what their mission is. What are their goals? What's their brand?

The world runs on branding and identity. Everyone we work with, deal with; everything we buy, consume, watch, listen to; everywhere we go and every activity we engage in; everything has a narrative. Everything has a story of what or who it is. It's a brand.

And if we want to be a part of that story or identity, if we want that story to be us, then we consume, partner, hire, buy, or become part of that "thing" that says: 'This is who I am.'

Think about the labels on your clothes, your phone and computer, and the car you drive. They have a story, and if you want to be part of that story, you buy them. You want to be part of the "scene" that is Apple. You like their brand and that complements who you are.

The most successful marketers are the ones who simply tell a story. And that story has two components — value and identity.

Obviously, the product needs to provide value on a core level. Someone will pay for a $200 widget if the perceived value is $300, for example. So they are buying perceived value of $100. That's the fundamental psychology in terms of pricing. You view that cup of coffee as worth $5 based on your time, your location, and your need, so you gladly pay $4 for the coffee. To you, that coffee establishment is handing you a $1 bill. You tell your friends and colleagues about that coffee place because you want them to line up and get their $1 bill, too.

But this value in monetary terms is secondary to the value of identity. The story a product or service tells about your identity is the most important value for which people will gladly pay.

We can drive any car. It has four wheels and it goes. We can wear any shirt. It keeps us warm and covers our nakedness. We can go to any gym. It has resistance functions of some kind. We can go to almost any college. Within range, the education is relatively the same.

But we choose to drive the car we drive, the shirt we wear, the gym we frequent, and are proud to wear the logos from the college we went to because we like the story that they tell about us. They let the world know who we are, what we stand for, and how we want to be perceived.

There are a quite a few people who actually have Apple Computer tattoos. It speaks to who they are so much that they literally brand themselves with Apple. Does anyone have an IBM or Dell tattoo?

Produce Yourself

Do you really need to drive a Tesla rather than a Honda? Not really. But you are willing to pay extra for that Tesla because it tells a specific story about you. It says you are successful, you are progressive, you care about the environment. True or not, this is the story it broadcasts.

Ditto for food. Where and what you eat has to fit your story. If you're consuming food or eating at places that don't fit your brand, then you hide that food or don't tell your family that you just ate at McDonald's. But you'll socially share a check-in of a restaurant that you want people to know is part of your brand. "This is me, everyone. Check it out, I'm here."

Social media posts and check-ins are kinds of temporary tattoos. You want people to associate slogans, vacation photos, and places with you. They help tell the story of who you are.

The stories that products and services tell are so powerful they become part of our Hero's Journey. We strive to be a website designer, an accountant, or a contractor because we like the branding. We want that identity to be our identity. We buy into and happily pay for story inclusion.

I didn't know yet exactly what movie producers did, but I bought into the story of one. I liked the branding. I liked how it made me feel. So I made it part of my journey.

But I, in turn, am a part of others' journeys, and I failed to make that clear. As an eager person shooting emails or résumés, I failed to reveal my brand. Plus, I revealed I didn't know theirs. I was simply regurgitating mass quantity to get someone's attention.

Cut to today. The majority of my quick afternoon email deletes look something like this: "Dear Sir: I wrote a great screenplay and want to make it into a movie. Will you read it?" Or there's: "I have the best idea for a TV show ever; call me."

Those emails usually continue on for a few paragraphs, but I never get that far. The first lost opportunity they had to gain my attention was proof they didn't research my brand and didn't reveal theirs. They made no personal request or provision of vital information.

I once produced a teen-comedy movie with a producing partner. We were casting for one of the lead roles. A young actor who is now famous came in to audition. I couldn't name the 50 or so guys we saw over a week since there were so many. But I am still reminded of his audition whenever I see him on TV. He's been part of one of the most successful TV franchises for over 12 years.

He didn't end up getting the part for our movie, even though he was amazing and would have nailed the role. It had more to do with chemistry and balance with another already-cast actor. The two of them were probably too similar.

Before he exited the audition, he pulled out a mixed tape.

He wrote a little accompanying note that laid out all of the songs and bands he thought would be perfect for the film's soundtrack. From his colorful doodling on the cassette and note, you could tell he spent some thought on this. And, unlike dragging-and-dropping MP3s into a folder or streaming links today, it took time to make that tape.

The soundtrack was an important component of the movie. We had some major bands on the soundtrack and prominent labels involved, a full-time music supervisor, etc. But this actor was the first to acknowledge and remind us how important the soundtrack was. He relayed to us that he knew our brand.

No actor needed to do this. It's not part of the audition. And why would an actor be thinking about the music in a film when they are showing up to read a few lines to get hired for a role?

Produce Yourself

But that tape made him memorable.

In a week of seeing the same performance day in day out with the same lines being read, his submission stayed with us, after all these years. This is a guy who researched and showed us he knew the identity and narrative of our film.

I wouldn't be surprised if it was this kind of value that he gave in his auditions that ultimately landed him a starring role in TV. 97 percent of the actors in Hollywood would kill to be on this show (let alone for 12 years running with the millions of dollars and residual benefits that accompany that). He's a fraction of 1 percent right now of all actors who are working and making money. All of this, possibly, for the focused work he did understanding others' story and providing value to their process.

While continuing to send out résumés and missing the mark, I bussed tables at an upscale restaurant for one summer. While there, I worked with a waiter, Z, who had been there over 20 years.

Z was a screenwriter. This restaurant gig was his day-job. That was his story. So we would discuss film when it was slow. I couldn't help but feel sad that this guy had been writing screenplays for the last 20 years and here he was still serving food in a restaurant. I would later learn this is typical of the majority of screenwriters in Hollywood. No different than an actor hustling for auditions in between barista jobs. It's highly competitive.

Dreaming is romantic. It puts a smile on our face. It takes no effort. We all do it. What if... some day... one day. This is what makes us human — always trying to better our situations. But dreaming without doing only makes for temporary mood enhancement. There's nothing substantial. It's a merry-go-round of wish fulfillment that never transpires. This was my observation of Z.

Z was a world-class dreamer. I was inspired by his knowledge and stories about writing and old Hollywood. I like to think he was toiling at night on his computer, writing furiously, which he probably was. But maybe that was his comfort zone. Similar to my 200 résumés, maybe he felt safe, alone in his house, writing, confusing his volume of productivity for effectiveness.

Hollywood is a beast — perhaps more ferocious than MGM's Leo — and regardless how hard or often you work, she doesn't necessarily reward you. She looks for brands, identities, and really wants value.

Z had the determination and courage to actually write screenplays. I read several and found them extremely well executed. But he was sending them out to production companies, just as I had those résumés. And today, being on the receiving end of screenplays, an unsolicited screenplay is the last thing I want from someone I don't know.

Like me, Z misinterpreted repetitive function as progress. It may have been productive, but was highly ineffectual.

There's no responsibility and no traction. We all find busy tasks which make us feel productive. We feel we're at least accomplishing something to advance our goals. But the problem is that we're often doing only the easy, passive tasks that require little effort or thinking — not necessarily the right ones. That makes us feel better but gets us nowhere.

That dopamine boost we get when we get a lot done gets mislabeled in our minds as progress.

I give Z props for having written the screenplays. I don't want to discount that. I commend him. Completing one screenplay is an enormous task; he'd written several. I have no idea what struggles he had to overcome to write what he did. That in itself is a Hero's Journey he took and completed.

Produce Yourself

But Z needed to rewrite his personal journey, wherein he would have the bravery to overcome his reluctance to continue wading in a pool of complacency. Simply writing and sending out more screenplays wasn't the answer.

Had Z stepped back and observed his own movie, he might have realized that the one character whose heroic arc he was overlooking was his own. As a screenwriter, you become so adept at the stages of character development you know exactly where your character needs to be. I doubt he wanted his lead character to be stuck waiting tables for 20 years.

This is partly why I conceived the concept of this book. Here was a writer, Z, who could craft and structure the perfect heroic character. He knew what traits and stages of advancement needed to be. So why not cast himself in his own script and write his way toward the life he wanted?

I say with confidence there's no way — none at all — he would sit down and write the fictional version of himself as a lifetime waiter. I know he has more talent than that. I know he wants more than that. His acorn is to become an oak; it's in his DNA. But here he was stuck as a dandelion at a restaurant on the beach.

Z was my first cautionary tale of Hollywood. He motivated me to take actions that were effective and purposeful. This was that moment in the movie where I saw my future on an alternate timeline. I didn't want to look in the mirror and see Z staring back at me.

I couldn't become Z. Z never even left his Ordinary World. It terrified me. As much as I needed my mentor BR to help me overcome the long gestating reluctance period, I ended up equally needing my anti-mentor Z. BR showed me what was possible. But so did Z. BR was the fairy tale. Z was the cautionary one.

It was time to upgrade my approach.

One of the numerous gates leading onto the Warner Bros. lot in Burbank, CA sat across an alleyway from a lunch commissary. Cars were often lined up to get in, have their license plates recorded, IDs checked, and go through a semi-TSA experience.

This was all pre 9/11 so security was more about protecting talent from paparazzi and tourists than it was for potential terrorist threat, as is the case today.

I noticed, at lunchtime, executives and employees walked through this same gate to eat lunch somewhere off the lot. Everyone seemed to have passes or badges around their necks, but many didn't, and many weren't stopped by the guards. I would just see a "wave" that whispered "back to the grind" as they wended their way, scripts under arms.

I realized this was my ticket onto the lot. We had this same system in college. We called it the Pepperdine Wave because you could drive onto Campus by going through the always open "permit lane" rather than the gated "visitor lane" simply by waving to the guard and looking like a student.

I figured the Warner Bros. guards were so busy with the lineup of cars they wouldn't bother with a returning lunch employee if they had a semblance of legitimacy.

So I made a faux script (all blank pages), donned a sports coat, and carried a shoulder bag with my résumés. Only this time I was prepared.

I had researched every production company on the studio lot I was targeting. I knew what movies they had produced, were producing, were developing, and names of the executives who recently got promoted or hired. Everything I could gather at the time. And I tailored each letter as if the given person were my best friend and I was simply saying, "Hey, here's what I'm up to right now. I see what you're up to. Let's work together. We can help each other."

Produce Yourself

Their Identity. My Identity. Story. Value.

We intrinsically protect ourselves by avoiding stakes, but we require them to stimulate change. For me, if I didn't recognize my stakeless sub-par submissions weren't working, my chances of success were indeed slim.

I walked behind 4 or 5 employees with purpose, carrying my fake script and bag of bios. I cast myself as the employee who was late to return to the office so I moved swiftly, scarfing half a sandwich — props for my ruse. I couldn't even tell you what the guard was doing, if he looked in my direction or what. I just walked. And suddenly, there I was, on the lot. I crossed the threshold quite literally where my outer hero was now catching up to my inner one. Usually, it's the opposite.

If you've never been on a studio lot, here's what's great about its logistics: all the production companies who have deals with the studio are housed in sort of Army style bungalows or rows of outhouses where you can walk straight up to the front doors from the pavement. You rarely have to enter any type of building, go through elevators or pass through additional security, as is typical for many traditional offices.

I proceeded to enter door after door, saying "Hello" to whoever was in the lobby of each office. I acted as if it was completely normal to walk into their office and ask if they needed help. "What can I do for you?" I would ask, then drop some names and info based on my research, as if I were in the know.

I badly wanted to just slide these résumés under the door. It was painful opening each door to give a song and dance and leave a résumé. But I repeated the mantra to work effectively, not hard. I wanted to resort to passivity, but I had already attempted that and failed. I also had visions of becoming Z.

During the next week, I received close to a dozen phone calls. This eventually landed me 3 solid interviews, which landed me an internship and then later a full-time job. What it also did was give me lifelong contacts who would later become friends and colleagues. Many assistants and receptionists I've met remember me busting in that day to introduce myself.

My internship started out "covering" scripts for Lauren Shuler Donner's company ("X-Men," "Deadpool," "Lethal Weapon"). Covering a script is the most basic entry-level task on the creative side. There's nothing lower. And this is what I did for free — read scripts, analyze, break them down, and write summaries so Lauren and her development executives wouldn't have to waste 2 hours on every submission. Rather, I would "waste" 5 to 6 hours reading and then writing for each one. My time was cheap. Theirs was not.

I would arrive at the office, grab 10 screenplays, go home and write coverage. Rinse and Repeat for about a month. As valuable as I found the experience, I didn't have the patience to continue it for long (to this day I still dislike reading scripts). So I contacted one of the other interviews I had received and requested a full-time job.

There was a partnership of two bigwig producers who were developing tons of films. I didn't see that they were making any at the moment, but they sure had their hand in developing a lot of big budget movies, big brands, with well-known writers and directors. They hired me as an assistant for their creative executives in the office.

I was the one in the desk right by the front door. I answered phones, wrote coverage, updated their phone lists, and picked up lunch. It was lame, as are virtually all entry-level positions. But I was getting some exposure to their world — meetings, budgets, scripts — everything that had to do with development. And I occasionally fielded the random résumé that was pushed through the door at night.

Produce Yourself

I wasn't nuts about being in an office, even though it was fun and "sexy" to be on a major studio lot. What I realized was that "Hollywood," at least this studio side of it, was all about deal making. I wasn't seeing a lot of making movies, just contemplating making movies. I wasn't seeing actual movies get produced; it was obviously happening somewhere. But I wasn't seeing much of it.

It was a lot of circulating scripts, seeing if the studio wanted to finance it. Then finding new scripts, sending those to the studio. A lot of THAT, which reminded me of my damn 200 résumés.

This was integral to how Hollywood works, and it's something I still struggle with. 90 percent of Hollywood is development. It's also why I eventually moved into TV where shows are made lickety-split. But that wouldn't happen for over a decade.

I would learn, years later, that, on average, a film released theatrically has had a road of 7-11 years to get there. Pick almost any movie in your top 10 list, and there's a lengthy story of development hell: lawsuits; director changes; actor rotations; studio changes; turnaround; financing problems; rewrite after rewrite with sometimes a dozen writers coming and going; starts and stops; and then even shelving until the right weekend to launch. All of that, for maybe 4-8 weeks in theaters.

So, after what amounted to a short stint working for others, first as an unpaid intern reading scripts, and then as a minimum wage office assistant watching producers wheel-and-deal and develop (but never make) projects, I decided, with my college education and business degree, I could hack and improve this process. I could bypass this and go make my own movie.

I was misguided. I let my ego get in the way. I should have given it more time and milked the relationships. But the youthful and ignorant hero in me didn't want to enter this new world in such an unheroic way stuck doing something I could have done in my prior, Ordinary World; sitting in an office answering phones and setting up meetings.

I quit after 3 months.

That was the last time in my life I was an "employee."

-

CHAPTER 11

Tests: Risk · Struggle
(Stage 6 - Part 1)

"It's what you do right now that makes a difference."

- Brian Van Holt in *Black Hawk Down*

THE STAGE OF "TESTS, ALLIES, AND ENEMIES" is where the hero will reside the longest on her journey. No longer in her Ordinary World, common occurrences and encounters will feel like obstacles, even if they're not. This is a new world, with new challenges. Once there, she has to learn new approaches or unlearn bad habits in order to survive and hopefully thrive. Since she isn't a native of this new world, the twists and turns increase in frequency, and perhaps intensity.

If you examine "The Wizard of Oz," the film is largely Dorothy journeying the yellow-brick road, cautiously deflecting every foreign and new hindrance thrown at her. To aid her, she has allies in the Tin-man, Scarecrow, and Lion. But she must also battle enemies in the form of the Wicked Witch of the West and flying monkeys. As she advances into other stages, she is still being tested. The tests never end.

Jon Snow clearly emerges as a hero of HBO's "Game of Thrones." But only because of the never-ending tests he must overcome again and again. Whereas everyone else in the 7 kingdoms has a name or gold stash attached to royalty, Jon Snow is but a mere bastard child. He is born with the ultimate test in a world where your name is your destiny.

This stage 6 is less a step between stage 5 and 7, and more a parallel course that coincides with the entire journey, from stage 1 to 12. It occurs simultaneous to most of the other stages, as a hero, Like Dorothy or Jon Snow, is never done being tested. She's steadily aligning with allies and identifying and avoiding enemies. This never subsides. You acquire better habits to alleviate issues and you learn to recognize peril. But these elements never disappear.

For this reason, I'm breaking up this stage's 3 elements — tests, allies, enemies — each into its own section. I begin with Tests.

This is what I faced when I quit and drove off the Warner Bros. lot. What in the world had I done? Was I crazy? I thought I'd overcome my fears and doubts, met my mentor, and Crossed the Threshold. After learning I inhabited the Refusal stage for 4 to 5 years already, I couldn't believe I was now exiting the Promised Land I'd fought so hard to find.

But this would be just one of the gazillion tests that would be thrown at me. They continue to come to this day.

The tests reveal what a hero is really made of, and, more important, capable of. The audience gains a deeper insight into her strength of character because of the challenges she must confront. They see her ability to find solutions to numerous problems. They witness her agility in adapting to internal forces, doubts, and insecurities.

Produce Yourself

In Jennifer Lawrence's "Joy," the protagonist is destined to do great things. We see it from the opening scene when, as a little girl, she cuts out dolls and makes her own toys. But even after leaving her dysfunctional family to sell her mop idea on QVC, she is tested and fumbles in every way possible from product design to selling to getting kicked out of parking lots. She wants to unleash the entrepreneur within, but obstacles keep weighing on her.

The test for Joy isn't so much physical obstacles as inner obstacles. Her inner hero has to overcome her own insecurities and Ordinary World at the same time in order to advance. This, not her crazy family or camera shyness, is her true test. Those are just manifestations of her undeveloped inner hero not catching up to her outer hero. Without enduring and passing these tests, she would be ill-prepared for what is to come.

This analogy is true for just about anything you want to accomplish. Were it not for these tough assessments, anyone/everyone could obtain/achieve everything they thought of. We need the struggle even though we don't want it.

We naturally want to find the quick route and the easy play. How do I instantly get from point A to B with the least resistance? These are good questions to ask when solving problems and seeking simplicity in complexity.

But without impediment and counteraction of any kind, we will never truly arrive. Without tests to strengthen and formulate our mindset for what lies ahead, we walk into battle unprotected. We need the training that only comes from having to surmount setbacks and learn from failures.

This is key to your journey.

Although it might sound dreamy to waltz into a liquor store, purchase a lottery ticket and win, few lottery players ever actually win. The odds of winning at lottery are only slightly better IF you play. Of course, there's nothing at stake.

Developing habits that help us overcome hurdles allows us to seek the stakes. Just about anything with no "cost" or risk to entry won't be fulfilling when you arrive. It continues to always be about the journey, not the destination.

Otherwise, without the stakes, there's no compelling reason for us to excel or remain in this new world. Plus we don't have the requisite tools to handle the world if just plunked down, discombobulated in a new environment.

I produced a show on Travel Channel called "Planet Primetime," for which I received an Emmy nomination. It's a fun show that explores different countries via their primetime television shows. We book a host/actress onto their shows and she learns about the culture and people.

One of the 14 episodes we aired was in the Philippines. I learned just how poor the majority of that country is. Several of their biggest shows are about lottery winners. One, in particular, is about a family that won the lottery, only to fritter it away. They are now dumpster diving.

Our host learned through interviews with the show's producers that this is a widespread common problem in the Philippines. The country's people are so poor that when millions of dollars suddenly land in their laps, they don't know what to do with it. They didn't earn it. Easy come, easy go.

This is true of lotteries across the world. We have data and analysis. It's an aberration to find a lottery winner who is happier and more successful 12 months later than they were before they won.

You're going to have to work for everything you want — at least anything that's important to you.

Produce Yourself

Maybe a few of us got lucky and met our soulmates on day one. But others, like myself, had to go through 30 girlfriends and endless online dating sites before finding someone to be with longer than 3 months. It took work. And for that, I appreciate the one I found (or possibly the one that found me) every day.

You don't have to work hard. That's not smart. I worked hard a lot in my past. I grew up in a culture and zeitgeist from the 1980s of "No pain, no gain" slogans and Michael Douglas' mantra in "Wall Street" that "Greed is good," which taught me the winner was the one who worked the hardest, sweat the most, strained, bled, sacrificed sleep, etc. But this was a terrible slogan to live by. It may have some immediate, short-term effects, but the long-term results are unsustainable and will wear you down.

Those steroid-jacked weight lifters and Terminator wannabes from the 1980s are now limping and having trouble breathing. They've completely hijacked their organs for some temporary physical attributes — ones which unfortunately not only age but may go out of style.

In television or film, if a character's task, approach, habit, or goal can easily be procured without friction or sweat, then this character isn't the hero. It's impossible to identify or sympathize with him. It literally doesn't work. The expedition has to be special. It has to be exclusive.

That's what you want. You may not think you want it, but you do. This is why the most common and simple forms of work don't pay much and attract less motivated people.

It's why some of the highest paid people have interesting job titles and interesting back stories of how they maneuvered through multiple failures to get there. They have a hybrid of acquired skills and a colorful background that, mixed together, gives them an edge that provides unique value. And people will pay for that.

The hero seeks an exclusive expedition. It's a challenge. It's special. If anyone can do it and there's no barrier to get there, then the hero has recast herself as the atmosphere. She's just background noise.

Julia Roberts in "Erin Brockovich" isn't background noise. She is tested beyond belief to fight for justice. And she prevails against all odds of small-town mentality, male chauvinism, and the legal system.

I can wake up tomorrow and start a plant watering business. I need water. I pour it out of a bucket or hose and water the plant. That's it. There's no education needed, no special skills required, no complicated logistics or resources to figure out.

You show up at someone's apartment or home and water the plants. Done. And that's why there's no reward. That's why there's no substantial business model. There's no demand, so who would want your supply?

In essence, the Hero's Journey to become a professional plant waterer is incomplete. The stage of being tested is absent. And that's a problem. A fundamental block in the foundation is missing. That in itself helps you recast yourself so you fit the Hero's Journey, as you must pass through every stage.

You must pass through every stage in the Hero's Journey. A skipped step is the one step that will debilitate you later.

And it's not just businesses. We can skip the heroic stage of being tested with our emotions. We can be a baby and just cry or be angry. It's easy. It's a default without filters or without the desire to be better. We can be short with our children. We can be dismissive with our co-workers. We can be angry with our clients. We can be critical or jealous of our competition. We can be the Internet trolls who spew hate because it's an easy path with perceived short-term benefits.

Produce Yourself

All those behaviors are easy. There's no hurdle to overcome. We can be spoiled brats or we can be compassionate and empathetic while nurturing ambition. It's effortless to be lazy with your reactions. It's an easily accessible response. But you'll loathe yourself after exhibiting that behavior (if you don't, then you really have a problem).

It takes courage and security to rise above the lowest common denominator of emotions and primitive reactions. That's when you are tested when you cut off the reptilian reaction to external, irritating stimuli and substitute progressive reactions that support, rather than attack.

If tests don't come, if you don't have doubts, fears or reticence because of steep walls in front of you, keeping you from seeing the entirety of this new world, then you have veered off the hero's path. Something is amiss, and you need your compass.

The only reason someone else is doing what you wish you could is they faced these tests, fought adversity and continued on. And they used their time wisely to accomplish this. They planted seeds. They grew trees.

And now you see their fruit. And you think, "I'll never have that fruit." That thought is a test. And you want that. You want the struggle. It is in this struggle, this test that the essence of your identity will be revealed.

Benjamin Franklin's parents couldn't afford to pay for his schooling beyond 10th grade. This setback only motivated little Ben to read voraciously and teach himself. He went on to co-found a little start-up called "America."

Stephen King's first book was rejected over 30 times, so he threw it away. But his wife pulled it out of the trash and told him to muster on. That first book became "Carrie."

Have you heard about the girl who was molested by her cousin, uncle, and other family members? Her situation was so dire, she ran away from home and at age 14 then had a son, who later died. She struggled beyond belief. Today that girl is Oprah Winfrey.

There was a wannabe film director who wanted to make movies so bad he applied to USC for college, arguably one of the best film schools in the world. But not once, not twice, but 3 times he was rejected for not having the proper skills or grades. So he enrolled in Cal State Long Beach, a local state school, and studied everything he could learn about film. That eager student's name is Steven Spielberg (he's now a trustee at USC).

And Thomas Edison famously said, after revealing that he didn't discover electricity on his first attempt (or 9,999th attempt): "I have not failed. I have just found 10,000 ways that did not work."

I wanted to be in control of my destiny and not beholden to what seemed like years and years ahead of me to produce a movie. And, although at times I want to slap my 22-year old self for growing impatient after 3 months of answering phones, I know that there was also power in my naiveté.

There's benefit in ignorance. You will be naive to many facets in the new world. You have to relearn what has been commonplace to you in your Ordinary World. You are once again a deer in headlights, getting your bearings and worried what is out there. But you have crossed and should let your purpose guide you.

Try to harness that simplicity of desire without fear of failure. This is why so many young people find early success and why older people settle for complacency.

If you are older, you now have more resources, a stronger safety net, and greater wisdom than when young. You've learned from many failures. If you don't have many failures, then you've not tried hard enough.

Produce Yourself

Youth may not have some of these elements, but it has passion and drive. The older version of you has these things but allows fear and insecurity to be the sentries and gatekeepers of innovation.

Here's one way to look at it that helps me when I'm feeling reticent and facing risk:

You're going to eat no matter what. I don't care how poor, in debt, or what your situation is. You're going to eat. It's going to happen. You have resources. You're also going to sleep with a roof over your head. Again, I don't care if you can't afford rent, have 8 roommates or are couch hopping every other night. You're going to sleep. You have clothes. And if I wanted to take your money I'd wager that you have more clothes than you need and probably 50 percent or more of your clothes you never even wear. Donate them.

We all know Maslow's hierarchy. I'm sure you've got the basic needs and fundamentals of the pyramid's first tier. It may not be easy or as smooth as you'd like. But you have it. You're not going to lose it. You might lose a house, a job, a car, or not be able to afford gluten-free locally grown consciously harvested ethically sustainable meals. But you'll eat. You'll live.

All the fancy stuff that you think you need in the first place is just marketing and branding. You don't have to have those products to broadcast to others who you are.

So as short as life is, if you want to ascend Maslow's hierarchy up to the stages of self-esteem and self-actualization, you have to take the risk and leave the basic stages at the bottom where they aren't going anywhere. You have to. You're safe. You're secure. You have family, friends, neighbors, spouses, children, who love you. You have a support system. It's going to be okay. You can climb.

But you'll never know what it could be if you don't take that risk. This is why you're on the Hero's Journey.

The creator of what became the Hero's Journey, Joseph Campbell, wrote: "We must let go of the life we have planned, so as to accept the one that is waiting for us."

We can do this when we take risks. And I don't mean reckless risks. I mean risks mitigated by analysis, research, and contemplation. But take it. This is a test you will face daily. Do you take the risk for something or not? Only you can decide.

I am writing this book knowing full well it may suck. It may bomb big time. This is my first book. I realize that no one may buy it, and no one may read it. I haven't, at this very moment writing this sentence, given much thought yet to the economics of it. Because I know results will eventually follow purpose.

I know I'm giving up significant amounts of money I normally make in film or TV production to accomplish this. I know I'm sacrificing brain power from other creative projects to focus on this book. I know, in the end, I may have spent an aggregate of 6 months writing only to have a piece of excrement buried in my bio somewhere. There's a potentially large opportunity cost to this endeavor.

I am fully cognizant of these inherent risks in writing an unsolicited book.

But, I'm also aware of the greater risk in not writing this book. That's the risk I want to diminish.

I'm aware of the brain occupation that occurs, and the thought thieves that trouble my days if I don't pursue this book. I'm aware of the risk in not expressing myself and fulfilling a purpose, especially when everything is obtainable. Everything. There are no excuses.

Produce Yourself

I'm aware what it feels like to want something and not pursue it. I'm aware of regret. I don't want regret. I don't want any "what ifs" in my life. I would rather try and die than die wishing I'd tried.

Candidly, I could not care less if this book flops famously or not. Truth. It's the process, not the result. It's the journey that I want my hero to take in this task, not worrying so much about the endgame, the destination. I know I will gain special powers along this hike. I know I will return to my normal village when I'm finished with this book with insight and wisdom I've gained in the process of writing.

Push yourself. Test yourself. Take risks.

A new world awaits you.

-

CHAPTER 12

Tests: Quitting · Sacrifice Options · Indolence Announcement
(Stage 6 - Part 2)

"The past can hurt. But you can either run from it or learn from it."

- Rafiki in *The Lion King*

Keanu Reeves is put through a series of tests in his new Special World in "The Matrix." He has to learn to spar and jump from building to building at a level that's impossible back in his Ordinary World.

In "Rain Man," the metaphorical and literal roadblocks Tom Cruise encounters due to Dustin Hoffman's condition constantly test his character. From initially unwilling to jump on an airplane to then not going outside because it's raining, Dustin Hoffman tests Tom's inner hero in the Special World.

My first major test was getting my bearings in Hollywood and assessing if it was what I really wanted. Whereas before all I could think about was getting there, now that I was there, it was figuring out the geography.

Everything I had dreamed and imagined was apparently in front of me. I was standing on the Warner Bros. lot where everything from "Friends" and "E.R." to classics like "Blade Runner" and "All The President's Men" had been filmed. I went in and out of old bunkers and ate sandwiches on sets being built for "Batman Returns" or "A Few Good Men."

The smells, the sounds, the visuals — everything appeared to me in Technicolor. But as I walked around and dreamt of producing movies, reality started to set in that the divide that separated where I was and where I wanted to be was just too great. I know, ignorance and hubris. I'd figured I could just produce a movie. But every producer I had met or heard of was two decades older.

The glamour of physically being on a studio lot wore off and disillusionment set in. I was answering phones in an office with producers who were potentially years away from going into production (and that was optimistic).

My bosses soon split, and one of them would produce a movie around 10 years later. The other would take 12 years or so to produce his next one. They were, of course, closing amazing deals and probably producing other content or businesses I was unaware of. But that didn't help my journey.

I had been aware that there was an independent side to filmmaking. There were rabble-rousers who bucked the system and didn't wait for corporate executives to validate their ideas. They didn't ask for permission. They just did it. Having an entrepreneurial bent, this spoke to me.

I had read articles and heard stories about a local video store clerk named Quentin Tarantino, who made "Reservoir Dogs" on a budget; and Steven Soderberg with his "Sex Lies and Videotape," literally shooting it himself (he still does this, by the way); and Kevin Smith's black and white "Clerks."

And then there's Robert Rodriguez's infamous $7,000 "El Mariachi," which he wrote after making a list of free resources (I have an old bus; great, put it in the script. There's a friend's bar; great, that's a location, and so on). He has since built an entire brand and now his own cable network, El Rey, all stemming from his initial $7,000 "El Mariachi." I continue to run into many filmmakers today who were inspired by this ridiculously inexpensive film.

There had been excitement over this attitude that you could just go out and do it.

It was liberating to discover there were others before me who also wanted to make movies, who didn't simmer in the studio's lengthy development cooker. They somehow got movies made and into theaters.

I was also aware of the many others who went broke throwing caution to the wind. They maxed out their credit cards or bar mitzvah money, tried, failed, and were on the next bus back to Omaha. That scared me. But I admired that they went for it (if they literally went back to Omaha, hopefully, they aligned with Warren Buffett and the joke is on us).

The failures of some led to success. Some producers are quite prolific today, because they attempted once more, took one more step, learned from their mistakes, and asked lots of questions to improve their craft. They didn't ignore the invitation to fail.

Sometimes the difference between someone who makes it and someone who doesn't is less about skill and talent, and more about tenacity and timing — knowing when not to give up.

Most of these iconoclastic filmmakers fell into the category of not giving up. They knew to quit ahead rather than behind. It doesn't work for everyone. But you have to give yourself permission to disrupt, innovate, and find creative detours to progress.

If you quit behind, if you quit when you're down, then you've already lost, and you've lost the benefit of learning from failure.

But equally, it's finessing the fine line of when to give up. Soderberg has teased quitting a couple of times (he keeps coming back, however, but each time more on his own terms, more independent than before). Tarantino has said he may have one or two films left in him. Actor Daniel Day Lewis said he was done acting. All three of these artists are still relatively young and capable. But regardless the other purposes and passions they want to tackle on their journey, they are quitting ahead (or at least contemplating it).

There's also the issue of knowing when to quit before greed sets in. You can go too far, like Bernie Madoff, not knowing when enough is enough.

Companies like Countrywide Financial, once the largest mortgage originator in America, got too greedy and imploded (I personally lost close to $30k on Countrywide stock because I too was greedy. I knew it was a gamble. I accept full responsibility).

Blackberry, being the first in, should have cornered the market on smart phones. But they have floundered and been reduced to nothing by not knowing when to either pivot, re-innovate, or quit. Like Blockbuster, they should have quit when they were ahead.

Everyone was shocked when George Clooney left E.R. He was perhaps one of the biggest TV stars at the time, in one of the biggest shows on

Produce Yourself

NBC's "Prime Time TV" campaign. But who's having the last laugh now? The remaining stragglers, or George Clooney, mega movie star?

Jerry Seinfeld also knows the value in quitting when you're ahead. He purposefully chose to end "Seinfeld" when it was the biggest show in the world. He and Larry David were offered tens of millions for just ONE more episode. But the value in quitting ahead gave both of them multiples of those millions in the form of other opportunities by keeping their cachet, rebooting, and finding fresh passions ("Curb Your Enthusiasm" - David) and muses ("Comedians in Cars Getting Coffee" - Seinfeld).

Rocky Marciano went out on top.

Las Vegas could be broke in less than a month if everyone who gambled in Vegas during that period had the dedication and restraint to quit when they're ahead. But in gambling, few quit when they're up. Most quit when they're down. And that's why Las Vegas thrives as an industry.

True, there are odds, and depending on the game, the house has a slight advantage. So over time, the house always wins. Always. But this can be hacked by gamblers if they simply stopped when they were up. Because, when the odds are as close as they are, gamblers are usually up at some point during play (think about the times you've gambled. Do you recall being up? Even if only a few bucks at some point?). But that's the key, stopping when you're up. And it rarely happens.

Here's the hack where you can almost always win in Vegas. The caveat is that it's not fun, at all. I wouldn't call it gambling. But you can win. And it's as simple as this: Quit when you're ahead. Keep playing when you're down. And when you're down, double the amount of your bet.

You sit down at a table, make a bet of 5 bucks, and win your first hand. Stop. Done. Are you in Vegas for 3 more days? I doesn't matter. If you stop now, you're up. You've won. You're done. Again, not fun, but you technically won. And if everyone did this over, say, a 30-day period, there'd be no business model left for Las Vegas.

Take the converse: if you lose a $5 bet (makes no difference what you're playing) then another, then another, then another, keep playing. Even if you switch tables or games, it makes no difference. Just play obviously within your responsibly allotted budget, but play until you're back up. Then you've won. Done. Stop.

Here's how that scenario above would look. $5 bet and lose. So you make a $10 bet (double whenever you lose) and lose. So you make a $20 bet and lose. So you make a $40 bet and lose. So you make an $80 bet and you finally win, after a losing streak of 5 times in a row. If you do the math, you're now $5 up (5+10+20+40+80= $155 in bets. But your last bet was $80, so you won $160. You doubled your original $5).

This is why gambling tables have maximum limits. They're very aware of this gambling strategy. You can search this online as the Martingale System. Or you can use any betting system you want.

This is less about a betting system and how to take down Vegas because you can't. They know what you're up to. It's about knowing when to stop (and definitely don't use the above analogy beyond what you can afford to lose. This is not gambling advice!).

This is a theoretical concept I learned in statistics classes in business school. And it's what helped me realize that this is what has separated many in Hollywood from making it in its Special World vs. heading back home to their ordinary one without the spoils. They quit when they were down.

Again, never quit behind. Quit ahead. But monitor when you're ahead. Then it's time to quit and move on.

I eventually concluded that it wasn't Hollywood that I wanted. It was being a movie producer — that's what I wanted. I wanted to produce. I wanted to create story, rally the troops, organize and manage the whole production. I wanted to lead. I wanted to deliver.

My reasoning was that I would do it for free. Looking back, the common thread in my endeavors was that I enjoyed building things. I would lose a sense of time when I was creating something bigger than and beyond me. I loved that total immersion and obsession when putting on a play or organizing an event or starting a little business that would continue with or without me.

Passion and Purpose first. Money second. Of course, I had to pay the bills, so I wasn't sure how this was going to work. But as short as life is, I just had to give it my best shot.

Entrepreneurs are frequently misidentified as risk takers. They are risk mitigators. You have to take risks. But you can mitigate them upfront.

If I had stayed on the studio lot and worked my way up or around town in a creative or corporate role, I would have had a certain stability (regular salary, benefits, retirement). Certainly more than that provided by the entrepreneurial and freelance path I took instead. This approach would have definitely mitigated my risks. Or would it have?

How risky is it when companies merge, go belly-up, or have to downsize? This happens all the time in Hollywood and other industries. What risk would I have taken in going the safe route by staying at a company and hoping to climb the ladder, if I were laid off or became obsolete (like my friends in the music industry after Napster disrupted and redefined it)?

Jim Carrey gave an excellent graduation speech in 2014 to the Maharishi University of Management.

A portion I find relevant to mitigating risks:

"So many of us choose our path out of fear disguised as practicality. My father could have been a great comedian, but he didn't believe that was possible for him, and so he made a conservative choice. Instead, he got a safe job as an accountant, and when I was 12 years old, he was let go from that safe job and our family had to do whatever we could to survive.

I learned many great lessons from my father, not the least of which was that you can fail at what you don't want, so you might as well take a chance on doing what you love."

This was exactly how I felt and why I had to leave the Warner Bros lot.

The other part of mitigating risks is more practical. How bad do you want it? What are you willing to sacrifice?

For me, it meant giving up my apartment, moving back home with my parents and working out of my childhood bedroom. It meant avoiding dinners and get-togethers with friends who were pulling down regular, albeit small paychecks. It meant I was still driving an older car rather than the newer ones some of my colleagues had. It meant I was hunkering down, spending my time on high-impact work rather than golfing, drinking, shopping, tripping to Las Vegas, or doing whatever other leisure distractions were available on any given weekend.

The value of what you sacrifice becomes the proxy value of your pursuit. If you aren't sacrificing much for your purpose, then perhaps you're not putting a high enough value on it. Perhaps other comforts of your life are more important to you. Or perhaps this in itself is a test, proving this isn't your true purpose.

There was a famous Stanford experiment done in the 1960s with statistical significance on delayed gratification. In it, a child is in a room all alone with a marshmallow. The tester tells the child that she'll be back in 15 minutes. The child can eat the marshmallow while she's gone, or they can have two marshmallows if they are willing to wait the full 15 minutes when she returns.

Produce Yourself

This experiment followed the subjects for the next 30 years. It found that the majority of children who were able to wait those 15 minutes all alone and not eat the marshmallow ended up healthier, with better BMI indices, higher SAT scores, stronger relationships, etc.

Your hero, when in alignment with her purpose, will sacrifice instant gratification. She'll think long term, not short. She'll walk away from negative relationships (friends or family). She'll simplify her lifestyle so choices are focused on her purpose rather than frivolity.

You will feel your purpose in your bones. You will want to take risks. You need to mitigate those, but you will want to take them. And you will make tremendous sacrifices to get there.

Every great product, service, company, or person you admire fits this in some respect. You'll find a back-story of incredible sacrifice and risk to reach their purpose.

Now camped out at my parents' house, I bought books on the filmmaking process (ones like "Feature Filmmaking at Used Car Prices," "Nuts and Bolts Filmmaking," "The Movie Producer," and "Independent Filmmaking"), learned about budgets, schedules, equipment, functions of crew and staff, distribution, marketing. Everything I could find, I consumed fervently and religiously.

Meanwhile, I contacted film schools and asked to meet with their graduate writers and directors, reading their scripts, viewing their shorts. It was a tough, penniless process of making a lot of elements come together. I had no experience doing any of it.

I quickly saw why BR cautioned me about being a movie producer rather than (the more structured path of) an agent or studio exec. A producer isn't a hireable position. But I didn't want to be an agent. That was too buttoned up for me. I struggled with this reality. I debated. I had sleepless nights. These were my tests.

If you want to be a producer, you have to wake up one day and call yourself a "Producer." No one is going to give you that title. It's a critical and frightening step to put yourself out there, brand yourself as something when you're not really there. But that's what was required.

And, as simple as opening a balloon shop and saying you are a "Balloonist," that's exactly what I did. I made cards, I told people to send me their ideas. I was now a producer. I was going to magically make a movie happen out of thin air. Somehow.

That might have been the scariest step in the entire journey. I see people frozen by this step with their dreams and ideas. No one wants to broadcast that they are suddenly official until they are sure they can pull it off. They don't want to fail in front of an audience on the big stage.

This was another important lesson I learned. Sometimes, what holds us back, what prevents us from becoming whom we want to be, is fear of pulling the trigger.

There's a singular action that will finally expose us to the world:

- clicking "Publish" on that website
- updating your LinkedIn with your new business identity
- exposing to your community that you are a closet painter and want to sell paintings
- opening the doors to your new boutique
- bringing your secret boyfriend to meet your parents
- posting on social media that you have a new podcast or new book
- revealing to everyone that you've quit your job

This moment makes the hero vulnerable. She's saying, "This is who I am. This is what I want to do with my life." It's scary for her to broadcast herself. But that's the difference between her — the hero — and everyone else who ends up admiring her when she's immersed in her purpose.

Produce Yourself

It's a therapeutic moment to emerge from the closet, so to speak, and to let the world know what you're doing. It's liberating. And although the mental mindset is an important level to achieve, it's also the physical catalyst that will keep you motivated to proceed.

Once you've released your narrative and brand outside of yourself, you are in a sense "Open for business." And any shopkeeper or sole proprietor will tell you, the minute you turn that sign from "Closed" to "Open," there's a shift in mindset that propels you to be the person you need to be to accept customers. You won't be sleeping on the couch or hiding in the back room. Your shoulders will fall back and down. You'll stand a little taller. And you are ready to present yourself as the person you want to be.

It's difficult to call yourself a producer and have people take you seriously when you haven't produced anything. It becomes a game of smoke and mirrors, reframing, and talking fast enough with enough name-dropping of what you're developing to steer focus away from the fact that you've not produced anything yet.

I quickly found myself in this juggle, drifting between calling myself a producer who had money to attract writers/directors/actors, and then calling myself a producer who had writers/directors/actors to attract money. Chicken and egg.

I knew one, literally ONE, writer in college. Again, having gone to just business school, Hollywood and the like was out of my reach. But due to a sociology class I had taken, I met a PR major who had said he had written a script. For me, that was it. I needed that script. I didn't even care if it was good or not. My focus had shifted to getting a film, any film, made in order to be taken seriously. So I optioned his screenplay.

For me, as a neophyte with no money, optioning was a godsend (I have since optioned at least 100 screenplays, stories, books). It's standard Hollywood practice, wherein a producer pays a fractional amount upfront to have the exclusive right to later purchase and own the entirety of the script.

So rather than pay $250,000 to buy 110 pages of paper, one would pay $5000 upfront and have 12-months' exclusivity to gain traction and then pay the difference at the end of the term. During this period, a producer is able to see if others like the script, if he can attach actors, financing, etc.

All those figures and terms are completely negotiable. I was able to option that first screenplay for $1. My pitch to the writer was that I would work tirelessly night and day to try to get his story to the big screen. I would take meetings, I would reach out to directors, actors, and other producers to partner with. I would go rogue, get creative, and do everything in my power to make sure everyone read his screenplay.

At the end of my pitch, he actually wanted to pay me rather than the other way around. I pitched him value, which is why he, in turn, gave me value. $1.

The concept of options is a utilitarian tool that applies to many industries and pursuits. It's an applicable concept that can give you the seemingly unattainable by leveraging your initial foothold.

We've all heard about lease-option-to-buy contracts with cars or houses. Same concept.

You have no obligation, but you get that opportunity by having the option. So rather than go full bore owning a car, house, stock or movie script, for a tiny fraction, you get the opportunity. You can now source and research your way to the finish line. And if it doesn't happen, your outlay is minimal.

One of my favorite independent films is: "My Life's In Turnaround." In it, the male lead is a cab driver pursuing a beautiful woman he picked up in his cab. She's flattered by his flirtations but reveals she's already got a

Produce Yourself

boyfriend. It's apparent she's out of his league. But he makes a persuasive argument, basically an option, to convince her to give him a shot.

He basically tells her (I'm paraphrasing):

"You're already with your boyfriend. You know him. If he's the one, he's not going anywhere. Give me 3 weeks. Just 3 weeks with me. Take a break from your boyfriend for just 3 weeks and if it isn't the best 3 weeks of your life, then go back to him. No harm, no foul. Give yourself a chance. You'll never know otherwise."

After some contemplating, she reluctantly agrees and a whirlwind romance ensues. The hero in the movie used the strategy of options to get a girl who is unattainable and out of his league. It worked. More on this filmmaker later; he plays a prominent role in my own journey (Chapter 17).

You've probably seen those late night get-rich-quick infomercials touting the purchase of real estate with no money down. Most are simply options.

A great deal is a great deal, period. If you ever see a business opportunity or financial deal to be had, don't let your lack of funds keep you from pursuing it. Money will always find a good deal, and vice-versa. Think about options, just like in Hollywood. Control the link between opportunity and availability and you'll prosper. This is even truer today, as we live in the connection economy.

The script I had optioned was an ensemble drama about a group of friends who would meet once a month and read open-ended questions from a box that prompted them to open up and share. As this post-collegiate clique tackled relationships, dreams, misfortune, and existentialism, they each had their own Hero's Journey to navigate.

It had limited locations, a small cast, no special effects. This felt tangible. So I sent one-page investment letters out to dozens of my relatives and my parents' friends. I laid out a simple plan of needing

$40,000 to make this little movie and hoped I could get it distributed and make money. My reasoning was that the film was so infinitesimally small, it barely needed any revenue to break even. Of course, I was making the assumption I could actually make a good movie for $40k in the first place. In hindsight, the $40k would not have been enough (not to mention cost of marketing and distribution).

Today, I don't blame anyone or take it personally, but no one accepted my offer.

- "We're currently redoing our kitchen."
- "We just got back from a trip to Europe."
- "Good luck, but we are all tapped out right now."

The responses were respectful but clear passes. It began an important set of 3 lessons for me that I carried throughout my film career.

1: Just because someone has money doesn't mean they'll easily part with it. There's a misconception among the ignorant — I was definitely in this group — that if people seemingly have lots of money, they should be willing to part with it. "It's nothing to them," one could reason. "They're a perfect target."

But it's actually something to them, which is why they have it in the first place. It means nothing to those who don't have it. Probably why they don't have it.

People tend to think those who have money must make a lot of money. Sometimes that's the case. But more often than not, people who have money know how to keep it, invest it, save it, and not spend it on questionable, depreciable, and insignificant things.

People with wealth come in all shapes and sizes. They take the bus, rent an apartment, or sometimes work for 30 years as a janitor.

2: Raising money would end up being my main function for as long as I was in Hollywood making movies. Strip away all the fancy meetings, creative brainstorms, teased collaborations, must-tell-stories, etc., and you're left without validation until you have the money.

The converse is also true. You can come into Hollywood with a bag of money, not know a thing about filmmaking or the development process, and everyone will welcome you to the club. You have the VIP ticket.

Once you have the money, as a producer, your managerial and leadership skills kick in to make the best movie. You keep your corral of artists humming in unison and playing nice in the sandbox together. But take too long to find the money, and they'll look for other sandboxes.

Aside from possibly an auteur director or someone just dying to make their opus, no one will work for free. Artists they are. Philanthropists they are not.

3: Familiarity breeds indolence. I wasted months with an ineffective business plan that didn't communicate value to the recipient or speak to their brand, all because I knew the potential "investors." I tragically traded deliberate and effective work for an uncooked plea to give money so I could go make a movie.

I had merely typed an informal one-page letter since I was reaching out to childhood connections telling them what I was doing, what I was going to make. It was all about me. I didn't speak to them. I didn't tell a story acknowledging them. I didn't provide value to them.

The irony is that these are the people with whom I should have been deliberately forming a special story, providing unique value that spoke directly to them. How would this film benefit them? Could they participate or gain other insight with their investment?

I already had the stage. I had their attention. I believe most of them respected and considered me somewhat savvy and responsible. But I wasted that opportunity.

Had I spent the time and written a screenplay about our world, one particular to all of us, I may have had a different response. And had I done my homework with a proper business plan with budgets, projections, accounting and tax advantages, etc., I may have had some positive reception.

But I failed. I failed at what I knew deep down was necessary, but I allowed familiarity to breed indolence.

In Malcolm Gladwell's "Blink," one of my favorite books, his theory is that in that initial blink-of-an-eye, your intuition (your gut instinct) is usually right. It usually cuts to the chase, jumping time and space, forecasting what you will later come to know. But for various reasons, you ignore your own initial understanding due to external factors.

You get in the way of yourself. I got in the way of myself not giving my own group of people the due diligence I would give to strangers. And I had my hand out with a story and script that had nothing to do with them or their journeys.

I knew when I sent out those form letters this simple process would not procure me $40k. I knew it. Looking back, I wouldn't have invested in my movie if I could have. I hadn't done my homework. And homework is the entrance fee.

So where I may have thought I was saving time with my form letters and casual approach to friends, I was actually wasting significant time and delaying attainment of my goals.

This continued to be one of my tests, as I had already encountered this before with the 200 résumés. There I learned the pursuit of saving time is merely a time waste in disguise if it's not effectual.

Produce Yourself

Saving time to raise money for this movie would have been doing my homework and addressing everyone's questions before they even knew they had questions.

Today I still think of that embarrassing disaster whenever I'm about to present something to investors. I ask myself if I've done my homework, have already addressed the obvious questions, and am not just presenting at this very moment due to laziness or excitement, thinking it will be an easy extraction.

First impressions really do last forever. Anyone from whom you are requesting something, be it money, time, product or service, doesn't have the patience to watch you grow and improve your process with subsequent proposals until you get it right.

It's difficult to raise money or request something of someone.

As the requestor, you need to provide value to the requestee. If they have too many questions or simply don't respond, you didn't tell them a story, you didn't speak to their brand, you didn't provide value, and you potentially soured a valuable source for future pursuits.

The tests never stopped coming. I am still tested to this day. It's a challenge to remember lessons from your past and apply them to your present. But eventually, we build better habits from the ashes of our failures. With hope, like the phoenix, we will rise from those ashes.

We journal. We analyze. We measure. We pivot. And we find the answers to our questions. We are our own best asset if we give ourselves permission to be and don't get in the way of ourselves.

Sometimes, it's helpful to have friends to keep us in check.

-

CHAPTER 13

Allies:
Friends · Tools · Support
(Stage 6 - Part 3)

"Some people can't believe in themselves until someone else believes in them first."

- Robin Williams in *Good Will Hunting*

THE SPECIAL WORLD OWED ME NOTHING, and I hadn't proven myself a worthy member yet. There was no scarcity of the services or value that I offered. So why would anyone need me? Hollywood needed another average producer like it needed another bomb at the box office.

The stage of Tests, Allies, and Enemies was challenging. For most people, it's finding the Call to Adventure or eventually Crossing The Threshold. It took me almost 5 years of my Refusal stage in college, but the level of difficulty with those stages was minuscule compared to my Tests, Allies, and Enemies.

After my first set of tests with unfavorable outcomes, I sought refuge and support in my allies. But having left my one and only job so early, I didn't have any allies with much leverage.

I found community and support in other newbies like myself, but as assistants and interns, few had any opportunity I could seize. We met weekly and shared information. But a lot of it was just talk and gossip to make us feel better.

When daily trades ('Variety' and 'The Hollywood Reporter') touted the mega deals being done, it was disheartening when that wasn't you. Like Facebook, the trades are the biggest envy architects there are. They're toxic. I had to do my best to ignore the trades so I could compete with myself rather than others' accomplishments and good fortune. Their journey has nothing to do with mine.

I wanted results. And having left the structured confines of the studio system where there's a clear road map, I felt the pressure to prove worthy of the risk I was assuming. I exuded confidence and assurance. But my inner hero felt the Sisyphean weight of my attempt to make a movie.

I realized that even though I was now in the Special World, I didn't need to limit my search to its allies and tools. I still had such from my Ordinary World. But I didn't think to engage them.

This is something every hero faces. Sometimes it's a trade she brought from back home on the farm or village. Sometimes it's a quirky friend who can help her solve a puzzle, give her a map, or get her information. Other times it's a tool or device she carries with her from the old world to the new one — one she took for granted but now finds life-saving.

Every hero has that epiphany or "Aha" moment where her old skills or allies may suddenly become useful. I was starting to realize that the one unique asset, the special "power," I had that could separate me from my immediate competition in Hollywood was my business education.

Produce Yourself

Whereas a number of Hollywood entrants at the time were English, film, or history majors, I had the formal training to build and grow businesses.

So, similar to the hero's reaction in almost any narrative at this point in the journey, I dusted off my Ordinary World skills and contacts.

Throughout Forest Gump's journey, he continues to return to the advice and wisdom of his Momma in his ordinary Savannah, Georgia world. In "Baby Driver," Ansel Elgort retreats to his deaf foster dad, CJ Jones, for his moral compass. In "Titanic," Leonardo Di Caprio shows Kate Winslet his old world, taking her down into the hold of the boat with his people, which ultimately wins her over. In "E.T. The Extra-Terrestrial," Henry Thomas' skills of bike riding and allies from the neighborhood help him pilot and evade the authorities in his new supernatural experience. Or in a film like "The Pianist," Adrien Brody's entire survival in his new world of the Holocaust depends on his piano skills from his Ordinary World.

I needed the wisdom, tools, and support from my Ordinary World. I was too new in the Special World and hadn't optimized my initial situation to give me any leverage.

I needed a legit office to be taken seriously. So I asked a high school buddy, S, a childhood ally, if I could crash at his dad's office. I immediately had a desk and a phone inside a back-room copy office. Instantly, I had an address, a receptionist who answered the phone, and a machine to make unlimited copies of scripts (probably my largest expense at the time, pre-PDF), all for free.

I needed help with my business plan, brainstorming actors, and someone to bounce ideas off of. Another buddy, P, from 7th grade became that guy for me. He, too, was starting to get the Hollywood bug. He helped me manage enthusiasm and maintain perspective.

And then there was my friend J, the guy I left Pepperdine to move down to San Diego with. J convinced his Dad, G — one of the parents who received my first ill-conceived pitch — to have a look at a new version of the business plan that I was working on. That was huge for me, as I completely fumbled the ball the first. I didn't think I would get a second chance.

Three concepts I held close to me had harmonized:

Preparation + Allies + Seeds = Results

I prepared. I finally realized the difference between effectual work and busy work, having now made that mistake twice. I made a business plan that spoke to investors, not friends. This was a tool I had left to rust in my Ordinary World.

I was so intoxicated and seduced by Hollywood that my focus was adoption and emulation of the Special World's ways. But I needed my trusty Indiana Jones whip from my bag of tricks. I needed my business sense to give me clout and influence rather than just another guy wanting to make a movie.

S, P, and J were my allies.

And I didn't think I could carry them into my Special World with me. But like the secret closet of "The Lion, The Witch, and The Wardrobe," there's always access to your former world's family. Being in one doesn't preclude the other.

They became my support group at a time when I was severely being tested, I had left a job others would kill for, and one I worked hard to get. I was living at my parent's house. And although I never displayed it, this zone of independence took emotional and mental dexterity to maintain.

I had to constantly remind myself that I was on the right path, that I had made the right decision, and that I was sacrificing short-term amenities for longer-term benefits.

Fortunately, what little I had at the time was the fruit from seeds planted earlier. This strategy has, currently does, and will in the future serve me well as it might be the single most important strategy I have learned and activated. Plant those seeds today, right now.

I had tutored J in Algebra, tried to get him into Pepperdine, and then moved to San Diego with him. These actions may have earned some favor with his dad, who agreed to take another look at my business plan. He knew me as a friend to his son, but also someone who provided value.

Same with S's dad in handing me a lease-free office. Back when I had formed a small painting company, I hired S for a summer and paid him well. His dad knew me as a dependable friend to his son.

And my third cohort, P, had a wise aura that helped me process and solve deeper concerns and issues on my journey. He too had been bitten by the Hollywood bug because I shared my notes and homework from BR's college class.

To this day, P's colorful and successful journey in Hollywood started with information he didn't have access to. I provided value. He, in turn, was my ally and pseudo-mentor, advocating my pursuit, but also asking thought-provoking questions. Today we work together, co-hosting a podcast and building a new company.

It sounds anachronistic, but without Google, as it exists today, information was more scarce and limited. The Ordinary World that my friends and I grew up in, had zero knowledge or access to anything Hollywood. Funny, because we lived but 6 miles from it. But it was a world away for us.

Later on, when P wanted to officially enter Hollywood as an agent, I also helped get him a job at a major agency, the same agency BR was a partner of and wanted me to work for. This has served him well, as he is now the President of a major tech-meets-Hollywood company that forecasts movie receipts for investors and producers. But I know him as the kid sitting in my childhood bedroom contemplating with me what to do with our lives while my mom made us veggie dogs downstairs (I was born and raised vegetarian).

On one hand, this is nothing more than my saying I had friends whom I turned to, as they had earlier turned to me. Hopefully, we all have that, regardless what stage we're at.

But on the other hand, I'm emphasizing the need to resource and activate those connections that are easy to dismiss or recall when you're in a new world. It's easy to think the tools and strategies you need in your Special World can only be found there.

When called to adventure, you don't have to tread naked and alone. Find your allies in the new world, if you can. But don't shy away from your allies in your Ordinary World. Don't forget about them.

Perhaps a great representation of this is the blending of Dorothy's special allies she meets in Oz — The Tin Man, The Lion, and The Scarecrow; who happen to also be the farmhands Hickory, Zeke, and Hunk from her Ordinary World in Kansas. It's literally a combination of her new and old allies that assist her through the undulating stages, as they are one and the same.

And, again, plant those seeds. Every single day. Every day you will be growing fruit, fruit that in turn provides more seeds to plant. Incremental. Compounding.

This is when an ally-adjacent in my old world, G, decided to become an ally-proper in my new world. G was a well-to-do CPA in my hometown. He had a yacht, a Porsche, and all those toys that you wish you had when you were a 16-year old boy.

After re-formulating and approaching my business plan properly, I sat down with him for an official lunch meeting. I pitched my heart out on the benefits of him investing in my movie.

Produce Yourself

He told me in so many words that he wasn't interested in the film per se. He wasn't interested in products. He was only interested in businesses.

He revealed to me how, as an accountant, he had access and entry into managing and buying businesses, helping them grow and become more profitable. Numbers often tell the truth, and, as an accountant, he could see where businesses were leaking.

That's the function he'd perfected. It was his forté. Accounting was just the ante to be privy to investing, buying, managing businesses. So although he appreciated my gumption and desire to make my little movie, he thought I was taking the wrong approach.

He wanted to start and administer a whole company for me. Why concentrate on one risky movie that may never even get made, he reasoned. Why not build a company, develop numerous projects, and increase your odds of not only getting something produced but making a return?

He was absolutely right. I knew this to be true. It was business 101 — diversification and the portfolio effect. But I had again vacated the significance of my business knowledge, thinking it had little utility in the Special World.

So reaching back into my old world for help, I partnered with G and formed Terence Michael Productions, Inc. I was suddenly a CEO at age 23. This, of course, was a mere technicality as I was also the intern and the receptionist.

The deal was that G would provide funds to help me option scripts, and I would work my ass off to develop screenplays and package them. I didn't take a salary. There was no staff and no payroll. But I had some limited funds to option and cultivate projects.

Also, my parents were my surrogate silent partners as they continued to take care of my living expenses. I was fortunate not to have to worry about rent or food at the time (much as I wasn't crazy about living at home at age 23).

But 12 months later the production company wasn't working out for G. He was losing money and the experiment with this production company was over for him. He didn't want to spend any more money and it was time to move on. He was right.

In "Broadcast News," Peter Hackes tells Holly Hunter: "It must be nice to always believe you know better, to always think you're the smartest person in the room." To which Holly replies: "No. It's awful."

You've probably heard this concept of standing next to the smartest person in the room. It's better than being the smartest person in the room.

Steve Jobs stood next to Steve Wozniak. Jobs wasn't even a coder. He dreamt big, but he needed Wozniak to help create Apple. Wozniak made it happen. He worked out the details to move along Jobs' vision.

Bill Gates stood next to Paul Allen. It was Paul Allen who actually came up with "Micro-Soft" and convinced Bill to drop out of Harvard to pursue this computer idea they had.

Kathleen Kennedy, who is now the president of Lucasfilm and brand manager for the entire Star Wars universe, stood next to Steven Spielberg. Starting out as his assistant, she worked her way up on almost every single film he made since "Raiders of The Lost Ark." There are very few Spielberg films where Kathleen is not credited as a producer or executive producer. Today she is "the" producer on all of the Star Wars films (she coincidentally went to SDSU in San Diego, where I'm guessing her surroundings were a bit different than mine).

Brian Grazer stood next to director Ron Howard. Brian is now one of the most prolific and successful producers in Hollywood. But he got there by aligning himself with Ron Howard, giving Ron his very first directing job on "Night Shift" and then "Splash." The rest is history as the two partnered and have done almost every single project together as a team from "A Beautiful Mind" and "Da Vinci Code" to the TV show "Arrested Development."

I, unfortunately, wasn't the smartest guy in the room for G If his sole purpose was to get into Hollywood, I was not the guy to bet on at this stage in my non-existent career.

And he wasn't that for me. He was a silent, behind-the-scenes partner with money. That was critical and helpful to have. I learned so much from him and I admired him as a businessman. I have new allies today because of him. But he had no connections, insight, or leverage to help me with my pursuits. I don't fault him at all.

But I think we had a partnership based on history, rather than culture. We each needed different partners, quite frankly, or at a different point in time.

G wasn't standing next to me, and I wasn't standing next to him. So for me, I was the only person standing in the room, and it was lonely.

In "American Gangster," Denzel Washington says: "The loudest one in the room is the weakest one in the room." Sometimes if you're the only one in the room, you are by default, the loudest.

The partnership was mostly optics. I was still nowhere closer to actually producing movies than I was before. In fact, I was somewhat farther because my concentration was now diluted. I was trying to build a slate and portfolio of films rather than just the original script I had optioned. I still needed more allies to collaborate with.

Over the next 2 years, I developed probably 40 film projects, took countless meetings, met a lot of great executives, had money attached to various projects, paid for some rewrites, aligned with other producers, formed co-productions, met probably 100 directors and everyone in between.

It was Project Allies for me every single day. Build, connect, meet, build, connect, meet. Network. Rinse and repeat. And at the same time, I was basically broke, for the first time in my life going 2 years without meeting the requirements to file a tax return (you had to make at least $4k a year to file. That's how bad it was).

Actors would come and go per their availability. It was a continual matter of temporarily having one to lure another — and grabbing the only ones I could approach via friends of friends, meeting at a party or begging an assistant at a management company to pass it along.

If I showed you the list of whom I had involved at any one point on any of the projects, it would be a "Who's who" of some of today's Hollywood elite. But there's a huge divide in Hollywood between what artists want to do and what their management will allow them to do; and furthermore what available money can buy.

As much as producers need actors to get their films funded, actors are sometimes the worst barometers of a film's prospects. They often focus on the role (not a bad thing) and not the movie as a whole. And getting an unsolicited script without a firm start date or official offer is meaningless most of the time.

The challenge is to get past gatekeepers of agents, managers, publicists, and entourage, take numerous meetings, and then get them all to sign onto a film with no money so that you can go get the money.

Managers know you need their talent to raise the funds, and they don't want that attachment to dilute their client's value. They also want to protect their client from having to say "No" to contractual money-offers with firm start dates because they've already said "Yes" to your yet-to-be financed independent film.

Produce Yourself

The representatives know the value in saying "No" as much as possible so they can say "Yes" when the right project comes along.

That pretty much describes the process of independent movie producers: optioning scripts, finding meaningful directors, and spending forever attaching and re-attaching talent, so that you can then have a package to secure financing. And attempt to do all that without anyone paying you.

Knowing that, G was not the right partner for me. He was a godsend. He helped me immensely with his investment. He validated my pursuit into foreign territory. He spoke my language from my Ordinary World. But he was the wrong partner when you analyze and lay out the challenges and functions.

This is a crucial, fundamental problem with many start-ups today. I'll often coach or consult new companies or collaborations on devising a plan of attack. But sometimes, I have to pull the partner (even a husband or wife, which gets tricky) aside and say, "Listen. This is a great idea. But you have the wrong business partner."

It's devastating. People partner with co-workers, friends, family. And many times those are the best allies to have. But often, because of the history and relationship, critical flaws in communication, utility, and function are overlooked.

You don't need to literally stand next to the smartest person in the room. But you need to stand next to someone who increases your average and has separate buckets of access, resource, and expertise.

You need to be next to someone whose tool belt doesn't look like yours. As in "The Avengers," "Justice League," "X-Men," or "Fantastic Four," you should each bring a set of "powers" that benefits and complements the other's, creating a synergy and force amplification.

This is why I love partnerships, by the way: two people can each bring different qualities to the table, but also motivate each other to improve and progress. We all need those kinds of allies. We need to surround ourselves with the best people who are motivated to succeed.

Synergy happens when the whole is greater than the sum of the parts. If you plus your partner, each a 1, are not equaling 3 or greater, then you're doing something wrong. Quite possibly, you have the wrong partner.

When a partnership or collaboration becomes two people who like hanging out together, growth and ownership are sacrificed for the most expensive employee. It's a bonus when it happens among friends. But make that the exception rather than the go-to rule.

Don't dilute the advantage of being allies in the first place. Sometimes, friends or allies are so similar that the focus becomes myopic and redundant.

People like to joke that they simply need more of themselves. But that won't solve the problem. That would just give them more of the same problem. After all, the aggregate of their best choices and decisions got them in the bind in which they find themselves.

When it comes to collaborative endeavors, your allies don't have to be anyone you know or work with. Sometimes it's better if they're not. Call it coincidental if they happen to be your best friend and it works out but set that parameter aside in your search for allies. Those new allies might, in turn, become your friends and confidants.

But at this point in my journey, I was standing alone. And I would remain this way for years as I attempted to become ally-worthy myself.

-

CHAPTER 14

Enemies: Process · Function Input
(Stage 6 - Part 4)

"The past is just a story we tell ourselves."

- Scarlett Johansson in *Her*

ALL THREE ELEMENTS — tests, allies, and enemies — bind and oppose each other at once and continuously, which is why they are collectively one stage in the Hero's Journey. Together, they test friendships, alliances, reveal enemies. And test all over again. Endlessly.

You will always (should always) be looking for your allies. You will need them. You will always be tested — if you're not, you're in the wrong place, which diminishes your potential. Challenge yourself. And you will always be attracting enemies. They're necessary.

Every show or movie you watch has a villain or enemy. It won't satisfy without one. Just as success needs a series of failures to be recognized, a hero needs her enemies to validate the disparity in morals, mettle, and might.

In traditional story architecture, we see the exterior enemy — the co-worker, the boss, the competitor, the opposition, the ex, the neighbor, etc. And in fantasy, this takes on the form of evil overlords, monsters, aliens, White Walkers, etc. — obvious enemies, easy to identify.

These tropes thrive in a story where there's a finite running time and the beats have to satisfy the audience. Our hero is foiled by a nemesis who will stop at nothing to prevent her from obtaining her goals. This will always crescendo at the end of the narrative into a mano a mano (or womano a womano) set piece that finally personalizes the journey's lessons. The hero, finding strength within, can finally conquer her adversary face to face, hand to hand, and move past the disturbance.

The visuals and action of the hero vs. enemy are usually a cinematic manifestation of the true inner-battle of the hero — the enemy within. This is the decisive battle every hero must conquer along the journey.

Kathy Bates holds novelist James Caan prisoner in "Misery." He can't escape when he's been hobbled and a crazy woman is holding him hostage. But is she the enemy, or is it his complacent ego (that has led to his killing off a favorite protagonist in his novels) that has imprisoned him? Is she not just the personification of the prison he made for himself?

Is Michael Douglas the victim of Glen Close's psychotic rabbit-boiling meltdown in "Fatal Attraction"? Or is he a victim of his own infidelities and reckless actions? Is Glen Close not just a visual parallel of the inner torment Michael Douglas feels for cheating on his wife?

What about Theon Greyjoy in "Game of Thrones"? Surely, he has enemies from almost every kingdom in Westeros, as well as some of the neighboring islands. But it turns out he is his own worst enemy, paralyzed by his betrayal of the Starks and subsequent cowardice to defend his sister Yara. It isn't until he can confront and overcome his inner guilt that he's able to awake his sleeping hero and right his numerous wrongs.

Perhaps "Fight Club" is the best marriage of the outer and inner hero as Edward Norton fights with his antagonist, Brad Pitt. They are one and the same. Edward Norton is, quite literally, fighting his enemy within.

With G's exit, I would be able to keep the production company name and the projects we had in development (he was very generous). But I no longer had a checkbook. He gave it a solid year and bet on someone who was as close to Hollywood as he could find. As any good entrepreneur would, he mitigated his risk.

Every day I was making connections and headway. There was always progress. But it was at a glacial dance of two steps forward and 1.9 steps backward because I didn't have more impactful and leveraged relationships yet. I was still learning. And I was naive.

As a CPA, he was used to more traditional business models that showed measurable results within a specific time period. And, in hindsight, he invested in me 2 years prematurely.

As a neophyte in Hollywood, having only 3 months' history working for anyone in the industry, I had almost no credibility forming a production company.

Fortunately, the investment was minimal and G's involvement was strategic lensing for me at the time. The perception and optics that his advocacy created were authoritative reassurance to help me attract projects and grow my network.

Once I processed the specifics of owning 100 percent of the company's shares, I realized it was only an emotional setback. All of the contacts and progress I had made were still there. No one else would know of the ownership adjustment. It was purely backroom shuffling.

Enemies give you special tools — sometimes more purposeful and utilitarian than those from your allies. When Tom Cruise asks Cuba Gooding, Jr. in "Jerry Maguire" to "Help Me Help You," he is, in essence, summoning the enemy for help. Enemies help you help yourself. They reveal your weaknesses, keep you agile, motivate you to improve and lead you further down the path you want to travel.

If your enemies are standing in your way, you're on the right trail. They are in essence validating your chosen path. The closer you get, the more your enemies will appear. You're doing something right. You're heading toward treasure which the enemy wants to protect or unearth for themselves.

So you might see a pirate, a goblin, or school principal, but they're just an exhibition of a more critical enemy: the enemy within.

For this reason, I'm focusing less on the opponent in the corner office. Because once your enemy within is contained, the office jockeying becomes easy to manage.

You are the inconspicuous enemy you need to overcome — your mindset, your ego, your attitude, your emotions, your energy. The enemy is you complaining, justifying, resenting, resisting, ignoring and surrendering. This enemy can be crushed with measurement and improved habits.

I sometimes hear this abandonment of attempt: "Well, I don't have the resources. I can't do that." I hear excuses for not having enough money, time, education, or not being in the right place at the right time. But the real enemy is mindset.

People love to blame others for their current situation. This deflects from the inner enemy by outsourcing the criticism.

Some of us have to work much harder than others. Some of us weren't gifted the same opportunity or head start as others. We weren't born with a silver spoon, with the ability to dunk a basketball, with the voice of an angel, or with a river of oil ten feet below our house.

My biggest enemy in Hollywood was me. It was convenient for me to acknowledge I didn't have a trust fund or rich uncle to give me five million dollars to go and make a movie. I didn't go to Beverly Hills High with all the celebrities or have a cousin who was an executive at a studio. My sister wasn't the VP of a talent agency and my best friend's dad didn't own a camera or post house.

I didn't have the low-hanging, readily available resources that a lot of my colleagues had — reasons they were in the industry in the first place. To them, this was their Ordinary World.

Yet I'm sure there were many who didn't have the conveniences or incredible family support that I had. I wouldn't trade that for anything.

Everyone should only compete with themselves. Envy is toxic and debilitating. It's not constructive.

But I had one of the best resources of all. I had me. I just had to get out of the way of myself to allow me to use the tools I already had.

One of the ways to do this is through measurement.

I had to stop and assess what my core functions were in my journey so I could eventually re-prioritize my habits to optimize my approach.

For example, the largest time-suck for me was reading screenplays. But as a broke, new producer, that was the one thing I could do: read.

My situation was like a game of dominoes. I couldn't produce a movie without having a meaningful, bankable cast. I couldn't attract a meaningful cast without a name director. I couldn't attach a name director without an amazing script. I couldn't have an amazing script without first finding a solid concept or screenplay to develop and cultivate into an amazing script. I couldn't find a solid concept without saying "Yes" to all submissions that came my way from writers I met everywhere. And they were/are everywhere.

That means I had to do so much reading that it actually took more than half my day (and many days, the entire day). A script from beginning to end could take 1-1/2 to 2 hours to read if one focuses without distractions.

Then add calling back the writer or writer's agents and managers to say why you're passing or convince them to give it to you for a one-dollar option. Lots of time.

But here's what the facts told me after looking back over 2 years of records and data-measuring:

1. If a screenplay didn't excite me in the first 10 pages, I never ended up optioning it. Never. It simply never happened. Those were just the facts.

2. If a screenplay came to me from an agent or manager, I was never going to be able to option it for less than $1,000. Not facts, but odds.

3. No matter how much I liked the pitch or synopsis, I never took on a horror project, western, or period piece. Never. I'm not against those at all. This is just the data. These are the results.

So what this assessment revealed was that I should only look for comedies, dramas, and thrillers, and those directly from writers themselves due to the economics. Furthermore, I would stop reading after page 10 and ask myself if I absolutely loved what I had just read. If not, I tossed it aside.

Produce Yourself

For some, the opposite is true. And that process works for them and who they are. I have a manager/producer friend in the business who has made some big, major movies. His entire business model is simply to read everything. I mean everything. He has a team of interns who scour the internet and make sure to request practically every single script that has been written. He spends 12 hours a day, including most weekends, reading. And for that, for him, he finds hot properties that he can sell to the studios with himself attached as a producer.

That would never work for me. I can't suffer that input and process.

When you analyze, assess, and measure, you can strip away the politics and dressing. Core functions are revealed so improvement in approach becomes obvious.

I immediately freed up half my days, every single day, to network and magnify other areas of business outside of material. This opened up opportunity.

We have to recognize the approach to anything we are spending significant time pursuing. When it isn't working organically, and we're not making at least incremental progress, and we're not enjoying it, we have to change it. That's a non-starter.

Unless you want your progress to be a directionless pinball, bouncing off every obstacle it meets, you need to stop, gain perspective, record the activity and analyze the data.

If you're spending weeks and weeks (or even years) doing something, anything, that you know deep down isn't operative, yet you sustain it, you are officially your own worst enemy. You are feeding the beast. You, as captain of your own voyage, choose to sit back and let the big ship slowly float through the water until it eventually hits an iceberg. Obvious in story telling, not so obvious in your own daily approach.

Occam's Razor says that when presented with numerous complex options to solve a problem, often the most obvious and simplest is the best solution.

This is why sitting down with a financial planner works. He isn't telling you anything you don't know. You know how much you make. You know what you spend because you spent it already. You were the one at the mall buying a watch, and you were the one at dinner buying drinks. But he adds it up, shows it to you, and whoa — revelation in numbers. There's suddenly a clear picture. And you can make a clear decision.

We know we don't want to pay $15 a month for that subscription, but we're too lazy to cancel it. It's only $15. We know we should empty out that $250/month storage unit, but that requires getting dirty and renting a truck. We'd rather go watch a movie. We know we could be in advertising if we wanted to, but we have to make that portfolio. We know we could be in a band but we need to make a demo tape. We know our relationship could be stronger, but it means having that conversation we would rather avoid.

And, not surprisingly, these weekly or monthly excuses have a way of soon compounding into a decade of excuses, large expenses, and procrastinated emotions. All of the busy work we did in the name of avoidance could have built equity in our goals.

Pause to analyze your patterns. Measure them and compile the data. You will have an epiphany of how absurd and time-consuming your ineffectual methods are. You intellectually already know this.

Silicon Valley and the tech industry have proven how data can solve problems, big and small, that we've endured and accepted as part of everyday living.

Having exited the industrial age and entered the middle-class corporate culture age, Americans got complacent and were programmed to accept the safety of monotony and corporate climbing. But as the tech industry matured and the nerds and geeks of yesterday became the heroes and giants of today, we started to recognize the value in data they were compiling.

By analyzing how long someone had to wait to get a cab, and even find a cab that was available, big data was able to save the day. It's called Uber. It's called Lyft. Big data was able to aggregate all the empty seats whizzing by anyone at any given time by looking at real time traffic, and then overlapping that with geographic unemployment data. Bam.

Now the biggest taxi company in the world doesn't even own a single car. And the biggest hotelier in the world (Airbnb) doesn't own a single hotel room. And the biggest bookstore in the world (Amazon) doesn't own physical books.

Ditto for everything in the entire sharing and crowd-sourced connection economy. Silicon Valley has become the premier problem solver in the largest industries, from medicine to dating, from travel and accommodations to housekeeping, from storage and moving to entertainment consumption, from real estate shopping to crowd sourced investing. Data doesn't lie. Math doesn't lie. It seeks clarity and pinpoints the problem or opportunity, allowing you to see patterns that often reveal a solution.

We've had this information. It's always been there. But Silicon Valley decided to ask the simple question that every single successful start-up asks: "How can we improve the process?"

If you were an infrastructure or industry, this is how the tech industry would solve you. So do it for yourself. Do it for your hero. Kill the enemy within. What is the data on you?

I have friends who seemingly have the best careers. They have fancy job titles in interesting fields. But if you pull the fluff away to reveal the actual mechanics of what they technically do all day, you see why they either love their lives or hate them.

People convince themselves they are living their dream. And some are. But many aren't.

As a pure functioning being, as if you were a robot in a warehouse, what functions do you need to be programmed to technically do, day-in and day-out?

This is the complete opposite of a social media selfie or post. Whereas Internet profiles show you in the most optimal light with filters, primping, and placement, living the most enjoyable life, this exercise should show the opposite. What are the actual, mundane, repetitive, actions you perform that consume your day?

Take a Yoga instructor. Many might say that person settled or hasn't maximized peak performance in achieving success. Can't anyone just be a yoga teacher?

But I would argue otherwise. I generalize here, but the functions of this instructor are consuming his world in a peaceful environment, stretching, exercising, meeting new people, helping new people, wearing comfortable clothing, and making money.

The actual functions a yoga instructor performs for the bulk of his life is one of mind, body, health, spirit, and mostly positive social interaction. These are qualities people strive for.

All else being equal, this person is winning at life.

You might see Charlize Theron looking great and glamorous in "Atomic Blonde" during the 2 hours you're in the theater. But ask her about the months of rehearsals, months of training, months of 18-hour days shooting, months of seclusion in a trailer waiting for camera set-ups, and months of press she had to conduct so you would see the movie.

The big secret that all of us in Hollywood know is that it's actually the most unglamorous business that exists. Ask anyone in front of or behind the camera and they'll confirm this. You see the final cake with its frosting, but not the mixing and baking we do while sweating and swearing with flour all over our face.

The red carpet isn't just for the premiere and press. Everyone involved in the film is just as in awe and excited to be walking the carpet. It is not a regular occurrence. It's just as foreign and odd to them as it is to you.

I'm going to borrow my girlfriend's industry and break down the actual mechanics of what an average therapist might spend the majority of his days performing.

This is what it takes (from my non-professional perspective) to be an average therapist.

You have to love to read journals, studies, and keep up with current trends, medications, procedures, treatments, disorders, new laws, and continuing education. Personally, I love this. But not everyone does.

Outsiders may romanticize about sitting in a cozy office with a fireplace and talking with someone in need. But those outsiders don't know the hours spent with pre and post paperwork, red tape, insurance form filings, court filings, and procedure. You have to deal with a lot of administration, billing, third party reporting, and license compliance. And then there are merchant services, payroll; and supervising, hiring, and firing associates and interns.

As a therapist, unless you're also writing books, teaching seminars, building a video series, consulting, or launching other adjacent businesses, you are an employee of your private practice. You only make money when you perform actual therapy. Nothing is being earned while you sleep. Nothing is being earned with the paperwork and administration. There is no equity growth from ownership. So it's a grind, day in and day out, having to fill your calendar if you want to eat.

You are an emotional sponge for your clients' venting, anxiety, depression, complaints, anger, sadness, and unleashing whatever is troubling them. As a therapist, you absorb that. You generously take all that in to help them process, gain perspective, and acquire tools to cope and improve.

You reverse cold-call, as you field the calls and do intakes of new potential clients daily. You spend an aggregate of hours a week you'll never get back talking to and assessing potential clients that may never come to you.

You're a detective, an interpreter, a scientist, and an artist all at once. You're using science and behavioral research, but there's an art to excavating the client's pretense to discover the issues. No two therapists will approach this identically.

Therapy is tremendously rewarding and prestigious. It's a socially conscious, commendable, and respected field. That goes without noting. Therapists are superheroes in my book for the input they have to endure for the eventual output.

When you strip all the kudos and emotions away, these are the daily functions of a psychologist.

Sitting in that office and listening is but a fraction of the behind-the-scenes infrastructure to keep it alive. Most prestigious careers are similar.

None of this is good or bad. It's simply the truth.

Produce Yourself

Much like Charlize Theron, an actress should only choose to act if she can endure the input and the mechanics of what it takes — auditions, rejection, memorization, vulnerability, study, living frugally, etc.

If you were to land on a farm and were told you had to work there for a month performing one of the several available jobs (milking cows, feeding horses, chopping firewood, or bringing water from a well), you'd choose it based on the function, not the perception. You don't care what your title is on the farm. You're on a farm.

But the world is your farm. Choose what will obviously bring meaning and satisfaction, but don't sweep under the rug the mechanics of what you have to do every day. It's difficult to choose happiness if you dislike what you do, or choose it for an outcome that may never transpire.

Next, you need to know how long you spend doing each of those functions. That's where the data starts to really reveal itself.

If you've ever worked in accounting or legal you know how to do this. They bill in 6-minute increments, dividing each hour by 10. How long are you spending doing each separate task throughout your day, both personal and work?

Look at all of these like activity packets. Each packet is a time period of doing one thing. There's the:

- driving packet (add up driving to and from work, and your to-and-from anywhere else so that driving packet has one unit — say 2.4 hours every day, which now tells you that's 10 percent of your day)
- sleeping packet (include the nap, if there is one)
- brushing your teeth packet
- texting funny GIFs packet (the sum of the dozen minutes you spent doing this will be revealing)

Over a weeklong period, you want to summate these packets and know how long you spend on each subject's packet so you can calculate averages.

Not only do you want a clear picture of how much time you actually spend doing various tasks or in down time, you want to see how many of these various packets you have. Perhaps you are spending way too much time doing something that isn't progressing. But perhaps you simply aren't prioritizing. Maybe you're trying to pursue too many things simultaneously. You might need to eliminate some of your activity packets or shift them to a different time of day.

I'm not going to detail what to do with this info. You will know. It will reveal itself based on your specific situation. But you have to do it.

This is why it's called the Hero's Journey, not the Hero's Destination. It's the process of doing it. It's in the journey where you will find the answers.

Now, apply this same concept to your finances — another enemy most of us have. It was certainly an enemy of mine when I made no money. So my dwindling savings account needed preservation at every leak.

I developed a simple spreadsheet back then, which I still use today. It asks the simple question: How much does it cost me to be alive for one day?

If you want to know how much it costs you to have your personal car, for example, you can figure it out fairly easily. The goal is to simply convert any payment, whether yearly, monthly or weekly, into a daily amount that has to do with your car. So if you have a car on which you put $3,000 down, with a $500/month lease, and spend $40/week in gas, $450/year in maintenance, $300/year in registration, $20 in smog check, $800 in washings, and $200 a year other miscellaneous, that would come to:

3000 down payment/365 = 8.22

500 lease/30 = 16.67

40 gas/7 = 5.7

450 maintenance/365 = 1.23

300 registration/365 = .82

20 smog/365 = .05

800 washings/365 = 2.19

100 misc/365 = .55

The daily cost of the car = $35.43.

This project will take time. But you will save potentially thousands of dollars a year plugging the leaks, eliminating forgotten subscriptions, overages, and negotiating better deals.

You will have to go through your credit card statements, your Quicken or "check book" or whatever you use to track all of your expenses. Go back over 2 years to get accurate averages. You have a monthly gas bill. What are all 24 bills over the last 2 years? Write that average down and convert it into a daily. Now you know how much it costs you per day to use gas.

I recently did this and was astonished to discover that my average dining-out cost was $46/day. That doesn't include the weekly groceries. That doesn't include my almost-daily business meeting lunches, dinners, etc. That's just my going out to eat tacos or enjoying meals on weekends with my girlfriend. That's $1,400 a month.

Numbers are very revealing. I can't emphasize enough the benefit of this exercise.

Do this with everything. Netflix, magazines, online accounts, recurring expenses, rent, utilities, insurance, mortgages, student debt, groceries. Everything that you spend money on. And if it's sporadic, like going to the movies or traveling, just average over a 2-year period and convert it to days. 365 days a year, 30 days in a month, for calculation purposes.

I typically end up shaving off at least a thousand dollars every year because of this. Those thousand dollars compound and produce fruit worth tens of thousands of dollars for Future Me.

A myth that annoys me to no end is that one has to make more money to have what you want.

It's about how much you spend, not how much you earn. And this was critical to me at the time. So by taking the time to analyze and measure my expenses, I was able to in effect make phantom income by eliminating and streamlining my expenses.

You may be surprised to discover that it costs, for example, $415 a day for you to be alive. It sounds crazy, but many people are at even double or triple that amount. But even if it were only $415, you would have to make $638 a day to sustain this pre-tax (assuming a modest 25 percent federal and 10 percent state tax rate). Are you making $638 a day? $4,460 a week? $223,000 a year, if you worked 50 weeks a year? If not, you may be in debt.

The best way to stop a leak is to plug the leak, not get a bigger boat. You don't have to make more money. That's nice and a great emblem of success if it happens. But it's not the answer, as the vicious pattern repeats itself — more money, more expenses, ad infinitum. Ad nauseum.

Produce Yourself

Go through your spreadsheet and see which expenses can be completely eliminated, which ones you can pare. Some competitors may have better rates, etc.

Knowing the goal is to lower your daily cost, it helps you switch things from a monthly to a pre-paid annual expense if it saves you money. You might have a website service that charges $20 a month for hosting. But if you prepay annually, they'll give it to you for $90 a year, which is $7.50 a month. $12.50 a month savings. Small. But it adds up.

Half the revelation is finding expenses that you forgot are on auto subscription. There's a reason some of the most profitable companies have subscriptions (Netflix, anyone?).

Today, as a mortgage broker, I see this narrative with over 90 percent of my clients. When I help them with their scores by looking over their credit reports, they can't even remember about 20 percent of their recurring expenses. So, in the process, separate from even needing a mortgage, they end up cutting their monthly expenses.

Here's another way of looking at how much more important your expenses are than your income.

According to the U.S. Census report in 2015 (most current available), the average income in the U.S. was $56,000 a year. That's not a ton of money, at least in Los Angeles. However, would you believe me if I said the person who makes this salary could be a millionaire with just modest savings?

As of 2017, if you're single making $117k or less, or married making $184k or less, then you can contribute $5,500 to a Roth-IRA (your retirement account) and have it grow tax-free. That's saving less than 10 percent of your entire year's income, which everyone should be able to do.

Always pay yourself first. Pay Future You, then Present You. This should be the first check you write every time you receive money — 10 percent to Future You.

Warren Buffett said, "Do not save what is left after spending, but spend what is left after saving." And by saving he means first paying Future You (retirement savings with tax benefits).

Since the history of its existence, the stock market has returned at least 8 percent on average with a conservative index equity fund. Putting in $5,500 a year, less than 10 percent of your income if you make the country's average of $56k a year, this would compound to $1.1 million after 35 years. Of course, hold on just 5 more years longer and that's over $1.6 million — the power of compounding, and the power of incremental steady and auto investing. Give Future You the best gift you ever could. Cut your costs. Invest regularly. And let it grow.

Ever read about the story of two immigrants who came to this country, worked hard — he a janitor, she a maid — and put 4 kids through college, then retired in their mid-60s? It's a common story and quite prevalent among many of America's hard-working immigrants. Their seeds were cutting costs and religiously investing. Their water was compounding. And the fruits of their labor? 4 educated kids and a comfortable retirement.

Perhaps the biggest enemy within is laziness in the form of busy-ness.

People think portraying the identity of "busy" equates to achievement (a sad byproduct of the post-WWII assembly line and corporate ladder culture). But it doesn't. It projects an inability to equip and command their own life effectively.

You can be in charge of your day. You can own it. You can be the boss. Or you can be an employee of your day, constantly fighting to catch up answering the numerous interruptions you get bombarded with.

Produce Yourself

If you start off your day, for example, opening your email, you are immediately allowing someone else's to-do list and tasks to become your top priority. You are starting off your day having to do unexpected work for someone else — notifications that jolt you out of the zone, questions that need responding to, an attachment you have to forward to someone. You are starting off on your knees, asking: "Master, what can I do for you?"

You've been hibernating overnight and this is how you reward a refreshed and uncluttered mind and body, by slamming sporadic, fractured demands and requests at it, at the inception of the day.

I know you need to:

- get a jump on what's happening at work, making sure your boss or partner isn't awaiting a response from you.
- see how the stock market is doing or if a client deposited a check.
- find out who liked or responded to your post, if an e-Bay item sold, or if your favorite celebrity is going to jail.
- check the texts from your aunt that are driving you crazy; you want to address that.

But answer this:

- Are all of these questions and requests coming from dictators and bullies who will punish you if they don't hear from you right away?
- And what's the definition of "immediately?"
- Are they expecting you to be a monotonous robot whose productivity is tethered, and subject, to subservience?
- Is your alarm set so you can wake up to respond to emails and text messages the minute they come in over night?
- What if you woke up an hour later? Two hours later?
- What if you lived in a different time zone?

- Do those notifications and requests disappear because you haven't looked at it within a specific window of time? Do they expire?

Have you placed a value on your time so low that you've conditioned others to contact you 24/7 and set a precedent with immediate responses? That nothing you do has the level of complexity or significance that requires any type of deep concentration, careful preparation, or focused process?

You're the enemy if this is how you value your willpower, priorities, and allow others to engage you in this manner. All questions can get answered. All problems can get solved. But you can do it right and do it once with thought and processing rather than via a dozen back and forth emails as if you're a fireman responding to a blaze.

Every time there is a distraction, however tiny or insignificant, that takes you out of the moment, a residual ghosting effect occurs. You may exit your task for 10 seconds to quickly respond to a text, but when you return to your task, there are imprinted leftovers from the distraction. You may not realize it, but it's taking its toll on your present task with a lingering ghost effect. Your brain is still flashing back to the distraction while you try to advance.

You're fighting and working against your own best optimization when you think about how you'll respond to an email rather than give 100 percent to the task at hand.

What should be tackled first are your high-functioning prioritized important steps, not the mislabeled "urgent" emails from a friend who is at the bank and needs your opinion as to whether they should set up direct deposit. Someone else's ill preparation is not your emergency. And you can respond in due time when you arrive at your low priority, low impact items.

Ever try to reach someone "important" and it takes them awhile to get back to you? They already understand that you are a distraction and they'll return when they've allocated time to address distractions. But it's lower on their priority list. It's how they became important in the first place — by understanding the difference.

People mistake constant disruption for effective communication. If everyone simply drops what they're creating in offense mode to consume in defense mode, then nothing gets created. Everything just gets consumed and reacted upon.

You shouldn't have to fly in an airplane without Wi-Fi to find leveraged focus. You can be proactive. You don't need logistics to be the scapegoat for your prioritization. Blueprint the bigger picture. Many of the smaller diagrams from that blueprint may now be irrelevant or solve themselves by the time you are able to reach them.

Ignoring the exponential multiplier mode at which your brain has the capacity to perform is a waste. Escape from busy defense mode, which is nothing more than "accomplishment" by fracturing your brain into numerous little tasks. Don't click from one email to the next, like a robot playing Tetris, thinking that's productive. That doesn't accomplish anything dynamic or effectual. People who are "too busy" mistake this for progress.

Look at any teenager on their phone, tapping away furiously, jumping from one conversation to the next, frenetic with selfies, posts, stories, furiously engaging and accepting requests that fly in every 5 seconds.

I predict this if someone else hasn't already: you're going to see a complete 180-degree shift from this in the next generation that follows Gen-Z or the centennials. These habits will very quickly manifest themselves as unhealthy, depressed and overwhelmed adults who are too attention-deficient to focus on anything of quality. There will be a huge gap in the ability to contribute any meaningful thought, creativity, or perspective. These teenagers aren't being productive. They're being busy. In their world "busy" is misinterpreted as "popularity." Busy is their enemy.

Productivity's definition has skewed over the years. People use that term as a euphemism for doing a lot of little things quickly, multitasking their way to a sense of achievement. But this is just busy work. If you're too "busy" you are procrastinating the important accelerators for your goals and replacing them with trivial breaks — that quickly become brakes.

Winston Churchill said, "You will never reach your destination if you stop and throw stones at every dog that barks." Choosing that one important impactful task and then hammering it to death will bring exponential benefits over multitasking.

Multitasking, moving fast, talking fast, checking the clock, fighting time in the day, all create hard work as a result of the actual hard work. You want to be in business, not busy-ness. Many people confuse these concepts.

Working effectively has short-term plus multiple long-term benefits, giving you time for anything you want.

Productivity quite literally is, according to Webster: "the effectiveness of productive effort... as measured in terms of rate of output per unit of input." I think the last part of this definition is what has gotten lost in translation over the years.

If you want to be busy, then do whatever you're doing. Don't change. Just walk through your day in defense mode, trying to address everything that is thrown at you, the minute it's thrown at you, so you can survive — every question, concern, email, phone call, tag, notification, text. The moment any one of those comes your way, drop everything and address it. You will indeed be busy.

You will be too busy for anything important and too busy for any of your long-term goals. You can't turn the boat around when 12 people in the boat are heaving demands at you and you need to respond. But if you shut them down, turn the boat, and then set it on autopilot, you can respond to any of them in due time. Nothing needs to be done this second. Half of those demands and questions will probably go away or will have answered themselves by the time you get the boat turned around.

It seems counterintuitive to some that airlines instruct you to first put on your oxygen mask before helping a child next to you. But when you take care of yourself first you can then think clearly and handle the next task. Don't deprive yourself of oxygen because you're immediately responding to other requests.

H. Jackson Brown Jr. said, "You have exactly the same number of hours per day that were given to Helen Keller, Pasteur, Michelangelo, Mother Teresa, Leonardo da Vinci, Thomas Jefferson, and Albert Einstein."

But they didn't wake up texting and posting. They lived their lives deliberately, taking care of their purpose first.

Your mind and body are always communicating with you. Listen to them. If there's a task that scares you or makes you uncomfortable, there's a reason. And if it's something you intellectually know needs to take place in the flow of your progress, then that is a productive and impactful step you must take.

Your mindset and resources are the most important asset you have. They give you utility. If you just let them run willy-nilly without thought, schedule, or order, you will always be "too busy." Without a plan, without a budget, without a schedule, you will feel fragmented, distracted, and be on the defense all day, every day.

Even telling someone you are "too busy" is a defensive play. You are having to shield yourself from a request. "I'm so sorry. I can't. I'm just really busy right now."

Kierkegaard said: "Of all ridiculous things the most ridiculous [is] to be busy."

You are the boss. Now pretend you are your own assistant and you want to impress yourself. What would you do for yourself to improve your days, both today and in the future? You have a list of what your boss wants to accomplish. You know where she wants to be in 1 month, 6 months, 2 years from now. What can you do for her that will help her? What can you remove from her life, what can you help her focus on, and where do you need to intervene? Help get the turbulent and cluttered distraction out of her life and get her into beast mode.

You are the hero. But you are also the enemy and you need to recognize that when you think you don't have what it takes. Analyze, measure, and change the things that are getting in the way. You already have the answers.

Edward Norton figured this out in "Fight Club." As the hero, he had to battle the enemy, which happened to be himself.

The biggest enemy in front of you is you.

Confront you.

CHAPTER 15

Approach To The Inmost Cave: Identity-Broadcast Muse-Monetization
(Stage 7 - Part 1)

"Sometimes you have to take a leap of faith first. The trust part comes later."

- Coburn Goss in *Man of Steel*

A PPROACHING THE INMOST CAVE is the stage in a hero's progression where she makes final preparations before plunging headfirst into even greater danger.

She's traveled far enough, deep enough, into the new world and is accepting the risks. She's open to the possibility of failure. But without acknowledging and accepting the possibility of defeat, she'll never be able to get close to her true identity.

In "Birdman," Michael Keaton puts his mental state on the line. He hallucinates having a conversation with Birdman and then starts flying around, knowing he may flail and die, or he may soar. He struggles with his identity.

In "The Breakfast Club," detained students sit and open up, revealing their identities. Anthony Michael Hall cries as he retells how he bullied a kid. Molly Ringwald reveals she's a virgin. Ally Sheedy proves she's a pathological liar. All of them want to move beyond these identities into their new ones, so they begin by revealing who they really are.

In "Close Encounters of the Third Kind," Richard Dreyfuss approaches the inmost cave in the form of Devils Tower. He journeys to the mountain which replicates his plate of mashed potatoes. He knows it is there where he will discover his identity or die; his obsession is weakening him.

When you transition into a new role, adopting new habits or systems, creating a new brand, or switching careers, there's that Matrix moment where time freezes, allowing cognizance of your evolving identity. You become hyperaware of your departure from one label to another.

We usually hear others voice their new habits or approaches when they start using them for the first time because they're excited to share. Thus the excitement. We should be proud of their dedication to their new identity.

- I don't eat meat.
- I no longer drink.
- I'm now a blogger.
- I take cold showers in the morning
- I meditate every day.

- I run every night.

I hear these statements all the time, but often when the habit has just begun, not 5 years into it.

Woody Allen said, "80 percent of success is just showing up." You have to show up. Most people never show up. They can envision their new selves, the new job, or the new habit they want. But they find every excuse possible to not show up. They protect themselves in their own comfortable routine, resorting to complacency and mediocrity.

One strategy that makes showing up easier is announcing to the world you're showing up, even before you have. You're going to show up. And that release helps obligate you. It also makes you culpable to your new accession.

How many smokers do you know who say "I quit smoking," yet they're now smoking again? Does this make them weak? Conversely, saying it may strengthen them. They know they can't quit on their own and seek moral obligation. They announce they are quitting, fully aware of the possible impermanence of the habit. But to give it their all, they broadcast this new identity to gain support and culpability.

Psychologically, we motivate ourselves to continue with the new augmentation we're initiating. It cements who we are by stamping a new sign on our forehead. It's a positive and necessary thing. It's also frightening.

Logically, you'd think no one should espouse the benefits of an approach or tell the world they have refined their process unless they have enough time behind it. But it's that skydiver's leap that people need to finally take. It's that galvanizing self-motivator that keeps our identity on track.

Not long ago I was producing a TV show. I was giving a roomful of writers and story producers some life advice. The topic of peak performance came up. One of the head writers said to me, "You should write an advice book; you seem to have a lot of information."

I involuntarily replied, "I am."

I caught myself off guard, blurting that out. I wasn't writing a book at all. I was guilty of mendacity. I felt like Steve Carell, having my voice controlled by Jim Carrey, in "Bruce Almighty."

The idea of writing a book had been germinating for a couple of years now, and it was starting to wake me up periodically. But I never took that first step. I hadn't given myself permission.

I had no excuses. I wasn't listening to my self. I was swimming through junk and reasoning that life was getting in the way. My brain was knocking on my morning door, waking me up, and I still wasn't listening. It took an audible in a room full of people stating a new identity for me to wake up and take note of this emerging purpose.

And as simple as that two-word sentence was to enunciate, I officially described myself as someone who was writing a book. And a room full of co-workers all heard me say it. There was confirmation.

I barely walked 50 feet over to my office, sat down and began writing.

It took me transmitting what I was doing, before I was actually doing it, to get me to do it. I wrote an entire chapter in about 20 minutes. It was liberating. It was terrible, rough (I've since amputated it from this book entirely), and every other disclaimer a writer gives for a first draft, but the process started. I was building a pyramid and I could immediately see its progress of the building blocks.

Produce Yourself

That group of story producers and writers have bound my testament. They check on my progress: "How's the book coming? When can I read it?"

That motivates me to show up as often as possible as a writer. And I've been showing up little by little, at least 3 times a week since then. Sometimes I write nothing more than the title of a new chapter, or just two or three paragraphs. But words become sentences, which become paragraphs, which become chapters, which become this book. The baby steps add up and compound into something with substantial momentum.

More recently, a colleague of mine told me about a business idea he was toying with. There was absolutely nothing novel about it. He wanted to start an Amazon store, of which there are probably thousands. Click, click, click. Anyone can have one.

It started out just as brief mentions-in-passing, at a random dinner, and later a salutation on the phone. I didn't think much of it until I asked him more details. As he started to explain how he had been researching a way to improve upon online sales for products, regardless of the product, I started to get intrigued. I thought it was a great business idea. Everyone uses Amazon. Why not be a seller?

He had read lots of articles, had had meetings with people, and had analyzed a few different strategies how to identify profitable products and sell them online.

But as I learned more, I wondered why he hadn't opened the store yet. It was a lot of talk and research for months. When I asked him why he hadn't started, he didn't have an answer. He acknowledged that. He wasn't the absent-minded professor, but he was so caught up studying how to approach and gaining never-ending information available online, he was paralyzed to initiate that first step.

He never gave himself permission. And so he never showed up.

Terence Michael

I asked if I could partner with him, 50-50.

To oversimplify, my friend was dreaming. And it was necessary. Without it, this business may have never reached my contemplation. I wanted to do. And he recognized that.

Within days of saying we'd partner, we were able to promptly proclaim to friends and family that we were now e-commerce sellers on Amazon. Bring us product ideas. We disclosed we hadn't sold a single item. Our store wasn't even officially open. I was still applying for seller permits and forming the LLC. But combined, we showed up and then wanted to prove ourselves. To everyone, but especially to ourselves.

The wisdom of not putting the cart before the horse is obvious. But if you want to have a cart and horse, it's okay to first tell people you have a cart. They'll soon be asking where the horse is, which will motivate you to get a horse.

You have to start somewhere, and sometimes, in a backward sort of way, there's no better strategy to start your identity than publicize it, even before you're fully immersed and established. We had to put the cart (quite literally shopping cart) out there before our own horsepower of ideas so that we could hold ourselves liable and have the platform to do rather than just dream.

Accept the identity you want. Broadcast it. And then start taking the steps.

I had to say I was a writing a book before I wrote the first sentence. And I had to call myself a producer before I ever produced a movie. If you wait for everything to align perfectly, you'll be waiting until you're in a coffin. At that point, you may be perfectly aligned, but no one will care.

Produce Yourself

The best time for anything is almost always yesterday, not tomorrow. So compromise and make today the perfect time. Kill the paralysis of analysis and stagnation of procrastination.

Here I was, calling myself a producer, yet I had not produced anything. I had opened and closed shop with the CPA. I had a handful of projects in development. But no one was paying me. I had no salary. I was cutting my minimal expenses down to practically nothing, yet putting on a sports coat and taking meetings at Hollywood's top agencies and studios all over town.

I found I wasn't the only one in this predicament. The majority of young Hollywood was juggling and jostling the same obstacles. The unglamorous side is that everyone is hungry and jockeying for position to get their breakthrough.

I started investing when I was 12 years old. I would ride my BMX bike down the street to the bank and put in 20 bucks or so I would get from washing cars, cleaning pools, pulling weeds, etc. That never stopped. All through high school and college, I continued this with my little business endeavors, always paying my Future Self first by way of investing.

My savings was small and dwindled quickly. But I couldn't project that I was a wannabe, broke producer. That doesn't instill much confidence in those who put faith in me to get a movie made. So I put the cart before the horse. I was a "producer," period.

But I was facing complete financial failure on top of having to wiggle out of having zero credits. I found comfort in knowing I was taking the risk and pursuing my purpose. That's what fed me. That's what kept me going.

But it was scary. No one wants to fail.

I have since learned the incredible value of failure. That we should actually seek and embrace it. Failure is nothing more than a step toward success. Not only does it help you eliminate what doesn't work, it prepares you for what does.

In "Iron Man 3," Guy Pearce says: "Failure is the fog through which we glimpse triumph."

If I want to roll a 6 on a die, I don't stop after rolling a 2. I keep rolling. That 6 will come up. Failure should become motivation, not excuse. Regardless how many failures find you, think about this: You are light years ahead of all the others who aren't even trying because they're afraid of failure.

Friends were already getting promoted 2 years out of college. Some had 401k plans with medical benefits. Me? I was still painting houses occasionally on weekends. I still did some "extra" work (background actor work in movies or TV shows), making $50 a day plus a free lunch. And I was doing market research here and there, and was paid $200 for a few hours of your time talking about phone service, my car, etc.

Had I come of age a generation later, I would have eaten up the gig economy that exists today. I feel that was made for my energy and diverse interests. The Internet was very alive and well, but the connection economy we have with Lyft, Airbnb, TaskRabbit, and the like didn't exist. There was no Craigslist where I could have sold everything I owned to buy more months on the timeline.

Today you don't have to get a real job. No one does. The Internet has equalized the sharing-crowd-sourced-access-gig-connection economy to the point that now over 40 percent of adults under 35 are making the majority of their income from the Internet. As they age and the economy ages this percentage will only increase.

Produce Yourself

This has made pursuing your purpose so much easier, as you can simultaneously remain a solo-prenuer and monetize other passions and talents.

I think that's the key overall strategy in life: pursue your purpose. Nothing is more meaningful or matters more than that. But in the meantime, monetize your passions and hobbies. Find a muse that you can hustle on the side.

Today we have incredible computations and algorithms that will put need and supply together faster than you can say Freelancer.com.

Here are just some of the platforms I wish had been available to me (if you want a complete list, visit SideHustleNation. I have discovered and vetted many of these sites from this extensive blog).

Do you love making jewelry, or love building tables, or love sewing scarves, or always wanted to sell your hand-made hats? There's Etsy, Shopify, Zibbet, and StoreEnvy where you can open your "store" with a click, plug-n-play, and done. You don't even need inventory, just made-to-order.

There are numerous millionaires online right now, including stay-at-home moms and dads who never even touch or see their product. Their store is a portal for orders wherein they are digital nomads connecting manufacturers to distributors to someone's mailbox at home.

Do you love travel, photography, writing, drawing, or painting? You can get paid to do any of those. Companies will sponsor you, blogs will hire you to write, share photos, and promote products. From Artsicle and TurningArt to RedBubble you have platforms with customers looking for your talents.

And you've likely heard about some of the early access platforms like Cafepress and Zazzle. I've personally used both numerous times. You can upload your designs on top of just about any blank product and sell it, like coffee mugs, plates, calendars or clocks. I once put my TV show's logo on skateboard decks and handed them out to the crew.

If you have a great idea for a T-shirt slogan, there's Teespring, Teechip, or Threadless. Had these existed when I was in high school, I could have hawked a lot of T-shirts.

Or maybe you love your city, like I do, and want to share it with others. Did you know Airbnb isn't just for renting out an extra room or your house? You now can make money sharing "Experiences." You can offer classes, tours, a skateboard lesson, a basket-weaving or cooking class, or a hike up to the Hollywood sign. Whatever you love to do, if you love people and sharing, this is suddenly a business where you can make money doing something you already do and love. But now many people join and pay you to follow your lead. I personally have a house on Airbnb and have recently launched an Experience for fun.

Do you love to design, doodle, or brand? You can make graphics and logos on DesignCrowd, LogoTournament, 99Designs, ZillionDesigns, and CrowdSpring. All of my company logos have come from these sites. And I will most likely get a book cover design for this book through one of them. I simply upload my ideas and get hundreds of submissions from around the world wanting my business.

Do you like to teach? There's Udemy. Make a course, videotape it once. Charge $50 or whatever. Work once. Earn forever. Skillshare, Coursmos, Rocketlearn — all places you can set prices and sell your course. Teach anything. As well, you can learn from these sites for fairly cheap.

Do you like snapping photos with your phone? Pond5, SnapWire, Foap, PhotoDune and many others. Upload your photos once. Make money every time someone buys it. Whenever I'm traveling or out on a walk and I happen to grab a cool video, I upload it to one of these sites where, to this day, I still make money when someone licenses the footage. It's small but it adds up. Do it once, earn forever.

Produce Yourself

Do you code, like to build websites, 3D modeling, 3D printing, build apps, or any technical computer experience? Visit Freelancer. And related, if you have an idea to build an app or anything you think you can't do, it's all hireable on Freelancer. Your mind is the only tool you need.

It's a great time for small or big swings, passion or purpose. No one has any excuse for not going after a dream or pursuit we may have set on the shelf years ago. There's a way. You don't have to wonder how you could ever become a talk personality on a radio show. You can open up your computer and start recording a podcast with the free tools available today.

Today, if you have skills, the Internet has you covered. Make money on the side and pursue your purpose.

But that wasn't the case for me as I attempted to reach the inmost cave of Hollywood while bringing in very little money. Muses and side-hustles were much more difficult to access.

So time was against me. I was fully aware that complete shutdown was a possibility, as much as I wanted to resist that scenario.

But what would I do? Go and get a "job"? I felt like that ship had sailed already, with most places wanting people right out of college. Here I was now a couple of years out of college and barely treading water.

My inner hero had reached a critical tipping point. I knew I had to launch myself in a big way, do or die, in one final attempt into the unknown. The pressure was on because I couldn't sustain another day of spinning my wheels.

What did I have to lose? I'd already lost if I resigned.

So further into the cave I ventured.

-

CHAPTER 16

Approach To The Inmost Cave: Fake-It-Till-You-Make-It
(Stage 7 - Part 2)

"The greatest single human gift — the ability to chase down our dreams."

- William Hurt in *A.I. Artificial Intelligence*

A FEW YEARS AGO I was having breakfast with my agent at CAA. I wasn't crazy about some of the projects I was being offered and wanted to try to pinpoint what I was interested in. But I was kind of all over the place. I gravitated to so many formats and spaces that it was tough for networks to sense what was right for me.

My agent told me, "Terence, it's all about your narrative. Networks want to know everyone's story. What's your story? Tell me, so I can tell them and then the right projects will flow to you since you will then be that guy."

He was so right. I had dipped my brush in so many different palettes, from music to sports, transaction to transformation, docu-comedy to docu-soap, red-neck to white-collar. Networks simply wanted to know who I was. When I went after a concept myself, I got it. But if I wanted the network to consider me, they had to picture me as someone specific. They needed to be able to pinpoint my brand.

I sometimes pride myself on having varied interests and being sort of a Swiss Army knife of producers. But that doesn't help when you need to broadcast to others why you are special. The Swiss Army knife doesn't cut it.

I decided that I was the docu-comedy guy. I could soft script due to my feature experience; my brand was comedy. Within weeks I was offered to show run and executive produce "Duck Dynasty."

It was one of the most fun experiences I've ever had. And if I never produce another minute of TV, I will forever cherish and remember my "Duck Dynasty" crew, staff, and cast.

This strategy of narrowing my narrative is what I was now facing with film, over a decade prior to entering the TV side.

Like me, other novice filmmakers were doing whatever they could to get their first films made. Some were blowing up credit cards; others were piggybacking resources from commercials or music video sets they worked on as assistants. There were a lot of different paths to get there.

But who was I? Why was I any different than everyone else hustling to make it happen? And not having any money, my options were limited.

I realized that when I broke it down, I was just playing the odds and fighting time. I was hoping that one day one of the projects I was developing would suddenly get chosen by money and celebrities. I might as well have played the lottery. My odds were not much better.

One evening, lying in my bed and staring at the ceiling in contemplation, it hit me. I'm not sure if it was out of desperation or I was able to clear my mind to find the answer, but I realized the flaw in my approach — and how to correct it.

I was sourcing and developing new material, for me, for my company. I was behaving as if I were a producer with a dozen credits looking for my next film. That's how you did it. That's what a producer did. But that was the wrong narrative for me. That was not a role I should have cast myself in.

I was at the bottom of the barrel with hundreds of other young producers trying to make it and get the first film going. What if I narrowed my ecosystem to just the bottom of that barrel?

In essence, could I carve a unique producer role for myself in an already existing film? Could I adjust my narrative ever so slightly as a producer wherein I helped other producers — those who had already found the money?

That was the big question. Since money was the obstacle, the challenge was finding a film that was already funded. But by eliminating that obstacle, I might be creating a new one in attaching myself to someone else's project.

The next morning, I made a strategic decision to pivot into a specialized type of producer, one that would accentuate my benefits and separate me from the pack of wannabes. It was a conscious decision in my latest attempt to dive deeper into the inner cave. I had exhausted alternatives.

Almost overnight, I branded myself as a finishing and sales producer. While not an official role, it is one of the many functions producers must perform in completing a film. Whereas all producers perform similar tasks in the beginning, toward the end, the fledgling producer simply doesn't have the contacts or experience to get a film distributed. Making a film is one thing. Marketing and sales is an entirely different animal (thus the purpose of most film festivals: access, networking, connections).

If someone was going soon into production, already in production, or looking for finishing-funds for postproduction and eventual distribution, I was the producer to collaborate with to help bring it home. That was my pitch. That was my new specialty.

Obviously, I had never done any of that. Again, I had zero credits. But in my 2 years now of developing and packaging projects, I had met all of the players. Everyone was lined up and ready when I finally made a movie.

There was a point where I had met practically someone from almost every company in the business. And I had memorized the staff rosters of every executive. I was obsessed, like going to a new high school and learning everyone's name.

Also, separating me from, say, an attorney or agency who effectively played in this same finishing and sales sandbox, I was a producer with projects actually set up at studios, with name actors, some half-financed. I'd been to all the film festivals, and spoke the language of a more seasoned producer. I just hadn't made anything. But so much was in the works.

My "store" signage: I'm one of you. I'm a producer making my own films, just like you are, but I also have the connections and know-how you need to get your film sold and seen. On top of that, I wasn't asking for 3, 5, or 10 percent of the sale, like an agent or attorney might. I was willing to do all of this free. I was working for credits. Because I knew credits had currency and that was worth more to me at the time than money — as much as I needed the money.

Produce Yourself

It was as if I had never driven a car, but I had read the manual backwards and forwards and analyzed reviews of the car. I'd watched videos of people driving it and talked to 50 people who had driven it. I had worked on my own cars, sat in them, and was prepared and itching to drive. But in the meantime, since I didn't have a car that started, maybe I could teach others to drive theirs. Let me sit in the passenger seat. That's all I ask.

Ultra-indie producers set out with lots of passion and what money they could scrounge up from relatives and investors, but find they didn't quite budget correctly, or just had to proceed based on the available resources. No one wants a lack of a music-budget or online-coloring to prevent commencement when crew and actors are in the wings. The "We'll fix it in post" phrase was, and still is, very much alive and well. And so projects frequently skidded toward the finish line running on fumes and desperate for help.

As expensive as a movie is to develop and produce, it's the postproduction process that makes the difference between a birthday party video and a gorgeous movie for the big screen. Coloring, audio mixing, editing, re-editing, composers, licensed songs, effects, graphics, etc. The story will never be any better. Ditto for the directing and the acting. It is what it is.

If you can't post it, it doesn't exist. It's incomplete; it's not a packaged product ready to be displayed on a shelf for a consumer to purchase. When it's done, it's done. And when it's not, it's not. And no distributor, no matter who they are, will look at it. Or look upon it favorably. Let alone distribute it.

Because I had worked at Warner Bros with legit "big-time" producers, and then run my own production company, the optics were there for producers newer than me. I was the guy who had Crossed the Threshold to the other side and would help pull them over. Ironic, I know. I emphasized my relationships with the studios and foreign sales agents, as well as investors I had acquired along the way.

Whereas an investor may not have committed $3 million to one of my own films, perhaps I might entice them to put up $120k to finish one that was practically done. Instant gratification for the investor who could assess the project based on shot footage, not just 110 pages of typed words.

New filmmakers were practically begging for anyone to assist them to the end zone. They had come down to the two-yard line, but couldn't cross the goal line. Giving up a credit, adding me to their film, wasn't a huge deal for them if I could help finance completion and bring them a distributor.

Perhaps their football game just needed me to come in the 4th quarter and kick them a field goal (interestingly, kickers are often the highest paid players of a football team per minute played. Their effectiveness comes from provided value, not how hard or long they play)

I remember meeting other young producers in this situation. I was envious. These producers had already made a movie. What I wouldn't give to be in their predicament. But rather than projecting elation and excitement, they projected anxiety, fear, and doubt. They had spent their investors' funds and were under immense pressure to finish the film.

It reminds me why we should never compare ourselves to others. We're all on our own journeys and dealing with our own set of obstacles.

For me, the obstacles were convincing other filmmakers that I was the guy to alleviate their fears. I was the guy with the solutions to their problems. But I also had to deliver. I had to kick that field goal.

Similar to many aspects of producing, it eventually required a balancing act of leverage, camouflage, and chutzpah to join the team.

Produce Yourself

While talking to Filmmakers #1, who needed funds to finish their film, I was meeting with Filmmakers #2 who had completed their film but didn't know how to sell it. Yet a third set, Filmmakers #3, was fresh out of college with their parents' money and getting ready to go make that film. I was talking to all three sets at the same time, just months from announcing my new narrative.

So, leveraging the legitimacy of each project as credibility for the others, I convinced Filmmakers #1 to bring me on board because of the information I shared about Filmmakers #2 and #3. Rinse and repeat a round robin with all three of them. To each, I was already producing two other movies — ones which capacitated the other.

In exchange for executive producer credits on all three, I would raise funds, help complete editing or postproduction, set up distributor screenings, and help negotiate final terms.

But I had to conceal the fact that I was just in discussions. I wasn't officially on Films #2 or #3. That is until I told Filmmakers #2 and #3 about Filmmakers #1. Leverage, perception, and camouflage.

I performed the functions exactly as promised. I provided value. I was a mentor. And I ultimately gave them what they needed in exchange for my credits. I never deceived anyone. But the juggling was precarious.

If you were to remove my veil during the initial stages, you'd see someone who had just enough knowledge to be helpful. But at the same time, I couldn't force any distributor to take a film they didn't want. I couldn't force them to write a check. But I could make connections and put the right people in the room.

Within 6 months of staring at that ceiling, I now had 3 executive producer credits. I was officially a movie producer.

An "executive producer" credit in a film can be anything. It sounds good but doesn't necessarily mean it was earned. Or, it is indeed more than earned, but you wouldn't know the difference simply from seeing the title and placement. People look up to it. But you're not the "producer."

In a film, it is the all important "Produced by" credit that is the person(s) who spearheads making the film come together and happen. Sometimes it's one person; many times it's several. But that's the main role. If a film wins an Oscar, it doesn't go to the executive producer(s), it goes to the producer(s).

I point this out only so you can understand my angling for a credit, but not taking credit for something I didn't do. The E.P. (executive producer) credit has no rules. That could be someone who provides funding, is maybe the manager of one of the actors, or as in my case, came in to help complete the film.

So it's an extremely well-respected credit. You're part of the club. But you haven't necessarily "made" the film.

To highlight how ambiguous this E.P. credit is, you could have been the one and the only person who made the film entirely and still have an executive producer credit, simply based on how the negotiations came down when you were sourcing the money or the intellectual rights to the idea. There is a myriad of scenarios; too many to describe. It's a fantastic credit to have. And fantastic hard working producers get that credit. But so do people who have never stepped foot on set or possibly even read the script.

To make things more confusing, switch over to the TV side a moment. In television, it's just the opposite. The E.P. is the top dog, the creator, the showrunner, or the person responsible for the whole series. Disorienting, I know.

And the "producer" in TV is a bit more subordinate, with functions that could be anything from directly producing for the E.P., to writing, to simply having that credit based on rights or part of management to the talent. In other words, the E.P. and producing credits are almost flip-flopped moving from film to TV.

But all of the above was now a good problem to decipher and navigate. I now was a producer with three credits. I could now return to my personal projects with renewed energy and experience to hopefully take them to the next step.

To me, these first three films weren't spectacular. I would have preferred spectacular. They were small, very indie, and two of them were barely seen by anyone outside of the cast and crew (a fate that befalls many first-time indie films). But one of them went theatrical and got some decent attention.

This temporary narrative into which I pivoted was in response to a seemingly insurmountable obstacle. Sometimes you have to reach unfavorable situations to force yourself into an alternate route. There's always a way. It's just not always obvious. In fact, it's never obvious for the hero.

The fake-it-till-you-make-it strategy is often employed by the hero during this approach to the innermost cave. There comes a time when traveling so deep into the special world, where the only tools available will be from the new world. She doesn't need to deceive, but she does need to project confidence in her new environment to remain alive. She needs to assuredly communicate that she can wield the weapons and tackle the beast. Like Wonder Woman, she is capable of retrieving the God-Killer sword.

I have a friend who is a high-level network television executive. He wasn't always. He transitioned from a completely different industry rather than work his way up.

I had drinks with him one evening and I asked how he was able to move laterally from a completely different industry. He said, "I faked it 'till I made it." He had no idea what half the systems and processes were in TV. He didn't know how he should be giving notes on cuts, assessing new potential projects, and the like. But he knew he could do it. Someone just had to give him a chance, allow him some slack to learn terminology, methods, etc.

While in his old profession, he had read voraciously and studied, interviewing people and scouring the Internet for info. He knew it could be him, but he had to present the lensing of being a network exec before he was, in fact, performing the functions of one. Today he's thriving and has worked at many of the top networks. He's learned the politics and dynamics of working at a network. It's not rocket science. And now he has the experience to back up his title.

When I was in college taking that class from BR, he told a story of how his agency once tried to sign a big-name actor. This actor came into their conference room which was filled with agents pitching why he should sign with them. Then the phone rang and an assistant chimed in that one of the agents was needed back in his office right away because Steven Spielberg was on the phone. The agent in question jumped from his chair and excused himself from the meeting.

The way BR told this story to our class, this actor was impressed that not only did Steven Spielberg call but that the agent jumped to immediately take his call. What this newly signed actor didn't know was that Spielberg hadn't called. The assistant who called was instructed to pretend. It was a fake call.

Deceptive? Yes. But only in a relative sense.

Spielberg did indeed work with BR's agency and had numerous conversations with agents there. But the agents couldn't guarantee he would call right when they were trying to sign the big-name actor.

Produce Yourself

So, to help present the credibility and access they had as agents, they manipulated perception to happen at a specific time. The agents weren't fabricating something inauthentic about whom they did business with or what their capabilities and reach were. But they needed the leverage of that relationship with Spielberg to reveal itself at a certain time on a certain day (a little manipulation, as in Reality TV).

In the end, the agency put this actor in a room with Spielberg to collaborate, doing exactly what they illustrated they could do.

I suppose it's possible BR made up this entire story to make a point. I don't know. Like Tom Hanks tells his son in "Radio Flyer": "Sometimes history is in the mind of the teller." We never questioned BR's Mr. Miyagi methods and wisdom.

You need to be true to your abilities. In the case of the network exec, BR, and me, we had the skills, knowledge, and contacts. But it took some temporary sleight-of-hand to get the opportunity to prove ourselves. We eventually did what we promised.

This approach to the inmost cave was one of the most challenging for me mentally. I was still far from finding the Holy Grail, yet I had dug deep, diving below my natural inhibitions to get a taste of possibility. But I wasn't there yet. I was still on the approach path to my ultimate career purpose.

I was grateful for staying in the game thus far. I came close to petering out. Too many of my colleagues didn't make it this far, and even fewer got past the first film.

It's almost a filter, like Darwin's concept of survival of the fittest, wherein voyagers are weeded out per their determination and purpose. How badly do you want it? Are you willing to show up every day, day after day? And are you willing to move laterally when needed, take a detour, or even make a U-turn?

What lurks beyond the next bend or over the next mountain could be the nirvana you've dreamed of. It takes courage and bravery to continue when the path you're on is barely navigable.

Every hero gets her shirt torn, her makeup smeared, hair tousled, and beaten down. She will plumb the depths of trenches and gutters before rising to streets paved with opportunity.

Success is nothing but the mathematical result of failure x 10.

- Keep failing.

- Welcome it.

- Keep striving.

- Keep at it.

- If it's you, and you feel it in your bones, you are on the right path.

You can have anything you want if it's your purpose.

-

CHAPTER 17

The Ordeal:
Networking · Permission
(Stage 8 - Part I)

"Every man dies, but not every man really lives."

- Mel Gibson in *Braveheart*

IT WAS NOW ONE YEAR after I obtained my first three credits, and I was standing on the set of a major motion picture. Sony Studios would soon be wide-releasing a romantic comedy starring Sarah Jessica Parker, Ben Stiller, and a young girl I absolutely adored named Scarlett Johansson. I was 25 and this was my first studio film to go into production. It was also my first time in New York City.

I was officially a Hollywood movie producer, doing everything I ever dreamed I could achieve, and at an age about 20 years younger than the average film producer. We were shutting down Times Square, Central Park, and even the Manhattan Bridge one night in 10-below-zero weather for a night scene. In essence, this was my first film from start to finish, and it was a hell of a way to jump in.

It would never have happened had I not pivoted and rewritten my narrative after staring at my bedroom ceiling of contemplation and predicament. I wouldn't have discovered the detour that eventually brought me to this point with a team of over 60 people standing in SoHo.

But as Deadpool would probably say, "We're getting ahead of ourselves. Let's rewind 6 months."

A crew member from one of those first three films I mentored to gain credits, introduced me to a friend of his, another first-timer wannabe producer, B.

She was interested in meeting me because her friend told her I helped first-timers.

I was barely ahead of her on the Hero's Journey toward moviedom. But now, having those three EP credits in my back pocket, (to her) I was the mentor she needed.

B knew two scrappy, iconoclastic NYC filmmakers and she desperately wanted to make their next movie. They were generating a lot of buzz around town after releasing their first movie.

In her career journey, she had been a model from London. But she had the determination to be a movie producer. And going through her own climb, she had left her Ordinary World with the call to become one. But she needed her mentor to help her Cross the Threshold. That's where I entered stage-right in her script.

I had approached the inner sanctum but not fully explored inside yet. I had traveled to the furthest recesses I could reach to learn and absorb everything about my Special World. But I was still barely skimming the surface. There was a deeper level that could only be obtained with experience and time.

Although I had faced many detours and impediments to get where I was, I had yet to face the ultimate Ordeal that a hero goes through along the journey.

Up to this point, I had epiphanies, doubts, pivots, misdirects, and subtle alterations in my approach and habits to becoming a producer. But none of my actions or experiences brought me yet to the point where I could fully prove my existence in this Special World. Nothing was absolute yet.

Now that I had some credits, I was labeled "one of them" in a world foreign to me just 3 years prior. I no longer felt like an alien among aliens, a stranger in a strange land. But I still had to prove myself. To me, if to nobody else.

Gaining the credits to advance is one thing. Taking on and physically making a movie happen from beginning to end is another. I hadn't technically done it, even though I was confident I could do it — blindfolded, with both arms tied behind my back. It was all I could think about.

B wanted guidance and needed me as leverage to get her first film going. I wanted to take my producing experience and exposure to the next level by having my own film from start to finish, development to box office. I wanted to be her guide — and, in turn, gain guidance myself. We both needed each other.

There's a common conception that to further progress or perfect what you are learning, you not only need to have a mentor, you need to be a mentor.

Remember when you'd form a study group in school? As much as I disliked the ideas of those groups because, quite frankly, there seemed to be more taking than giving, I learned the subject at hand more clearly and cogently by explaining the concepts to others, rather than just recite and memorize them myself.

If you take an idea or subject — one you are still learning yourself — and teach it to someone else, you will help cement it in memory. This goes for any task, habit, approach, or set of rules. When you become the instructor, you are at the same time the pupil of your own advisement.

This is partly why I enjoy dispensing advice about everything from healthy living to optimizing performance. You eventually do practice what you preach. Sometimes, until I verbalize a strategy to someone else, it doesn't become a regular habit for me.

Although I suspect there's a formal name for this concept, I like to simply call it 1-2-3, where you are always #2. As #2, you should be seeking and ingesting as much information from #1. #1 is ahead of you and has the knowledge you are seeking. That's why they are #1. #3 below you passionately wants the information you have. It's in this process of filtering and re-formulating the info from #1 to #3 that you, #2, educate and train yourself.

Information is power. But generously giving (money, love, knowledge, emotional support, anything) is empowerment. Big difference. This will not only embolden and fortify your own insight, it will expand your network, solidifying you as an expert. This, in turn, will help you reach peak fulfillment in an area, and it will engender opportunity as your tribe of colleagues recall your guidance later in life.

This is how that crew member came to recommend me to B in the first place. He viewed me as having a certain level of production dexterity, helping guide the crew on set toward completion. Honestly, I didn't have to do much. They mostly had their act together. Sometimes by stepping back from the detailed minutiae, the global lens can help identify overt mistakes. I was given that opportunity by being able to observe and supervise.

Nevertheless, this brought B to me.

I liked holding court for my meetings at Beverly Hills delis. A lot of the agencies were in Beverly Hills and it seemed a wasted lunch or coffee to not rub elbows with someone new, expanding my scene.

I still stick to this philosophy somewhat: that we all have to eat; most of us have afternoon coffee or tea; and many of us drink. The more you can make those three daily activities part of networking, the more you will cultivate contacts and opportunities.

Sure, there are times you need to scarf down the basics due to time constraints. But, although you are minimizing your time expenditure, you aren't maximizing your impact. You're saving a penny to lose a dollar. If your budgeted time isn't allowing for lunch meetings or coffee meetings (even within your own office), a Skype session, or while walking for 20 minutes in the park to share coffee, then there's a critical issue with mismanagement of your time.

There's too much administrative work and too many distractions and unimportant tasks eroding your daily schedule, making you "busy." But the cost of that is great if it keeps you from connecting with a potential mentor or ally.

By aligning my necessary functions with networking, I was able to attract others who came from other scenes of influence and resource — areas I would never be exposed to had I sat at home eating a sandwich or making a solo coffee.

When you're attempting the almost insurmountable task of getting a movie made (or insert whatever your purpose is here), you need every ounce of support you can find.

Dorothy would never have made it to Oz without the help of her friends. She needed them. And they needed her.

B's circle of influence was completely different than mine. We had almost no overlap. Her scope was club owners, photographers, artists, models, Wall-Streeters, et al. She could make calls and get people excited about assembling. She also knew NYC very well, which is where the film needed to be shot. She was also sticky. People gravitated toward her. They liked her. She was perfect for bringing people together and motivating them — signs of a great leader.

What she didn't have was the experience or knowledge to get a film made, She didn't have any rights, contracts, or attachments. But she had agency.

She found the filmmakers in NYC. And she found me.

That was enough. She had currency.

At our meeting, B insisted I drop everything and go see "My Life's In Turnaround" (first mentioned in Chapter 12). This was the film that was written, produced, directed by and starring the filmmakers she wanted to introduce me to. She wanted to produce their next film. And they needed a producer.

Watching "My Life's In Turnaround" proved to me an amazing movie could be made on a low budget. These guys spent a mere $40k (later an additional $160k when finishing funds were added) and made what I thought was one of the funniest comedies I had ever seen. But it also was filled with heart and spoke to my behind-the-scenes Hollywood fascination (everyone in Hollywood shares this same obsession).

The film was about two filmmakers trying to make the film we were actually watching, with them as the actors. It was a meta mash-up. The last scene in the film is with them making the first scene that we, the audience, originally viewed when the film started — creative, clever, and irreverently funny.

The kicker for me was that their film's budget was less than that of each of my first three films, none of which I felt could compare to this one.

Content is content. Story is story. This film enlightened me that execution, not budget, is crucial. Downstream, I never again let budget be a justification for subpar performance again.

Growing up in the suburbs with a Cineplex, I saw all the same movies as every other kid on the block, which was whatever was corporately spoon-fed in national TV ads and store merchandise.

This was really my first exposure to truly autonomous and unconstrained film that was not viewed as low-budget first, movie second. It was a movie first, period. Oh, and by the way, it was low-budget.

"Moonlight" was one of the lowest budget films of 2016 at under $2 million. But did you care? Phenomenal and beautiful, it won the 2017 Oscar for Best Picture.

After diving into the filmmakers' press articles on their film, I learned how they decided to finally reject rejection and start giving themselves permission.

Donny was a bartender for 10 years. Eric was a cabbie for 10 years. All while trying to write, pitch, sell and break in any way they could as writers, actors, whatever. But nothing.

Eric said he couldn't take one more day of lying on his bed, staring at the ceiling and wondering when it was going to happen for him (that same ceiling of contemplation I was all too familiar with).

When would the world allow him to make a movie? He just kept driving his cab, day in and day out, getting older, and making no headway. He just couldn't take it anymore. He said the pain of not making a movie was worse than the pain of having to live one more day staring at that ceiling. If you watch the film, he eloquently articulates this emotional epiphany, as he plays himself going through this exact stage.

Eric and I have always shared similar philosophies, and I think that's why we hit it off when we finally met for the first time. I had left the studio system when I was answering phones at a desk. It didn't take me 10 years, but I saw the writing on the wall, or maybe more accurately, the ceiling.

I, too, didn't want to wait for permission. You will never find me standing in line behind a velvet rope.

Eric took 10 years, but he was writing the entire time, honing his craft. He was prolific. He literally had a box of over 20 completed screenplays in it. It bought him meetings, contacts, and legitimacy as a writer to watch. But he was still never able to break through (very common in Hollywood).

Here was a guy who heard his call loud and clear. He obeyed it. But the obstacles were too great trying to climb the mountain with the same directions that were suggested for every writer in Hollywood. Do this, do that, send it here, send it there.

Eric found his ally along his pilgrimage in Donny, someone who was also living the same fate, albeit with a night job so he could write during the day. So together, they would align their synergy and hopefully triple their efforts. They gave themselves permission to Cross the Threshold and explore the spirit of their future identity.

It took 10 years of building habits that would enable them to leave their comfortable all-cash jobs. The passion burning inside them for so long was either going to kill or liberate them.

So they did it, on their own terms, moving laterally off the traditional path to make their own. The experience and the results of the film got them meetings with almost every studio, guest spots on every late night and magazine show. And it got them writing jobs at production companies. Networks wanted to develop TV shows. Producers wanted them to punch up their writing.

They made it. They stopped waiting for someone to give them an admission ticket. They green-lit themselves into production and into their new world, and they were now exploring the new landscape, tempted by its spoils.

But you know by now how the Hero's Journey goes; and it wasn't long before they encountered unforeseen obstacles, tests, and ordeals — some of which they may have brought upon themselves. For the hero's journey is often one of internal revelation and exposure to what is suppressing your progress. These obstructions manifest themselves as external events, but sometimes need to be recognized as internal circumstance.

Nevertheless, they finally realized the difference between dreams and goals.

Dreams are romantic and comfortable. They come in the night. It doesn't take much effort to dream. They come to us; we don't seek them.

Goals are stark and frightening; they require building daily, accountable habits to measure advancement. Self-reflection is required to:

- record and analyze how you're spending your time

- know if your steps and tasks are effectual

- sense if you need to pivot or dive deeper

- realign with new allies

- remove distraction

Eric and Donny quickly discovered the studio's tempting but slower-than-a-sloth development system. They were lured by the fancy lunches and studio-lot meetings. They rubbed elbows with celebrities and famous directors. They made money.

But what they didn't do was actually make another movie. Lots of development. No production. They encountered the same large wall that I once answered phones under.

This is when, and why, our hero paths collided and merged.

Eric and Donny were disillusioned by the process at this point in their journey. This is why they were ready to forge a relationship with me to make another independent film.

It's why almost anyone makes an independent film. It's why almost anyone strikes out on her own, becomes an entrepreneur and starts her own business.

The Hero's Journey is made for everyone who is ready to give themselves permission to do whatever they want. It's there for disruption. But it takes solid habits to do it effectively.

Everything holding a hero back can be overcome along the journey. It's a process. There are stages. It's not easy.

That's why it's called The Ordeal.

-

CHAPTER 18

The Ordeal: Momentum · Informality Collaboration · Instinct
(Stage 8 - Part 2)

"Life passes most people by while they're making grand plans for it ."

- Johnny Depp in *Blow*

THE STUDIO SYSTEM, although sexy and alluring as hell, is an extremely slow process of pitching, waiting, pitching, waiting, developing, waiting, re-pitching, waiting, etc. It involves a lot of talk, a lot of meetings.

What it's not for many is a lot of making movies. For a few, it is this, but for the majority, it is not.

I rejected exploring this approach early on for one where I could grant myself entry. This was the Ordeal Eric and Donny were currently experiencing, hot off their first theatrical release.

Waiting for their number to be called simply put them back in the same line they were in prior to making their first film. Why become successful in order to be back to square one? Why go through their entire 10-year struggle to be in charge of their own destiny, only to be at a place where someone else is in charge of it?

It's like the famous story of the Brazilian fisherman and the businessman (told in many languages and variations, so I'm extrapolating and re-interpreting as I recall it from business school):

A businessman is sitting on the beach in a beautiful Brazilian seaside town. He meets a local fisherman who is pulling up his little boat filled with large fish. Impressed, the businessman asks the fisherman how long it takes him to catch all these big fish. The fisherman replies that he does it in about 2 hours. Shocked, the businessman asked why he didn't simply stay out there longer and catch more. He could be rich.

The fisherman tells him that he doesn't need any more fish. This is more than enough to feed his whole family. And since it only takes him 2 hours, he's then able to return to his house, play with his kids, take a nap with his wife, join his buddies in the village for a drink, play guitar, sing and dance into the night.

The businessman can barely contain himself and explains how easily the fisherman could improve his process and be so much more effective. He should spend more time at sea, at least doubling or tripling his haul. Then he could buy a bigger boat, and then more boats, get crews of men, set up a cannery, have a whole distribution system of the best fresh Brazilian fish around. It would be so easy to upscale. He blows a huge opportunity by not realizing this.

Produce Yourself

The fisherman thinks about it for a few moments, then asks the businessman what it's all for. What's the purpose?

The businessman, frustrated by the fisherman's simple mind, tells him he could then retire rich. He could move somewhere by the ocean, buy a house, play with his kids, take a nap with his wife, join his buddies in the village for a drink, play guitar, sing and dance into the night. He wouldn't have to worry about money.

The fisherman asks the businessman, "Isn't that what I'm doing now?"

I love this story, true or not, because it highlights two principles for me:

One, although the story wasn't intended to have this effect, I partially agree with the businessman. To the extent that there are ways to monetize when doing something you love, that's nirvana. That's what it's all about. The entire Hero's Journey is about meaning and purpose. And if you can make money doing what you love, it doesn't get any better. So I understand where the businessman is coming from in his frustration.

But on the other hand, the story's lesson, which I also agree with, is that if upscaling to have and make more, simply costs you more, such that the end result is the same, it's an ineffective pointless process.

If I can make $5 today by selling one glass of lemonade on my front lawn and then go enjoy the rest of the day, wonderful.

Compare that to the guy across the street who has a line around the block. He's got trucks of lemons and 10 employees mixing batches for him, working 14-hour days. If he's selling $5,000 today but spending $4,995 to get there with advertising and overhead, he'll also end up with $5. The approach is obviously broken.

If those are the only two scenarios, which guy do you want to be?

Bigger isn't always better. It can be with the right approach. It many times is when optimized.

But it wasn't for Eric and Donny in terms of meaning. They did make some nice money when they arrived. They had lots of offers. But as you know by now, the majority of that lies in development.

When they stripped away driving onto the fancy lots and shaking hands with celebrities passing by in golf carts, they were just begging people to allow them to make a movie again. They didn't need to go through all the pomp and circumstance to arrive at the same spot they were in originally.

In an effort to keep altering my average of 5, making Donny and Eric part of my new scene would drastically change my sum-game in the indie world.

I always viewed myself as tenacious and resourceful. But I'm a wallflower compared to these guys. They approach people in the street. They ask for what they want. They tell you what they need. They cold call anyone and everyone they want to work with. And they do it with humor.

When I first met Eric, I was bummed to learn that Donny wouldn't be involved in this next film, but the script we chose from Eric's box of 20 had a single lead. It wasn't a buddy comedy.

Donny's journey was headed in a different direction within Hollywood, one equally as profound and prolific as Eric's, but now separate.

I was also confident I could help Eric, mentor B, get the film made, and, in-turn, help myself. I was still learning, but I was confident in my ability to produce, even if this would officially be my first film, beginning to end.

So over the next 3 months, I spent hours with Eric numerous times a day, breaking down the script, budgeting, scheduling, and seeing how we could make the film as cheaply as possible. That was the enticement since all of us had made films for cheap. But no one had done it as inexpensively as Eric had. It was inspiring and challenging to learn just how far he pushed a dollar on screen.

B eventually raised $30,000 privately, on her own (again, that network she had and her natural leadership skills), and Eric felt that was enough to get us going. It wasn't. Not even close.

But God bless Eric because, in many ways, it's what we needed to kick-start the project. Eric knows how to create momentum more than anyone I've ever met. He may only have one shoe on, but he'll start walking out the door anyway.

B and I hopped an airplane for NYC with the $30k in a paper bag as we continued to call all our investors. I think we were looking for about $300k, a little more than Eric had spent on his first film.

B also found us an amazing Upper West Side apartment from a friend of hers, so we made it our temporary production office. We went about securing locations, getting permits, licenses, and staffing.

Meanwhile, we needed name talent if we were to find the other $270,000. We met with and tried to attract everyone who was hot at the time. Fortunately, having Eric currently in the news with a film in theaters helped immensely.

I proceeded to contact all my finishing-funds contacts, distributors, sales agents, and even straight up studios to come in for the budget. Just as I had done with my first three E.P. credits, I was reaching out to the same contacts, but this time on the front end. I also had a solid business deck, having learned from past mistakes.

In hindsight, we didn't really have anything that special. We were just another project, another rom-com script looking for money. We had Eric, who was enjoying buzz, but so were dozens of other directors, most of whom had more credits and were better known.

But, like a boulder that descends a hill and picks up exponential speed, we had growing momentum. I learned how important momentum is, even if it's initially just perception. Eric's frenetic strategy was to set a date and tell everyone about it. This made it tangible and official. The solidification of concrete milestones to hit, even if they seemed impossible, helped broadcast the narrative we were serious.

I found this ironic coming from a guy who took a decade to break through. He was so impetuous and dismissive as to traditional preparation on this film, I feared we were headed for battle unprepared. But he was right. It was half optics and half sheer bravado. Given how tiny our budget was, we may have never been adequately prepared.

Making a movie is a huge endeavor: an average of 50 crew members, maybe 14 cast members, 18 locations, over 7 weeks of shooting. Not to mention having the funding in place to pay for those goods and services within a finite period, run payroll, stay out of trouble, and deliver the film to a distributor.

Like building a house or throwing a big wedding, it's a confluence of a lot of mini-events and occurrences that have to sync as they stack atop one another like a game of Tetris to complete the puzzle.

Because of this, choosing a start date for shooting is often the most difficult task. Rarely is this done until you know you have everything in place and have lined up everyone's schedules maybe 6 months from when you have your funding.

But, whether ballsy or irresponsible, Eric said the only way we were going to get our movie made was if we picked a date and went. That's what had worked for him on his first film, so that's what would work now. That's it. Do or die, little or a lot of money, big actors or small actors, rain or shine, that's it. This is the date of our party and we are throwing it, period.

This was contrary to everything I knew about preproduction, planning, budgeting, and being smart. It went against everything I, as a producer, had been reading and learning, and everything I knew from my Ordinary World about flow-charting progress.

After Eric proclaimed that we were absolutely shooting in 4 weeks, we notified the press. If actors aren't available, tough. We'll lose some great keys (heads of departments on set), locations, etc. But we're doing it. We're doing this, whether we shoot the entire film in Eric's apartment or in 20+ locations the script actually called for.

Everyone knows to avoid the cart-before-the-horse. Attempting to mitigate risks and maximize opportunity, this seemed counterintuitive to undertake something so complex before it was ready. In business, you set up steps, break down large goals into smaller, doable tasks, etc.

But, no longer needing consent after proving he could do it on his own terms, Eric was throwing caution to the wind. And since we still only had $30k in a paper bag at the time, the risk seemed minimal.

Eric quite simply did what his hero needed to do when faced with challenges that traditional insight couldn't conquer. And right or wrong, for his hero, it seemed to work.

I later adopted this approach when it came to critical junctures in projects or businesses where I was contemplating what to do next when staring at the mountain in front of me.

Just verbalizing you're doing something sometimes makes it a reality. As one of my fraternity brothers once told me (a quote attributed to Thomas Paine): "Lead, follow, or get out of the way."

Eric had been following, but been in his own way for too long. He was now leading, albeit somewhat haphazardly. This is why we became a great Yin and Yang for each other. I understood his fire and passion ("Just do it"). And he understood my value-benefit approach ("Let's help others... they'll help us"). We were on opposite sides of the spectrum and conflicted in pace. But together we coalesced into the impetus our film needed.

Eric understands that when he does something differently than everyone else, he in effect highlights what they were doing wrong. And people don't like that. However, it irks me when some people criticize Eric's approach. I understand where they're coming from. But they are mostly frustrated that they can't do what Eric does.

The masses don't like outliers. When someone resides on the fringes, he demonstrates others' lack of growth and gumption. The mediocre like to criticize and ridicule someone who colors outside the lines.

If you want to grow and upgrade your life, you need to be content with alienating yourself from the herd. Most don't like change. Most like policy.

Most in Hollywood would probably behave like Eric if they could. But the wheels of corporate Hollywood turn ever so slowly; everything must be in perfect alignment to begin. I understand this approach. This had been my normal until I met Eric.

So in 4 weeks, we would be shooting. Once our announcement hit the trades, we raised around $1.2 million within a couple weeks.

We shot the film and flipped it halfway through production to Sony for $3.5 million, immediately profiting. I could write an entire book about this film's production, as I could about any of my other 19 films. Each one has its own circuitous Hero's Journey, all equally crazy and miraculous that they got done. Most producers in Hollywood feel this way about their movies.

It goes without saying that I was standing on the shoulders of allies throughout this process (they also stood on mine). Everyone from Eric to B, from Sarah Jessica Parker to Ben Stiller, was immensely helpful in all aspects, on and off-camera. Even supermodel Elle Macpherson, who joined the cast, was enormously helpful in getting some product placement, locations, and music. And for me, I made a special friend in Scarlett Johansson. I was privileged to be able to watch her career evolve into a stellar one.

We also partnered with veteran producers (hot off of "Dumb and Dumber") who also owned a sales company to structure the sale to the studio for us.

I'd love to take credit for making everything happen. I can recall a couple dozen things that, had I not accomplished, the film wouldn't have gotten done. But the reality is that everyone probably has equal recollection. I can't take sole credit, ever, for any project I've done. Rather, it's always been a convergence of heroes on similar journeys who combine forces to support each other like rock climbers ascending a cliff. This might be one of my favorite aspects of movie making, besides telling story.

Fighting the reptilian brain's default to find the path of least resistance is a never-ending battle. Avoiding discomfort, failure, and shame are the main factors separating anyone's future identity from their present existence. These are the obstacles a hero must tackle with good daily habits. And sometimes (or all the time, in my case as a movie producer) you can't venture into battle alone.

I continue to see this autocratic, selfish problem in people still struggling to find their purpose. They feel they must keep the entire pie, assuming one day they will finally reach the top of the mountain and be able to enjoy the entire pie by themselves. Just them. No need to share.

But if they understood math, probability, and weighted averages a bit better, they'd know that sharing that pie with others — taking even just a slice of that pie and having 5 others help you carry it up that mountain — not only significantly increases your likelihood of success and shortens your time requirement, it will increase your reach and opportunity.

In addition to sharing in the tribal spirit and motivation that exudes from a group, you'll have the time to cook other pies of different flavors and sizes. You'll eventually have diversified pies and people with the same goal — getting up that mountain to enjoy pie.

If you think climbing the hill pushing one big boulder by yourself works for you, then great. Isolation and singular focus does indeed work for some people. But welcome perspective and collaboration as much as you can. Your horizons will expand and your average will increase with many fractions of one, rather than just one. For me, I'd rather find the five best partners possible and have us all carry pebbles up the hill, than haul a big rock myself.

As hot as Eric and the producers of "Dumb and Dumber" were at the time, as much as Ben and Sarah Jessica brought as actors, as tenacious and resourceful as B was, and as entrepreneurial and managerial as I was as a producer, it took the assemblage of all, including the entire 75-person cast, crew, and staff, to make this one film happen.

For Eric, he once again proved that giving himself permission to fail was the path to success. This was only his second film. But, it was his first big studio film, which only became a studio film after-the-fact because he partnered with B and me and others to help marry his talents with studio needs.

Produce Yourself

I learned a lot about instinct and informality from Eric. As much as I thought I knew from business school — looking at data, planning, scheduling, finance, and in general how to be "professional," Eric's foreign but fresh approach has stuck with me as a go-to fallback position when following the rules doesn't work.

Case in point: Eric — with all due respect to him as a short, quirky, neurotic New Yorker — could get any girl. I mean ANY girl. Models, celebrities, the hot girl in the supermarket, the yoga girl in the park, the girl on the train. And yeah, I'm pretty sure if he wanted her, the Girl with the Dragon Tattoo.

Talk about a lesson in courage. Talk about a lesson in setting your fears aside. The movie that Eric produced for his own life made him the hero every time he approached an attractive girl. He didn't have any stupid, slimy come-ons. He was honest. And he had the guts to take that first step, literally — the one most people shy away from, girls or otherwise.

I can't count the times Eric and I were at dinner or walking in the park, working on our films, and he'd see a pretty girl. He'd typically stop and say, "I'll be right back."

The scene was always the same for Eric. He cast himself as the guy who knows the answer is already "No" if he doesn't ask this girl out. It's "No" right now just standing there in the park, observing her. It's never going to be anything but "No" if he doesn't ask. "The worst thing that could happen," he would recite to me every time to pump himself up and look for a reassuring nod, "is that she says 'No'. But it's 'No' right now, so let me give myself the chance to find a 'Yes'."

So by going up to her and saying "Hi, I'm Eric. Can I take you to dinner?" he gave himself the chance. He imbued himself bravado and audacity.

Eric has sights of where his heroic self could be in an alternate future universe with that girl. For him, Crossing the Threshold, an obstacle most don't pass when approaching a stranger, was the easy part in his movie, or so it seemed as he eloquently and adroitly followed his own direction.

By producing himself as the guy who could do this, he permitted the hero in him to conveniently turn chance into good fortune.

There were times I heard the "No" from across the park or dining room. I could see the girl blushing or fluttering her hair, illustrating her flattery to his advances, even if she rebuffed him. He was always clever and charming, and would playfully walk away. I often smiled, somewhat jealous that he had such bravery to simply go up to anyone and start talking to them. She may not be the one. But he knows she never will be if he doesn't ask.

I came back from my first New York experience with Eric fueled with confidence to take on the world. I accomplished in film what I knew I was capable of, and I had a new ally who was drastically different in strategy and approach.

I learned nothing earth shattering from Eric, but his unique approach to his purpose helped crystallize the various junctures where I had pivoted, rebranded, or disrupted mine. Eric's buoyant attitude of certainty was a fresh contrast to mine of methodical independence but sometimes uncertainty.

Those girls? I'm guessing, but would say more than 50 percent of the time he got a date from those encounters. He has so many stories, he actually wrote a book about those moments and the relationships that followed (many with celebrities), called "I Can't Believe I'm Still Single." And together, Eric and I created and produced a TV show based on that book over a decade later. It ran for three seasons on Showtime.

Produce Yourself

Looking at him on the surface as a cab-driver shuttling people up and down Amsterdam and Broadway, Eric shouldn't have had the life he now had. But he stopped saying, "I can't." He stopped accepting: "You'll never." He bucked the system by producing his own independent system.

Eric's story isn't unique. This chapter is nothing but a metaphorical blip on the radar of heroes we look up to everywhere, in every field, at any point in time. From Ben Franklin, Thomas Edison, and Albert Einstein; to Richard Branson, Steve Jobs, and Elon Musk. None of the heroes you follow or hear about have done anything less dramatic than Eric.

Eric is just your average guy, potentially more average than you, with similar insecurities and flaws. Still, he did it. He showed up, signed up, and crushed it. He didn't allow circumstance to refute his purpose.

He will always be a hero. He will always be MY hero, which is why to this day we continue to work together.

–

CHAPTER 19

The Ordeal: Evaluation
(Stage 8 - Part 3)

"You're your problem and you're also your solution."

- Melissa McCarthy in *Bridesmaids*

IN CINEMA, ONCE THE HERO has spent some time in her new world, it starts to become her Ordinary World 2.0. She is no longer a deer in headlights, tiptoeing over branches so as not to scare the villagers. She has arrived with determination and resourcefulness. She's acclimated and is now resembling a native herself, able to not only survive but thrive.

This happens to Kevin Costner in Oscar-winner "Dances With Wolves" when he enters the world of the Lakota Indians to enjoy their simplicity of life. He forgets who he was in his Ordinary World as a civil war soldier. His new normal is that of a native Indian.

But our heroine shouldn't be fooled by environmental familiarity. The internal hero has yet to encounter her main ordeal. This is the stage needed to slingshot her metamorphosis towards full identity. It's a maturation that we all consume in real life as we evolve and grow — emotionally, spiritually, and mentally.

For me, producing movies was always the goal. But the precious prize was yet to come. I didn't know what it was at the time.

It's at this very stage that the hero needs to be careful. Gaining some traction and becoming comfortable in her new world is intoxicating. But sobriety will soon follow as she realizes there's more to it, a deeper knowledge and level that outsiders can't readily detect.

Perhaps what has driven your passion all this time regardless your goal is something more tangible or stereotypical — a better habit, a different job, a better relationship. And there's no way to know until you arrive.

I returned to Los Angeles with posters everywhere of my movie on buses, billboards, and buildings. And even though we were a studio film, we received news we were premiering at Sundance. It was a wonderful, albeit surreal experience.

Was I in this Special World for this one thing, this one feeling? Was this what it was all about — the special potion, the perfect moment, the sparkly treasure, the insight and knowledge I had since acquired? If so, I wanted more.

Or was this just a MacGuffin? Coined by Alfred Hitchcock, a MacGuffin is simply a plot device to advance the story but is itself completely irrelevant. It has no actual meaning or purpose. It's interchangeable.

In "Pulp Fiction" there is the mysterious briefcase that everyone pursues. But it's just a MacGuffin. We never learn what's inside that briefcase, and we don't care. The true search is how the cat and mouse of the characters help them all learn more about themselves as they overcome their Ordeals.

Or in "Raiders of the Lost Ark," the MacGuffin is the Ark. The whole movie is about the search for it. In "Citizen Kane," it's about the pursuit of Rosebud, a sled. But both are unimportant. They are just devices for the heroes to pursue and overcome their own inner Ordeals. You could replace the sled, the ark, or the briefcase with anything else and all three movies would work just as well.

Having now officially run the gamut, beginning to end, soup to nuts, top to bottom, I was a Hollywood producer. This is what I wanted. I had an office. I had a staff. I had an agent. I was being sent scripts. I was taking meetings with directors, having fulfilling creative sessions, etc.

This was me. This was my life. I could hardly believe it, often having déjà vu moments of what I had envisioned my identity as a producer would be back when I was writing letters in my bedroom to investors.

I was immediately developing a follow-up film with Eric, wanting to continue to water that garden. But I also put dozens of other projects into overdrive, accelerating their development.

It wasn't easy. It involved a lot of juggling and having to keep many projects in development for the chance that one of them would eventually be given a green light.

So, all pistons firing, I pushed from every angle possible, trying to capitalize on the fresh credibility I had earned.

Hollywood loves to find any reason to say "No" and to unearth your flaws, the better to discard you. I had to overcome those objections daily. With too much supply (movies wanting to get made) and not enough demand (money for those movies), every day in Hollywood is a constant default reaction to finding flaws and reasons to say "No."

There just isn't enough time to analyze every script and meet with every filmmaker. You have to winnow the list as quickly as you can. I've had to make this list as well as succumb to its fate.

Over the next few years, I managed to produce 12 films, most of which I cobbled together with a mixture of bank financing, foreign pre-sales, and private investors. I had a decent reputation for having some chutzpah and being resourceful. I was always open to collaboration. I was making good connections, networking, and basically stepping outside my comfort zone on a regular basis.

I was young, as far as producers go. But I knew how to woo talent and attract financing, even though I felt insecure and scared many times. I resorted to my newer identity as much as possible, studying my "producer" role and reminding myself that I was the confident ballsy producer who reassured others I could get things done.

The Ordeal for me at this juncture wasn't making the films. I was getting those made, and I loved it. The problem was that I found myself fundraising with such increasing regularity that I questioned why I was even producing in the first place. That was my biggest Ordeal.

My days started to have more angst and loneliness than I'd expected. I enjoyed the title of "producer." But when you pulled the curtain away and saw the wizard, it wasn't as glamorous as it seemed. I felt empty and creatively unfulfilled.

The irony is that my business background suited me perfectly for the financing of films. And I do love aspects of business and finance. But that was my prior, Ordinary World. Having traveled so far in my journey to arrive in this extraordinary world, I wasn't expecting to be doing so much fundraising.

I wanted to produce. I wanted to create. Whenever finances were locked in place, I got to be that creative person. I thrived whenever the money was put to bed and I could concentrate and play with all the artisans it took to make a movie.

But the percentage of time I spent creating vs. drumming up money was heavily lopsided. And I was starting to measurably notice the disparity — years fundraising, only months "producing."

Was it possible this new Special World wasn't so special? I started to think about my prior Ordinary World when I was simply full of hope and dreams before crossing over. Had I taken a wrong turn? Should I have listened to BR and become a writer? Should I have never jumped off on my own? Was the structured ladder system of the studio what I really needed but hadn't given it enough time? Did my impetuosity handicap me?

As a movie producer, unless you're aligned with, and already have a deal at, a studio, you're one of thousands of producers trying to get your film made any way possible. The allure and competition of Hollywood are great, the funnel tight, and the bulls eye small.

There's always a long history to get just one film made. Getting the rights, getting the screenplay perfect, hiring and firing and rehiring writers, getting the right director, finding the cast per their schedules and budget, and of course, raising funds. And that's all before anything is actually done.

The wind was constantly being taken out of my sails. Daily. I realized that, as a movie producer, I was very much a fundraiser — first and foremost. A lot of patience and strength is required to hold onto the emotional roller coaster of the hunt for money.

As long as I wanted to remain a producer, I would always, every day of my life, be chasing money, luring investors, putting together business plans, negotiating with banks, partitioning, and selling off rights, etc.

This is the name of the game. It finally sank in once I actually measured time spent doing what I loved — and what I didn't.

It's easy to default and fall into a trap of comfort. The almond-shaped amygdala in our brain keeps us in survival mode. It isn't there for us to analyze and process if our approach is optimal, or to seek success and happiness. Rather, it simply wants us to stay alive. So it allows us to settle into complacency.

As a surviving species, we humans settle by nature. It's in our DNA. It's how we are built. So we have to constantly fight the gravitational pull away from assessment and optimization, or we will never change our habits or approach to anything.

The first step in resisting this proclivity to the Stone Age is a measured evaluation. I had to sit down one day and do the math of where my time was being spent (and, as you know by now, this is a developed habit I have repeated throughout my journey. Still do today. It's revelatory).

That was when I had my epiphany.

This wasn't who I wanted to be. I was faced with the Ordeal of being exactly where I wanted to be on the outside, but not the inside.

This is the journey of the hero. She needs to have these epiphanies in order to improve her processes and systems. She needs to seek the agony in something she is doing so that it reaches a tipping point.

It's in the darkness and shadows where, lacking anything else to distract us, we see ourselves. It's here where the Ordeal we endure reveals its purpose.

-

CHAPTER 20

The Ordeal: Patterns · Ego · Ideas The Subconscious
(Stage 8 - Part 4)

"If I'm gonna die, I wanna still be me."

- Jennifer Lawrence in *The Hunger Games*

EVERY NIGHT, I'M HUMBLED when I lie in bed at night and think about what I learned that particular day. Not a single day goes by where I haven't learned something. I know so little.

Schools teach and measure hard skills — reading, writing, memorization, testing, application. But no traditional, formal entities teach soft skills — processing, reaction, emotional agility, mental awareness, compassion, optimism, generosity.

This might be why the hero's biggest transformation during her journey is the one of her inner hero.

There's no widely accepted infrastructure to improve ourselves. We can improve our knowledge and skills. But so can robots.

In a world of fast evolving industrialization, manufacturing, and productivity, the ladders of education and corporate advancement make sense.

Today there's a ubiquitous increase in self-improvement, self-awareness, and quest for peak-performance and optimization among the leaders of industry. Athletes, CEOs, inventors, and heroes everywhere understand the value of self-reflection and self-analysis.

We are never done learning. We are never done accumulating new perspectives, insight, and epiphanies. The wisdom we admire in our mentors is the consequence of self-examination, risk taking, answer seeking. We derive revelation from failures, insight from discovery. And benefit from the endless wonder of compound interest.

The lessons of a sage are there for the taking, like a ripe tomato in a well-tended garden. The wise have an advantage. If not in age, then in their cognition.

There are times when you are your own best mentor. Whether you take your own advice or not, consulting yourself is a habit worth developing. More often than not, you have answers to your concerns. They're not necessarily wrapped with a pretty bow and handed you as a gift. But they're a gift, nonetheless.

This sounds abstract and metaphysical. I assure you it is not.

It's applicable if you develop the routine of observing yourself. Some call this having intuition or trusting your gut. I think of it as recognizing patterns and interpreting their significance. The world and, indeed, the universe, is interconnected. Sometimes it is up to us to connect the dots. Then we will see a pattern emerge.

Patterns surface with proper self-reflection and honesty. When you're honest with yourself, when you keep your ego at bay, when you're not trying to impress or become someone else's definition of whom you should be — then you discover how to caution and complement yourself.

You know what you should or should not be doing. You know when something isn't right or not working. You know when you need to pursue something. You know when you have the answer and you just need to be honest with yourself, but you may be frightened.

You have the knowledge. It's there, but, like the nuts squirrels hide under fallen leaves in autumn for the following spring, it lies hidden beneath layers of consciousness and ego.

Fear holds you back, so you ignore your inner voice. Ego gets in the way and suppresses the organic you. Labels, titles, and accolades become the focus rather than the emotional, spiritual, and mental fulfillment you really desire.

In Marvel's "Dr. Strange," Benedict Cumberbatch is paralyzed from the nerve damage in his hands. He's trying to learn a new craft (sorcery), but his arrogance and ego keep him in his Ordinary World. His mentor, Tilda Swinton, tells him, "Surrender your ego and your power will rise." This is a major turning point in the film when the hero can find his purpose: transforming from hero to superhero.

Ego usually subsides at night, in your sleep. That's when your true self reveals itself. Quietness. Darkness. Solitude. So it's an effective time to discover and listen to your inner voice.

The demons of consciousness can often be overcome by the heroes of the subconscious. Consciousness and subconsciousness vie on a daily basis. Shrinking the disparity between those two has immense benefits, revealing knowledge that lurks beneath the surface.

An exercise I find useful is monitoring the communication at night between the inner and outer heroes. The ego has taken a nap, so communication is easier to detect.

This will take some determination on your part. It temporarily jolts you out of sleep, but it'll help you remember what your intuition whispers in the night.

Put a small pad of paper and pen on your nightstand next to your bed.

As you dream, you'll momentarily come out of REM stage when you shift positions or seek your covers. You're likely in a semicomatose state, barely functional, but, as quickly as possible, jot down what you were dreaming about — what you can remember.

Just scribble down what was mulling in your subconscious. Don't wake yourself up. It requires fine balance to quickly record your thoughts while borderline awake, yet get right back to bed without disturbing your sleep cycle. This will take some practice.

You might be surprised how revealing this exercise is. You might think you've resolved a certain issue, but find you're dreaming about it while rearranging your pillow or shuffling to the bathroom. You might think you're at peace with a discussion you had with a friend or colleague, but find you are replaying its highlights as you kick off the covers.

Unreconciled issues and controversies might weigh on you. If you're deliberating an old circumstance or current situation, it will find its way into your nighttime journey if your fears are battling your instinct.

Produce Yourself

Opportunities and entanglements that are meaningful to you, but unresolved or unrequited, are trying to penetrate your fear barrier. They are trying to remind you, "Hey, don't forget about me. I'm still here. I matter."

Listen to yourself. You have the answers. And when you set your ego aside, when you take cues from your subconscious at night, you gain the secret power of knowledge.

My subconscious advises there's an open-ended problem that needs a satisfactory outcome. It's significant enough that it won't give me complete peace at night. So I take my subconscious self's advice and get to work tackling it while conscious.

One thing that kept dancing in my head at night, in contrast to what I told myself and presented to friends and family, was that I aspired to make studio movies.

It's not as if I awoke one morning and my night stand note-pad read: "Studio movies." It was more of a puzzle that my conscious self had to figure out from weeks of various scribbles of colleagues' names, movies I had seen, and the like. When combined, it seemed to spell out a desire to give the studio system a fair chance.

I knew full well it was an uphill battle, which is why I pivoted into my indie-producing role. But my subconscious continued to poke during the night. And I would rather fail, knowing I tried, than simply discount the poke as a non-starter. I felt that would give me peace, if nothing else.

I also knew this would mean playing the painfully slow game of development. It was a different approach for me, even though many of my 12 films thus far had been distributed by studios.

There's a big difference between making a film for a studio from the outset, where financing is required upfront, vs. selling the film to the studio after you've made it independently.

Terence Michael

The angle into the studio system is rather simple. It involves almost single-handedly pitching an insanely high-concept to studios that has potential for franchise, merchandising, theme park, and ancillary spin-off. They fall in love with the concept and give you the money to write the script. You hope for a green light. If they give you a green light, you're funded and you go produce your movie. This is the glamorous version that rarely happens so smoothly. Nevertheless, that's it, in elementary form.

Movie studios are in the business of distributing movies and need good ideas to develop and feed their pipeline so they can make money at the box office. That's essentially all they do. They don't "make" or produce the movie; that's what producers do. They just give producers a venue for distribution by providing financing to produce that movie in the first place.

So, in an environment that has no shortage of ideas, I knew I couldn't walk in and simply pitch the same thing they hear all day long. I needed strong, cogent and sexy ideas they couldn't refuse. I needed to provide value. But my ideas and input up to this point were in the form of reworking, not inventing from scratch.

I had to ignite my idea machine and exercise a muscle that I had not flexed to this degree. I had never had to sit down and create new worlds out of thin air. Scenes, sure; endings, definitely, but never the whole movie, beat for beat. My contributions were more about adding characters, changing a scene, and fixing narrative paths that were already in an existing script by re-routing them.

This was a muscle I would come to depend on years later in television, and it has served (continues to serve) well. My decade-long television career dates back to this point in time when I finally took this creative muscle into the gym for conditioning. And it's been there ever since.

If you want to be more flexible, you have to stretch. If you want to be stronger you need weight resistance. If you want to have great ideas to pitch (whether movies or other), you need to come up with ideas. Every day. You need that repetition to build stamina, to build habit.

The farther away from a creative industry you are, the more you should generate ideas as much as possible, as you are less exposed to the "idea gym" on a regular basis. It's a simple exercise with massive benefits, and you already have the tools.

Many of us restrict the capacity and potential of our creative muscle. We have a schedule, we know where we need to be, and we push our brain no further than what is minimally required for primal functionality.

Our brains are so powerful and easily accessible, once we get them in shape, ideas will come pouring forth. You'll want to:

- start blogging
- invent a new product and sell it online
- teach a course you're passionate about
- learn a new skill
- patent an idea
- start a new business
- introduce a new system at work
- examine alternatives to solve problems at home

You'll eat better, sleep better, and in general be more optimistic and excited about possibility.

Your brain will start to react and behave in a more responsive and nimble way when you force it to work out of passion and fun rather than stress or fear.

It doesn't matter what your ideas are. It's the process of exercising that part of your brain that matters.

Try it for one week. Take time and just start jotting down ideas. That's the header on your piece of paper: "Ideas." And it can be anything. There are no rules. There's no test and there's no wrong way to do this. Just 3 completely random ideas. But shake the dust off and do it.

This may give you a head start:

- What product in your kitchen would you love to improve?
- How can you save an hour in your day?
- What's a better way to shop for food than you currently do?
- If you could invent anything, what would it be?
- If you could clone yourself, would you be friends with yourself?
- What character on TV do you wish you could be? Why?
- What do you wish could be delivered to you instantly with an app?
- What's your perfect vacation, and whom would you spend it with if it had to be someone from high school?
- What do you wish you could say to an ex?
- What features would your dream home have?
- What would your personal logo look like if you were a company?
- What do you want to tell your 20-year old self? Your 30-year old self?
- Who should you say "Thank you" to, just because? (and you know they deserve it). Do it now.
- What foods do you wish you could stop eating?
- If today was an extra day and you could do anything with no repercussions, what would you do? Describe that day in detail.

Just free form your thoughts and write — a little, a lot; it doesn't matter. But really think about it.

Your brain needs this, every day. It's powerful and you know it, but you don't fully exercise and stretch it. Give it the fuel it wants. Let it think and imagine. You can even do this when responding to an email that you want to give thought to. Use that email as your workout machine. Do a few reps on it.

This was the muscle that was shrinking for me. I was using it less and less as I got more and more immersed in film finance — basically more strategic and administrative tasks and less meaningful and fulfilling ones.

Creative sessions were amazing and intense when they occurred. And I was always chasing that high. I had carved out a pathway in my brain that became like an old scratched record. The needle just easily fell into the groove and went along for the ride. The problem with grooves is that they create walls on both sides, and become habit. But in this case, a bad one. Some grooves prove to be ruts.

On the surface, it's seductive to walk into a studio, tell an executive a story, and get a check to develop that story. It could be that. But once the trade announcements are yesterday's news, 95 percent of the time you're left with what is known as "development hell," and that's if you're lucky. That means your idea falls into a lengthy process of finding the right writers, ones with sexy credits who happen to be available to come on board and write your idea. Everyone reconvenes months later, gives notes, and often a new writer is brought in. This cycle continues, sometimes with as many as a dozen writers before the project has either collected too much debt to go forward, or you get a conditional greenlight if you can subsequently attract the right director and cast, get the budget down, etc.

I won't bore you with the 100+ ideas I had pitched around town, setting some up (always an initial high), getting paid off by others (a mixture of high and low), having several turned into 1st, 2nd... even 9th draft on others (one of those became Warner Bros.' "Chill Factor" with Cuba Gooding, Jr., which at one point was going to be a sequel to "Speed").

It's what I imagine drugs would feel like (I don't do them) — a roller coaster of emotions where you're always seeking that first-time feeling. It definitely plays a number on your nerves. I prefer my drugs to be ideas. That's my high.

I remember one of my first big studio pitches. I sat in my car, in the parking lot of Disney with my buddy, P, from high school. We were going in to pitch a concept my Dad came up with about a modern-day search for Noah's Ark on Mt. Ararat in Turkey — still one of my favorite stories.

We were both so young and so nervous that we slammed beers in the parking lot like we were heading to some college basketball game, just to calm our nerves.

The project never happened, but its typical labyrinthine route through development brought me life-long contacts and collaborations with everyone from Oliver Stone's company to actual adventurer-journalists who had traveled to Turkey and searched for the Ark themselves.

My day would be won if I was meeting with a hot writer or had a pitch meeting at a major studio. And my day would be lost as soon as my agent told me they were passing or putting my project out to pasture.

Nevertheless, the lure of spending days creating rather than raising funds was something that enticed. It was another facet, another area of my new world that I needed to explore.

What I discovered, somewhat to my surprise, was that producers who had studio deals (usually because of a recent film's success or rights they had obtained) were completely frustrated at the studio process as well. Other than the money — that part is nice — they were spinning their wheels and spending years with projects set-up around town. The chance of any one project getting a go-ahead was minimal.

Produce Yourself

Many writers and producers in Hollywood make a handsome living, but you never see their movies. Many of those people are extremely unsatisfied and unfulfilled. Several of them begged me to take their projects to the indie side and make them on the cheap. They desperately wanted to see their work on the big screen.

Development is a massive business, partly sustained on relationships and deals. But it's also a necessary evil, wherein the studios are part of conglomerates looking for the franchise that will help them sell merchandise and engender new rides at theme parks.

That's really what it comes down to for the studio mandate — a few smaller Oscar films for attention and acclaim, but primarily franchises, remakes, and established brands for the bottom line. What this means is that many in-demand writers and producers are disproportionately weighted in sci-fi, supernatural, big disaster, and high-concept material.

Outside of those tent-pole franchises, the only prevalent development deals are the "vanity" ones, where the studios will give housekeeping production deals to celebrities.

The value-strategy for me, as an independent producer, was increasingly difficult to employ from the pitch angle with studios. The entire game is very one-sided; studios hold the purse. And a variant of the Golden Rule applies: he with the gold makes the rules.

Even if they love your idea, even if they're holding a checkbook in their hands, the risk of their saying "No" to your project is paltry in comparison to their saying "Yes." A "Yes" triggers a speculative and treacherous set of events for the executive that immediately puts their job under scrutiny and possible jeopardy.

For these and many other reasons, the luster began to wear off. I became less motivated to don a sports coat, get jacked on caffeine, and drive all over town to pitch an idea that had a minuscule chance of ever making it to the silver screen.

Yet, similar to other detours and dead-ends along the Hero's Journey, these were lessons and building blocks in disguise. Complacency and optimization can't live together. It's one or the other. I had to experience rejection to become the optimized version of my hero.

I allowed myself to fail, over and over. I had to hear a lot of "No"s to eventually find the occasional "Yes." Without self-permission, I never would have taken the meetings, pitched ideas, and learned the skill and art of selling, something that I now do almost daily in every facet of life.

Without permission to fail, I wouldn't have developed the skills and proficiency to promote TV concepts, business ideas, real estate strategies, mortgage arrangements, investment opportunities, and even relationship habits.

In the back of my mind, I knew I could always go get a job at a large production company or at the studios and work my way up. That's how most people "worked" in Hollywood — all laboring ultimately for one of the big seven or eight studios. So, to be fair, there was that. But I discovered early on I'm happiest when I work for myself. And I wanted to choose to be happy. That was paramount.

I didn't want to spend my life pitching (to the studios) and wondering when my lottery ticket would get selected. I also didn't want to spend the majority of my life drumming up finance (in the independent world), with a hand out.

And if you don't want to do either of those, your producer career is dead.

That is the process. You have to be willing and able to do both of those, and do them well, if you want to be a producer. It may constitute only 5 percent of the functions you need to perform to produce a movie. But it consumes 95 percent of your time. I wasn't satisfied with that ratio.

I kept pivoting and still encountering approaches that didn't feel right. I felt like a pinball that bounced around to find the smoothest path possible.

Maybe it was time for the next chapter in my life. Maybe producing a dozen films was it for me. I didn't know.

I didn't feel the consummate love that initially brought me over into this Special World. So, whatever the case, I had to change my approach — again, for the umpteenth time. I told myself I loved producing. I loved the identity. I loved the output. I loved the narrative. But the input, the process? It seemed from whatever angle I approached it, I would always bump up against certain realities that weren't ideal.

So I decided to close the doors on my company. If there were an actual sign attached, it would read: "Under renovation. Please excuse our mess."

-

CHAPTER 21

The Reward: Input vs. Output
(Stage 9)

"You make me want to be a better man"

- Jack Nicholson in *As Good As It Gets*

CLOSING MY FIRST AND ONLY PRODUCTION COMPANY, now the company of record for a dozen films, was both depressing and liberating.

The approach and numerous course corrections, although engendering some decent output, weren't sustainable for my identity. The math didn't add up. And the process was problematic with each approach I took.

I realize I sound like a crybaby. Arnold Schwarzenegger would not be proud of me. How bad could it have really been? Honestly, it wasn't that bad. And many might have killed — or at least be willing to part with a limb — to be in my predicament.

But I wanted optimization.

I don't believe a current process should be justified because it's not as bad as another process. Anything can be worse. But anything can also be better.

Going this far on the journey usually brings more reflection and perspective for the hero. Things that were important at the beginning of the journey may be less important later.

This will happen as you journey further into almost any area of your life. From the outside, you often see a single goal, a bull's-eye. But as you go further into the forest and peek around trees, you see there are still more trees. There are other philosophies, nuances, and perhaps other dimensions you hadn't considered. Having been in this new foreign world for awhile, there may be new mini-worlds to be discovered within the larger one.

Toward the end of my Ordeal, when I was fully engaged in the pitch process with major movie studios, I met a writing duo, R & J. They were known around town as being among the most entertaining and energetic pitch masters. They were selling and writing scripts for everyone from Disney to Columbia Pictures, from Mel Gibson to Steven Spielberg. They had strategically branded themselves as the sci-fi guys who could verbally paint a detailed movie, beat for beat, as well as anyone.

Of my numerous pitches floating around town, a production company at Disney took a small spark to one but wanted me to bring on R & J to write the script. After introductions, the two writers acted as if I would be doing them a favor to enlist them. But the favor ended up being mine. R & J opened my eyes to the way movies were supposed to be pitched.

Produce Yourself

I recall a studio executive yelling to his assistant in the next room: "Bring us some popcorn; [R & J] are here to pitch!" One sat for the next 20 minutes and listened to them complete each other's sentences as their twin-headed beast pitched the beats of the film, drifting in and out of actual dialogue and tense description. It was amazing to witness not only their verbal facility and impeccable timing but also their ability to read the room and address concerns before they surfaced.

Watching them humbled me. Where I had been thinking about the final film and how to produce and market it, they had been thinking upfront about the tiny ingredients that give every great movie its flavor. They captured the pacing, tone, vibe, and mood, and, between the two, displayed an intoxicating linguistic dance. And the execs got drunk. I was pretty buzzed myself, even knowing exactly what they were pitching.

R & J focused on input. I was focused on output. And even though I align so many aspects of my life with math, and use math to solve complex issues and strategies, the analogy somehow escaped my approach to making a pitch.

Many entrepreneurs focus on output first, not input. And that's an amateur mistake. That was my mistake. I was selling, to executives, the movie that everyone would see, not the emotional moments and transformations that happen to the characters within the movie. I wanted to skip ahead and sell the finished product. I didn't want to break down the stages the characters inhabit — the Hero's Journey. But those are requirements for executives to feel a universal human connection. And ultimately, that's what they are buying.

R & J sold emotion. There are really only 7 movie plots. Just 7 stories make up every movie or TV show you've ever seen, which is why they all feel familiar on some level. And because of that, it was the emotional nuance and journey that I needed to sell, not another plot. The executives had already heard them all.

It's beyond obvious to me now. But back then, as a young entrepreneur, I made the same mistake of many startups, concentrating on output rather than input. Focus on 2 and then 5 and then 4. Those will add up to 11. It's math. Just build that 2, 5, and 4 and the 11 will result. But I was pitching 11, not 2, 5, and 4. If you build it, they may come. But you've got to build it right.

That project which introduced us, unfortunately, suffered the fate of most studio projects and languished in development hell. This contributed to my shuttering the Terence Michael Productions office. Plus R & J reached a point in their own writer journeys where they decided to separate, find new mentors and allies, and cross new thresholds apart from each other.

Coincidentally, as much money and success as R encountered pitching ideas for movies, he ultimately wasn't making them. The whole reason he joined this business (why everyone joins this business) was to make movies. He needed to change his average. He needed to alter his allies. He needed a different approach. So, as financially successful was his partnership with J, he saw the need for change.

This is where our journeys crisscrossed. This was the pinnacle of my Ordeal: closing the doors to my production company, and opening a new one — one with new potential and a new ally.

It wasn't my purpose to be stuck in development hell at the studios or to be fundraising 10 hours of a 12-hour day in the indie world. The imbalance was too great in the process versus my purpose, input vs. output.

Whenever your input is incongruent with your output, you suffer.

As painful or tragic as it is, the hero must endure the Ordeals before finding her Reward. This is why it's critical she take mitigated risks but also actively seek and invite failure. Shunning a viable but potentially treacherous approach will only prevent full attainment.

This Reward is the original goal the hero fantasized finding when back in her Ordinary World. It isn't necessarily the ultimate and final "prize." That may come later, arriving when least expected after returning to her Ordinary World.

The Reward could be something unimportant to the inner hero, but appealing to the outer hero (the secret formula, the briefcase, the gold chalice — the MacGuffin). It drives the hero on her quest in the first place. But having evolved and transformed throughout the journey, this Reward might take a back seat to an even greater, more meaningful and fulfilling surprise.

With the "death" phase behind her, the hero can transform during this Reward stage with improved clarity, strength, and agility in her purpose. Eventually, she is indemnified and compensated for the challenges and interferences she diligently conquered with good habits, mindset, and focus. Be it small wins or a gigantic one, she can relish her output at this stage of her approach and progress.

The fruits from her planted seeds, the knowledge and insight from her incremental steps, and the revelation from her resourceful search are all prosperous proof of her journey.

She challenged her identity. She stretched and reached beyond what seemed sustainable to defeat her inner demons. And for all of that, for everything she has fashioned thus far, she finds her Reward.

In "The Matrix," Keanu Reaves encounters his greatest Ordeal when he heads into Agent Smith's hideout. But, completely outnumbered by multiplying agents, Keanu is helpless until he changes his approach. He is rewarded with the revelation that he can dodge bullets and move just as fast as the agents can — something he never thought he could do with his prior approach to the Matrix. It was there all along, but he needed to face this insurmountable obstacle in order to seize his Reward.

In "Fight Club," Edward Norton's ordeal crescendos when Brad Pitt disappears from his life. Ed searches fight clubs all over the country and can't find the one person who is giving him purpose and pause. During this search, Ed is rewarded with the cognizance that he himself is actually Brad Pitt, and he's done some terrible things. It's in this consciousness that Ed is able to alter his mindset and approach and defeat his inner-demon (Brad Pitt).

And in "The Wizard of Oz," the lion, the scarecrow, and the tin-man all eventually get what they want — courage, brain, and heart, respectively. Yet they never really needed these. They needed the approach of the outer journey to reveal the inner qualities they had all along.

R had an upgraded goal to elevate his involvement, sow additional seeds, and diversify his human investment in the film business. He wanted to be a producer so he could control what happened to his projects once the pitch was over. He had no on-screen credits because he sold his ideas or came on board for rewrites. He didn't produce them so he had no voice. He had no control (typical of writers in Hollywood).

I produced movies. And I made them independently, so I had voice.

And, having just shuttered my company, I liked the idea of starting something new and fresh with a partner. Inasmuch as I believed in the power of synergy, collaborating, and sharing the pie, I felt isolated and alone with Terence Michael Productions.

R, now without his writing partner J, felt the same way. So we partnered and formed a new production company.

Together, over the next few years, we would produce 5 films and 2 television movies. We each become the ally and mentor of the other.

Produce Yourself

We increased our averages and realized an output exceeding the sum of inputs.

Whenever we see each other today, we annoy others just reminiscing about the halcyon days. It was an exciting time for us — film festivals, Cannes, back-to-back and simultaneous productions, new directors, new actors, having fun, living the dream. Constantly producing, pumping movies out like clockwork.

We were producing, which was the most important thing. We were performing the functions that I loved and that R desired. We were a team, and it was great to eliminate the isolation we'd both felt.

I was still having to drum up financing, but I did it with someone by my side who was in it with me. And, due to R's exceptional pitching talent, our development was quick and smooth. So the two areas that I'd had issues with — fundraising and development — were ameliorated by having a partner. Specifically, R.

I've always known the value in partnerships. But thus far in my journey, I hadn't fully embraced a full-time one. I had found good allies, mentors, and concentrated on my average of 5 on specific projects. But I was mostly a solitary pilgrim until now.

Partnerships can be tough. There are times when each side resents the other, feels they're carrying most of the burden. But there are other times you're glad someone has your back and is looking out for you. R and I motivated each other. We wanted to progress with more product, more films, more opportunity.

Harold and Kumar, Romy and Michelle, Beavis and Butthead, Dean Martin and Jerry Lewis, Will Ferrell and John C. Reilly, Mel Gibson and Danny Glover, Wayne and Garth, Cheech and Chong, Chris Farley and David Spade — all do better with each other than without.

Many pursuits, be it business, love, or life in general, are better with a partner. Not always. Sometimes it's worse. Many times someone should be an employee or steward, not a partner. But when you can each inspire and encourage the other to be their best, I think partnership merits consideration.

When you foster an environment where each side is progressing out of love rather than fear, then you can expect enormous strides. You both want to impress each other, report back with good news, and contribute so you're setting each other up for success.

I taught R how to produce. He taught me how to sell story. It was educational and fulfilling for both of us. We were effective as a team, whereas we may have been only productive separately. Big difference.

All things have a cycle. Eventually, a dry spell hit us. We were unable to get the next project going before money stopped coming in. For those reasons and others that collided at once, we had to officially close our office.

I don't recall exactly how it happened. It was very cordial. R and I were talking on the phone and it was just one of those very comfortable and casual conversations about having to let our lease go, empty out the business account, and, by the way, let's keep in touch (we do keep in touch).

We'd be fine. We were now, as young as we were, veterans in Hollywood. We could get anyone on the phone. We knew the players. We knew how to attract good material (or in R's case, he simply had to write it). All would be fine.

I would simply rekindle Terence Michael Productions and continue on. I had gained more experience, credits, and insight. I felt full and satisfied. This was my Reward.

Produce Yourself

And then, one morning while standing in the middle of a Century City weight room with 20 or so other early-morning strangers, I stared at a TV screen above the treadmills. A plane had just flown into the World Trade Center in New York. And then another. It was September 11.

Suddenly my Reward and everything I had worked for, seemed completely insignificant and utterly shallow compared to what was happening elsewhere in the world.

My quest for peak performance and optimization seemed completely selfish and inconsequential. Those poor people. Their families.

Walking out of that gym and aware that I was alive, breathing, and safe; that my family was alive, breathing and safe; the last thing I could think of was trying to produce another movie.

-

CHAPTER 22

The Road Back: Purpose · Your Why Proximity Potential
(Stage 10 - Part 1)

"There's no place like home."

- Dorothy in *The Wizard of Oz*

I'M NOT USUALLY AFFECTED BY NEWS EVENTS, even terrorist tragedies. It's easy to feel insulated in a safe bubble when it doesn't happen in my hometown or to people I know. It's not "real." But 9/11, although on the other side of the country, was an impactful wake-up call due to its magnitude.

As creative as I like to think I am, I can't conjure the pain the families of its victims must have experienced. It's unfathomable.

I don't want to hijack a horrific event and make it my own story. I was fortunate to have no degree of personal connection to the disaster whatsoever. But as geographically distant as I was, that seminal event accentuated the desire for deep reflection that needs to be activated along our journeys.

Realizing there were almost 3,000 people who could no longer continue on their own Hero's Journey — wherever they were, whatever battles they faced and obstacles they encountered — involuntarily made me take stock in a way I might not have otherwise. It was an organic reaction to having the freedom to make choices to be whatever version of myself I wanted. Those in the World Trade Towers no longer had that choice.

It was tragic these people were dead.

How much more tragic would it have been if any had been living an empty or soulless life? What if someone in the Twin Towers wasn't following their purpose? What if they were hiding their authenticity? What if they were meandering — just existing, complacent, repeating the motions, meeting the minimum?

What if they didn't take that one risk to reach their goal? What if they didn't take the time to find their goal? What if they could have, should have, would have? What if? And now, all of that was taken away.

No more opportunity. No more possibility. No more second chances.

I had so many second chances — pivots, course corrections, trials and errors, experiments. But what if I hadn't had those opportunities? What if SNAP, and that was it? Suddenly, the light at the end of the tunnel. That's what happened to those unwitting victims. Ashes to ashes. Dust to dust.

No one should be robbed of life. But almost more importantly, no one should rob their own life of potential and possibility, especially when they have a choice. If anyone were to know they would die on 9/11, what would they have changed 2 years prior? Or perhaps 5 or 10 years before?

Don't say they would just travel the world and lie on beaches. I don't believe that for 5 seconds. That's not a purpose. That doesn't explain why a person has passion, ambition, satisfaction, and, ultimately, esteem and actualization.

Everyone has dreams, goals, and a purpose. And for those who were fully living them, choosing to be happy, seeking peak performance, finding their Why, and loving themselves and those around them every day, 9/11 swindled them. They were squeezing all they could, only to have it stolen.

For them, maybe they would have escalated their timeline. Maybe they would have sought optimization and maximization sooner. When we think we have all the time in the world, there's no rush. That's why procrastinators work best with deadlines. The victims in the Twin Towers, unfortunately, didn't know when their deadline was coming.

It's an admonition for the living.

For those caught up in the event, who phoned it in, I weep. For those victims who didn't pursue a life of purpose, I'm saddened at the thought of what might have been.

But I also half-wonder if 9/11 only accelerated the inevitable for some poor souls. For some, they were already inert inside — refusing or unable to choose for themselves and the life they wanted.

And for them; for all the people who didn't make the choice and take the path they wanted; for all those trapped souls who were cheated of any future ability to experience advancement, change, improvement, fulfillment, and meaning; for those fellow humans whose journey was abruptly terminated, I had to expedite my journey.

I had to live to the fullest and multiply my relevance and meaning. For their sacrifice. For me. So I wouldn't be one of them — one who glimpsed their future essence but didn't get a chance to live it.

What if, on some grander scale, I was comparatively just the ant in the ant farm pushing a grain of sand from one side of the hill to the next? What if there was so much more, and it would take a 6-year old boy with a magnifying glass to burn my group to a crisp for me to realize I wanted more in this short life?

If life could be so transient and ephemeral, I wanted to seek and find more substance and congruity in my daily process sooner rather than later. After all, what is life but a summation of our daily processes, every day, day in, and day out?

I wanted to consciously live more deliberately. That was the takeaway message of 9/11 for me.

Storytelling was my raison d'etre, my ultimate purpose, why-I-was-here-doing-what-I-was-meant-to-be-doing.

The production company with R worked. And that was my Reward stage of the journey, wherein I finally learned so many lessons along the way to avail me of that opportunity. And there was a payoff.

Certainly, the process became smoother. I learned how to be more effective with my approach and accept the joys of collaboration and networking. But ultimately, I had chosen a path where no matter how much permission I granted myself to live fully within my purpose, I needed approval from new, third parties every time I wanted to tell a new story.

No matter how skilled a dancer I became, I still always had to get out on the dance floor, look around the room, and ask someone to accompany me.

Produce Yourself

Only the "dance floor" is a crowded ballroom hosting the longest wedding you've ever been to, with:

- sloppy drunks (investors who entice you but are irresponsible and don't have enough money to be investing)
- wedding crashers (investors looking to take lots of drink meetings and get to know you without ever committing)
- single bridesmaids (investors who verbally commit, but once the sun comes out, they're off taking the walk of shame home, hiding)
- out-of-town relatives (investors who just wanted to hear stories about stars rather than part with two dollars)
- the bartender (an investor who lost his shirt on a prior deal so no matter how different your project's analytics are, you will also be the representation of his misfortune... but he'll let you buy him a drink)
- the couple getting married (investors full of optimism and excitement to make a movie, but perpetually on vacation so you can never connect to solidify anything)

What I needed was the lonely girl or guy sitting at an empty table observing while everyone else was dancing. That's the smart person with the checkbook but who is often too shy to make themselves known.

Those were the realities. Combine those with the mood of the nation at the time, and I had little interest in thinking about movies.

I recall a moment of clarity: that the struggle and joy; the ups and downs of Hollywood; the arguments and negotiations over trailer size for stars; credit placement on screen; and backend points were all so petty and hollow. I was ashamed to be the guy who walked into parties telling people he was a movie producer, when, in fact, that was the plain truth.

The self-esteem and confidence I normally felt being a "movie producer" suddenly felt gaudy and crude. It felt like an embarrassment in a time when people had lost their lives. I knew it would be temporary. I knew it was a precious stretch to align my own mood with that of affected New Yorkers. But it was still an identity challenge I faced at the time.

Maybe I just needed to volunteer at a hospital or fire station and feel something substantial and selfless for a moment. I don't know. Maybe the timing was nothing but concomitance.

Hollywood can be a very selfish place. Me. Me. Me. That probably played into it too.

If you dislike your narrative or how you divulge it (say at a social event), take note. You should always be proud and excited when you tell your story. There may be a reason behind reluctance to tell your story. Your auto-response is revealing (just like those dreams at night).

The wallflower at a party who doesn't engage or desire to meet new people is usually shielding their narrative. They don't want to answer the dreaded "So what do you do?" It's a compelling barometer of your alignment — are you living your "Why"?

I found myself briefly hesitating, wondering whether to use humor to deflect the obligatory "What do you do" question. Here I was a "movie producer," which, where I live, is considered something of a pinnacle achievement. This was a source of conflict for me: I loved what I did and was immensely proud, but was also simultaneously embarrassed to mention it.

I knew my Why. I knew I loved (still love) storytelling. I discovered that it was my purpose early on. It's WHY I do what I do. But maybe there was yet another approach to reach my purpose. This is what resonated with me during my Road Back stage.

Why do you really do what you do? This is what I asked myself. Is it for the title? Are you trying to make someone proud? Perhaps that person would be just as proud of you regardless of your title. And that's what you're stressing over?

Is it for the money? What do you need the money for? Do you really need all those expenses, all that stuff? You might be abundantly happy with half the stuff and half the income. Most are, but their ego won't allow it. They continue to accumulate for presentation rather than meaning.

Is your Why because you like to help people? Is it because you like solving problems, like selling, analyzing? Is it because you like connecting people? We all have a Why. That's our purpose — why do we do what we do. And once we can pinpoint what that is, we can strip away the bullshit and fancy wrapping-paper that usually means nothing to anyone and get to what makes us who we are.

When George Clooney married his now wife Amal, I remember reading a post to this effect: Amal Alamuddin was a Lebanese-British international human rights attorney who represented Prime Ministers and other political figures, and rubbed elbows with the foreign elite. The next sentence was: "She is marrying George Clooney, an actor."

The Internet went wild with the contrast. The news wasn't about some actress lucky to be on George's arm. It was the opposite. George appeared to be the lucky one. Next to Amal's description, George looked like a simpleton. She was doing something "important." He was just an actor.

My reaction, however, was more speculative. Strip away labels, titles, good looks, and celebrity, and what do you have?

If Amal is immensely fulfilled and living within her purpose, then she is my hero. She is her hero. And a hero to young girls everywhere who hopefully transcends the antiquated notion of gender limits.

But just looking at her résumé and denigrating George in comparison constitutes the kind of social brainwashing that causes many people to pursue paths for the sake of others rather than themselves. They go for the label. They go for the reaction from others, but indubitably at their own expense.

They can't live deliberately and within their Why, if they are chasing a "standard" to impress others. The truth is others don't care.

Whether you think acting is "important" or not, George's profession appears to be his purpose. What you think about acting is irrelevant. He loves what he does. He's a ham, a performer, and a clown. This is well known. I have friends in common who have confirmed this. This is partially why his reputation is sterling. He has found his Why and is happy with his identity. For that, he is my hero. He is his hero.

Amal is a superhero saving the world. George is just the town's jester. I get the comparison. It's superficially funny.

But let's commend people for taking the Hero's Journey and achieving success — wherein success is defined as authenticity and purpose, not the placard on your door or the degree behind your name.

In most storytelling, The Road Back stage solidifies the Why. It's when 75 percent of the story has unfolded and it's reaching its big climax. The hero has already obtained her reward and is ready to journey home. But this is usually when an entirely new battle begins — a battle even bigger than what she's navigated so far. The forces that kept her from entering the Special World in the first place will now conspire to keep her from leaving it.

In the movie Wonder Woman, Gal Gadot spends the entire film following her purpose. She is very clear on her Why, which is to kill The God of War. But when she finishes going head to head with the evil German Captain, Ludendorff, and is ready to revel in the accomplishment, she discovers that nothing has changed. War is still progressing. Bad things are still happening. Humans are apparently evil.

Produce Yourself

Wonder Woman's reward is short-lived on her Road Back. Reality sets in that she has yet to face the real Ares. The God of War is someone completely different than she suspected. Her Why hasn't changed, but her process has to change if she is to defeat him.

In Fight Club, Edward Norton takes the Road Back to normalcy. That's his Why. He wants to rid himself of his disorder and be normal. He has to stop himself (in the form of his alter personality, Brad Pitt) from creating more damage than he already has. He already gained the reward of discovering whom he really is and that he's battling himself. So Ed attempts the Road Back to his Ordinary World, but not without evil Brad Pitt trying to prevent him.

And in "Baby Driver," Baby is ready to literally hit the Road Back, "in a car we can't afford, with a plan we don't have." But a new fierce battle begins when Jon Hamm will stop at nothing to prevent Baby from leaving this world of crime.

I began my Road Back in a reverse Call to Adventure partly because 9/11 made my career feel trivial against the backdrop of misfortune. But also because I was once again at another crossroads, floating in the mezzanine between the ground floor of hell and the first floor of heaven.

When one door closes, another opens. But I hadn't yet identified the next door after closing the one I shared with R. So I contemplated discontinuing this path altogether.

What I didn't know at the time is that this inner-space is the Road Back. It's a personal journey where the hero reflects on the Reward stage as she begins her return "home."

I decided to work on my house, refurbishing a practical teardown. So much had been destroyed in America at this particular time, it was refreshing to tangibly build something, and see immediate results. I didn't have to ask for permission or wait another day. I could effectuate this instantly, and it felt personal since I was doing it with my own hands. I was building something. I was producing.

So began a hiatus to find ugly neglected houses and transform them.

When some people asked what had happened to me and where I had gone. I told them I had retired.

It was an aggressive stance, and not entirely true, especially if the definition of retirement is that you're no longer "working." I'll be working until the day I die because what most people consider "work," I consider purpose. I don't work. I purpose.

I just wanted to press the pause button on Hollywood for a bit. I wanted to have a personal deep-dive away from the industry to assess what I was doing with my life. What would I regret 10 years down the line? I was in such a competitive 24/7 working environment that it was easy to be too laser focused, too insular, too myopic.

Backing up just a couple of years, I had bought my first house during the height of my production company with R. I learned over the weekends how meditative and relaxing it was to work on something tangible rather than abstract. I never had any construction skills but was always good with my hands (thanks, Lego). With home remodeling books and immense knowledge from my dad, I learned that anything is possible in home renovation.

It's actually very simple. It's all accessible and doable. It's arts and crafts. I mean really. It's just a bigger child's version of sitting in a sandbox building something. It's so basic and easy.

Plus the Home Depot near me was open 24/7. That became my Friday and Saturday night go-to. So I sacrificed getting drunk and partying with my colleagues to chip away, little by little, taking the house all the way down to its interior studs — incremental steps compounding results.

Produce Yourself

Upon selling that first house just 2 years after I purchased it, I learned about an amazing tax benefit. Here is a legitimate, completely legal way that the government invites you to take advantage of, to make money tax-free when you sell your house.

It's because of this tax code that I felt semi-confident in saying I was retired.

I refer to IRS Code 121. It basically says when you sell your principal residence (the one you live in, and have lived in at least 2 of the prior 5 years), you don't need to pay any taxes on the first $250k in profit if you are single, or $500k if you are married. That money is not taxed at all. It's effectively free money.

Where else can you earn that kind of money and pay no taxes? It's equivalent to having a whole separate shadow career and income to go with it, but one that runs largely on its own, untaxed.

If I could try to time matters so I got as close to starting that 2-year clock over as often as possible, I could in theory flip 5 houses over a decade, profiting $250k every 2 years tax-free. I had to be willing to move every 2 years, of course, but several times, that was literally just a block away.

Today, that may not sound like a ton of money, $125k a year. But again. tax-free! And you can earn it parallel to any other income stream. That same $125k is like earning $250k before taxes if you're in a combined 50 percent tax bracket (federal and state), as many are.

So that's effectively what I did for my first three houses in a row, getting very close to that $250k profit every time, buying the ugliest house I could find on any street and fixing it up. It didn't feel like a "job" because it was my choice.

I didn't have to produce movies. I loved producing movies. But I didn't have to. I could take a break and do something else. I could turn what might seem like a chore — like renovating a house — into a choice.

Whenever you can make or reframe a chore into a choice it changes your motivation. It wasn't that I was tired or bored of film at all. But whenever your "career" is your only source of income, it becomes a chore. Making it a choice gave me clear motivation to produce when I wanted to.

And because of that, during this retirement period, I actually took a short 4-month break and produced my 20th feature film. When I was done, I returned to painting walls, listening to the radio, and skateboarding at the beach.

My parallel narrative (I would always be a "producer" in some sense) was that of Entrepreneur. This identity would bring me closer to where I began; starting businesses in high school and college — my old identity from my Ordinary World.

This is why this stage is called The Road Back. The hero is not only reflecting on The Reward thus far but now glimpsing the Ordinary World she left behind. At a certain point, it's time to return home, but this in itself becomes a journey — one traveled now with more wisdom, using tools gathered and lessons learned from the Special World.

Deciding to refurbish a house was equivalent to green-lighting my own "productions," with zero interference from anyone else. And I had full "final cut" rights. I was a pure solo-preneur. If I didn't like the way a wall looked, I tore it down. If I hated the floors, I ripped them up. If I wanted to paint the walls blue or red, or both, I could do that. There were no rules. This was my new muse: rehabbing houses.

The best part is this became my Zen refuge. It was my contemplative sanctuary where I could ruminate and get aligned with my Why. It was healing for me. Not only was I devoid of financial stress, I found pride and satisfaction in learning new skills and got instant gratification daily.

This respite and launch of a separate stream of income really opened my mind to diversifying my pursuits and employing the concept of multiple income streams.

Because films have a long tail of revenue, even after spending years to finally get it made, the money will trickle in up to a decade later. Rights are constantly sold, royalties are earned, new media surfaces, licenses expire and are renegotiated or resold, etc. To this day I still receive checks — albeit some as tiny as $2, but others several hundred — as they trickle in from one of the 120 countries that project my films.

Technically, I still had my two production companies operational. Their physical presence was nil, but legally they existed to collect and distribute money. And now, with flipping homes, I was beginning a whole new revenue stream.

It was ingrained in me from early age that you choose an "Occupation" and that's how you made a living. My dad is a physician. My mom is a nurse. My sister is a dentist. This is what you did. You go to college and pick a major so you can be slotted into the right faction of industry and contribute to society. And that's how you earn money.

The entire classroom model as we know it today was largely created back during the Industrial Revolution, when children needed to be tested to see if they could handle the monotony of an assembly line. Then they were graded on patience and skill to see where on that line they'd be placed.

This compartmentalized, scholastic approach may be effective in identifying those who could follow instructions, complete homework assignments, solve problems, be team players, etc. But it rewards rigidity, mimicry, and memorization. It's gotten better, but it still tends to force square students into round holes of employment.

Fortunately, there's been a burgeoning growth away from this, as we've realized the outdated model isn't necessarily the best to foster passion, creativity, and encourage individuality — places that can lead to one's purpose.

An individual's skills and passion may not neatly align in basic job categories set out by the government or tax code. It's possible what someone is meant to do hasn't been created yet. It's possible an inefficiency or gap exists between two industries just waiting to embrace the person who is terrible at reading, writing, and arithmetic, but good at other things.

Today many are enmeshed in side hustles and finding their muse to make money and add additional revenue streams. But this wasn't taught traditionally to most people. I learned business and entrepreneurship in school, but it was mostly for a singular operation.

The idea of activating multiple streams of income came later, partly out of necessity and partly from experimentation (failures = experiments).

Having the time to reflect allowed me to concentrate on what I call "proximity potential" — assessing what additional, tangential pursuits I could monetize that might fall just outside my lane of familiarity. It's low-hanging fruit because of its proximity. It's close by. It's what's easily accessible or just a phone call or short walk away.

Proximity potential may be one of the most powerful tools you have to discover and grow an opportunity only you can access. Or you at least have easy access with minimal barrier because of who you are and where you're standing. Your education, environment, skills, and network figure in.

You might have a unique perspective or be in a special situation for a side business others would envy. Because you know of this job function and that occupation, you see a bridge that no one is building between the two occupations. There's a discrepancy that needs a solution. There's an opportunity to build a business and make a repetitive process or transaction more efficient and effective, and thus valuable.

For me, the obvious proximity potential was starting a mortgage business. I already knew how to build and run a business. And now with the homes I was fixing and flipping, I was dealing with a lot of realtors and banks for mortgages.

I was never an ideal candidate for a mortgage. I didn't have regular W2 income or salary from the same large corporation for 5 years with retirement and benefits. That's what banks want to see before granting a mortgage. They are wary of freelancers, entrepreneurs, and anyone who makes money sporadically and unconventionally (this applies to 80 percent of those in Hollywood).

But I knew I could build a bridge between the two. I wasn't the first or that unique in this thinking. But I had access. I knew Hollywood, and I was learning a lot about real estate. So I had proximity potential in melding the two. This was the key to providing value, which in turn made the business valuable.

Proximity potential allowed me to commingle ideas and create another revenue source for a niche market.

Perhaps you're a professional football player who was also a business major in college. You could provide a niche service of financial consulting only to football players. You can bridge the gap between two industries that are typically separate circles. Pro ballers make a ton of money, but, on average, only within a narrow window of 4 years. Because of their high salaries, they buy fancy, flashy toys, only to be broke 4 years later with little job prospects. But invested properly, their revenue aggregate is substantial and could last them more than one lifetime. Someone who speaks both football and business is in a unique situation to brand and market himself as the specialist for these young athletes.

Look at two archaic infrastructures — the U.S. Postal service and (what used to rent DVDs) Blockbuster, or other brick and mortar venues. Netflix's business model simply used already existing government mail for DVD rentals. That's it. They launched at a time when Blockbuster was asleep at the helm. Blockbuster hit an iceberg. Netflix was the iceberg.

What could have been easier than Netflix commingling ideas by combining two business models into one? They then took it a step further with proximity potential. They realized they, being a movie rental house, had all these movies. So they began uploading them to their own servers and providing instant downloads.

Currently, they are exercising proximity potential yet again, and now producing their own content, which began with the first season of "House of Cards." They realized they had all this data, exactly what people wanted to watch... so why not cut out the middlemen and make it themselves? Now they are literally the biggest player in Hollywood in terms of expenditures.

While taking a break from Hollywood, I worked on my homes. And while taking a break from my homes, I camped out at the Marina Del Rey Starbucks taking online courses to get my real estate broker's license. I figured I went there every day to get a coffee, anyway. Why not carve out an hour and take the required courses to get my license while sipping a joe?

After some basic online searching, I discovered the power of a broker's license. It would allow me to do numerous things. For one, I could open shop and hire a bunch of realtors if I wanted to have a realty company. I could also open an escrow company, a property management firm to manage rental properties, or — a mortgage company. That one I liked.

Produce Yourself

Smart or not, I never intended this new revenue stream to be a full-time endeavor. I strategically calculated a low-level word-of-mouth campaign to let others in Hollywood know that I started a company that could write mortgages for them. I wanted a slow burn; let it grow organically and under the cover of my main Hollywood identity. To this day I'm not sure that was the right strategy. But it reminded me how important it was that I remain attached to Hollywood.

Even with this sabbatical, I couldn't let go. I was still a movie producer at heart. I was simply taking a detour to bring the skills and talent of my old world into the void of my new world. I didn't want my Special World to get spooked that I was out of the business.

To this day I run the mortgage business remotely, in my underwear with a beer if I feel like it, on a weekend here and there, or over email when I choose to engage. Many clients I've never met in person. But I know their credits and they know mine. That gives me the credibility to understand their unique Swiss-cheese earning schedule. I then rewrite their story in a language banks can understand and voila! Mortgage, refinance, or debt-consolidation for them.

During the Road Back, the hero is always on the lookout. She's learned from her travels so far. She's always asking: "What if?" She's always contemplating a new approach, a new process, a new monetization, a pairing of ideas, talents, hobbies.

Put 12 of your favorite things to do on a pair of dice and roll it. What combo can you initiate today with baby steps to turn into a fruitful business tomorrow?

- Do you love to dance? But also love doing interior design? Great. Become the go-to interior designer for dance studios. Be that person that is so specialized that you are clearly the one to hire.

- Do you love hiking? Do you love food? Do you love photography? Great. Start an Experience on Airbnb and be the go-to for taking groups on your favorite hike to an awesome lunch spot where they can Instagram their hearts out.

- Do you love exercise? Are you an attorney? Awesome. Create a personal fitness business where the client can ask you legal questions while being trained by you. You effectively double-dip as both a trainer and legal consultant.

It may sound crazy, but so did every great idea out there before it became obvious. And don't think big. Think small. Narrowcast into a niche and target that niche's tribe. Word will spread. When you can narrowcast, you make those clients or customers feel extremely special. They will pay well for that kind of attention and service (or product). Don't make something for everyone. Make something for 20 people. That will grow to 200, which will become 2,000. Two thousand customers are one thousand more than just about any successful business needs. That's it. Want to get bigger? Fine, but perfect the program for 20 people and then hire someone to scale it for you. Move on to another stream of income.

I had three — movies, flipping houses, and now the mortgage business. But soon, proximity potential came calling again, adding a fourth income stream.

I may have never noticed this had I not taken The Road Back.

-

CHAPTER 23

The Road Back: The Now
(Stage 10 - Part 2)

"Every passing minute is another chance to turn it all around."

- Penelope Cruz in *Vanilla Sky*

O<small>N MY</small> R<small>OAD</small> B<small>ACK</small> from the movie business toward "home," I added the additional narratives of house flipper and mortgage broker. But I still kept a tiny toe pointed toward Hollywood.

I closed the film office. I let the staff go. I wasn't taking meetings. I rarely read a screenplay unless a friend slipped me one. People knew I was either "retired," or just taking a burnout break. Or they didn't care.

Hollywood is competitive and ruthless. You're easily forgotten. Everyone is in line at the ice cream truck, and if you leave that line, it just means someone else will get their Push-Up Pop sooner.

Hollywood eventually stopped bothering me. Maybe in part because I stopped bothering it.

Still, the gravitation toward my overall purpose, as storyteller, was strong. So it was probably just a matter of time before Hollywood called me. Sometimes it just took running into a director I knew or a call from an agent who wanted me to meet someone.

I'm opportunistic (is that a bad thing?), and even when I'm playing in one sandbox, it's tough to resist an invitation to another one. I do resist such invitations daily, but it's not easy. That's my saying "No" to focus with linearity, clarity, and purpose. But it's still tough to fight the "what if"s.

9/11 shed light on what I was missing. It took me personally designing and building my houses to fulfill me creatively. Ironic that, despite being in the movie business, I had to find creativity elsewhere. Working on houses became my temporary "productions." And they were just for me, no one else.

But then, with a mixture of serendipity and seduction, I discovered the most obvious proximity potential: television. It was staring me in the face. All the time I was inhabiting my special world, it was right there, yet I never gave it consideration.

Working in movies, I was always meeting people from the TV industry who were dying to get into film. Film was the perceived pinnacle. So, at a young age, that was my goal. I skipped over what I mistook as mere stepping-stones to the Holy Grail. But rather than a stepping-stone, TV is indeed its own treasured prize and growing more valuable every day.

TV was a lookout-point that BR, my original mentor from college, wanted me to visit on my journey. He said it was fine and good that I wanted to be a movie producer, but I should consider producing television by first becoming a TV writer. I interpreted his advice as misidentification of the essence of me.

But now, I found myself facing this TV rest stop during my Road Back to my Ordinary World. There it was — the sign with blinking lights that said: "Make TV" was right where it was before. But my hubris and adolescent ignorance blinded me to its attributes.

BR said: "TV is a producer's medium. Film is a director's." I didn't understand it then. I do now. Even though, as a movie producer, I would have ultimate decision-making as "the boss," creatively it was the director's sandbox.

As a producer in movies, I was building the box, pouring in sand, providing all the toys and playmates, putting an umbrella over the sandbox to provide shade, and even had an ice cream truck nearby for treats.

But it was the director of a movie who sat in the sandbox barefoot with her hands in the wet sand, pushing and moving it around to shape the landscape she wanted. After the director walked away, I preserved what she made and sold it to the masses by sprinkling glitter, bells, and whistles on it. But the director created it. I made it happen, but she created it.

In TV, it's quite different. The Executive Producer (EP) is often the creator. The EP writes, pitches and then runs the series, making the mounds, gullies, and roads in the sandbox.

The director in TV is usually more technical, working closely with the camera operators, lighting, coverage, look, and sometimes actor performance. But in general, it's the EP who gets to create the world, set the tone, and invent the characters in TV.

In TV it's the EP, not the director, who is god. He is both the boss (equivalent to the producer in film) and the creator (equivalent to the director in film). The EP, or showrunner, makes all the ultimate creative decisions. Not the director.

There are exceptions, especially when it comes to hour-long dramas that feel like mini-movies. Those directors definitely create, but usually just within their specific episode, not the series. The series belongs to the EP, the showrunner.

I didn't know this. Or I ignored it, thinking TV was just the bastard child to film. TV was accessible. It was easy to dismiss. We often tend to give short shrift to things that are easily accessible.

Movies were a special event. You had to invest and commit to a specific time, drive across town, and pay for parking. But in exchange, you sat in comfy seats with incredible surround sound and larger-than-life screens.

It's optics. And that lensing stuck with me since I was a little boy watching movies in a theater. I wanted to make that. I didn't consider making a TV show. TV was light, digestible noise that happened in the background while my mom was cooking or my dad was on the phone. It was a distraction.

Movies were fully immersive. You could shut out your Ordinary World and transport to a Special World.

That was my skewed perspective at the time. Of course, if you rip away the special packaging, it's really the same. The actors, the writers, the directors, the producers, the grips, makeup, location managers, and even the journeys of the heroes. The functions, the tropes, devices, stories are the same.

It ultimately comes down to story. We live the Hero's Journey every day. It's who we are as humans. It's all we know. It's in our DNA. Take away some fancy camera moves, an exotic location, and Ben Affleck's 3-stories' high visage on the silver screen, and you've got the same journey, whether it's in a dark theatre or a noisy kitchen with three kids trying to light each other on fire. You're telling and viewing the same stories, over and over again, small screen, big screen, around the campfire or on the wall of a cave.

Today, Netflix, Amazon, and Hulu have drastically changed the television space. Bingeing and personal headphones have now brought the special immersive experience home to television. A convergence of immersion and convenience have put TV front and center.

Film will always have its special place. But now, so will TV. It's a sibling to film, not a bastard child. Today, in 2017, the disparity between TV and film has shrunk. The audience is now largely the same and, due to the explosion of cable options, the choices in TV are immense.

It wasn't always this way.

Nevertheless, I was wrong to bypass the TV industry and head straight to film. For whom I am and what provides meaning to me, TV might have been where I wanted to be all along: in the sandbox. I was so myopic about Crossing the Threshold into my new extraordinary world I didn't consider the value in geography. I made it to the playground and planted my flag.

That was it.

I sort of took the elevator, rather than the stairs. I was fortunate for that on many levels. And perhaps I could have taken the elevator in TV as well. Perhaps my mistake was defining TV as a "step" when it was just another moon shining in a two-moon world of entertainment.

My resistance and refusal to listen to BR's original advice may have been counterproductive. It would take me almost a decade to appreciate his wisdom (it would also take Hollywood many years to understand this;

today just about everyone from film is now flocking to TV — in front of, and behind, the camera).

But with many pit stops, detours, and course-corrections along the Hero's Journey, we can't dwell on the paths not taken. It can be debilitating to undermine choices made in the past. We forget that at any one moment in time, we make a choice based on the circumstances at hand — where we are emotionally, physically, mentally, financially, spiritually. Mix in opportunity and risk. Stir. We can beat ourselves up regretting the 9 options we didn't make rather than accept the one we did.

It's worth mulling why we make the choices we do if there's a habitual pattern of making bad ones. But making one good choice over another good choice, only to scrutinize the unchosen choice in retrospect, is futile.

Nonetheless, I've done it. And so likely have you. I still do it. This is as much a reminder to myself as anything. As romantic and wistful the "what ifs" may be, they are also dispiriting.

It's why time travel movies are so popular. What if we could go back in time? What would we change? What would we have done differently?

- Can Arnold Schwarzenegger alter the future of mankind in "The Terminator"?

- Can Bill Murray finally optimize his daily process in "Groundhog Day"?

- Can Matthew McConaughey communicate with his daughter in "Interstellar"?

- What would happen if Michael J. Fox didn't hook up his parents at the Under The Sea high school dance in "Back To The Future"? What could have been? How would his life be different in the future?

As these stories often demonstrate (similar to Ashton Kutcher in "The Butterfly Effect"), changing one event may falsely discount the other positive consequences tied to that event.

- Who wouldn't you know because of your choices?

- Would you change the children you have for anything in the world?

- Would you change the experiences you had with that one person, colleague, hobby?

- Would you really be where you are today had this, that, and the other not happened, whether ideal or not?

Part of the problem continues to be emphasis on the destination rather than the journey. Because once we've arrived anywhere, we want more. Once we're at the party and have walked the whole place and seen everyone, we get bored. What's next? Where's the back room? Is there something outside I haven't seen?

Getting dressed and driving to the party is stimulating. Planning for a vacation, studies have shown, is more beneficial to the mind and body than taking the actual trip. The trip itself can sometimes be exhausting, throwing you off your sleep and diet schedule in exchange for a different view. Most travel is actually physically unhealthy. Of course, it can also be mentally challenging and healing.

When we underscore the destination rather than the journey, we reach into our bag of "what ifs," "could of," "should of," and "what's next." That's not a bag of choices that usually holds affirmative results.

You can make a good habit out of being present-moment as much as possible. Ruminating about the past or speculating about the future brings angst, nervousness, and stress. The harsh truth is you can't change the past. No matter what — good, bad, or neutral. What's done is done.

We all intellectually know this. And worrying about the future doesn't change its outcome.

Many times what one worries about never materializes anyway, so all that precious present-moment time you had was tainted by false worry. And what if your worry comes to fruition? That's proof worrying didn't quash it. So why worry? Admittedly more easily said than done.

You don't want to carry that big bag of "what ifs" around; and you equally don't want to obsess over the future. It's smart to learn from your failures, and it's smart to plan ahead. But both of those can be done in the Now.

When you're in the Now, you can calmly avoid noise, multitasking, and free up your mind with clarity. This clarity is what allows you to focus, appreciate, and build opportunity. It's a secret weapon we all have. But to find and recognize this skill, we have to declutter our mind's over-stuffed compartments and minimize our past/future fixations.

It's the difference between being mindful and mindless.

When mindless, we get distracted by what's next, what's upcoming. And, by the way, did we screw up that moment 2 hours ago? Mindlessness is when we allow the noxious fumes of multitasking and time-jumping to infiltrate the now.

When mindful, we take advantage of present stimuli, but the stimuli are curated for our purpose and protected from distraction. Mindfulness is accepting and enjoying the moment and all that it has to offer, in real time.

Although I probably failed daily, I consciously tried to live in the Now of the movie business. When I was on set in the thick of it, I couldn't think about anything else. I was the little kid engrossed in a coloring book, having forgotten what happened 10 minutes ago or what was to happen in the next 10 minutes. I rarely had to consciously strive for this flow state when I was physically in production.

But as therapeutic and meditative as house renovating was, it took conscious practice to have that little kid's monotasking mind while tiling a counter-top or installing cabinets. Of course hammering my thumb also brought me into the present.

That reminds me of a little film I executive produced. In it, the lead character is told to wear a rubber band around his wrist whenever he feels anxious. So when his mindlessness gets the best of him, he stretches the rubber band and releases it, snapping his wrist. This causes him to stop dwelling on the past or worrying about the future — sources of anxiety.

I have a close friend, Y, who was so anxious one day that it led to the beginning of my television career. And all I did was ask him a question.

Y has had an interesting journey. He was a technical lighting director for bands on tour, directed some local live news, became an Emmy-winning editor, and then started producing documentaries on TV. He traded traditional college for the University of Life and was able to start his career 4 years before his peers.

We became fast friends because when I ran the film company with R, we optioned a book from Y about gangster Pretty Boy Floyd that Y owned the rights to. R and I thought it would make a great movie.

That project ultimately was never made, but Y and I hit it off and became friends (Remember the online e-commerce business I started with a friend in Chapter 15? That friend is Y).

Y was also the first of all my friends to change my average of 5 with a weighting in TV. I didn't know anyone in TV. So during my Hollywood absence, I visited him one day for his first official TV production as a showrunner/EP. I walked into a cool art-deco space in an old building on Wilshire Boulevard and witnessed a creative sandstorm of activity.

Writers and comedians sat around a table spitting out jokes, pitching each other prank scenarios. There were skateboards everywhere (this was a comedy/prank show featuring professional skaters). It was more buttoned-down, youthful, and vibrant than I was used to in film production.

Mostly this was due to the type of show it was. Nevertheless, I was immediately captivated. Without having to raise a bunch of money and develop for years, Y was suddenly in official pre-production on a network TV show because his agent brought it to him.

Unlike film, there was no need to run around town and raise funding. Done. It was also about professional skateboarding — another love of mine. I've been a skateboarder almost my entire life.

I'm not sure Y saw actual drool from my mouth, but I wanted in, badly. Y was getting a dozen questions thrown at him, he was stressed about finances, and there were some administrative issues as well. He was newer to working with casting directors or writers. He had done more documentary-type work that is built more solitary and during post. So this being semi-scripted and for a major network, he just felt overwhelmed and a bit out of his element (he wasn't, by the way).

I simply asked Y, "Can I help you in any way?"

I looked at what he was doing and saw a big sandbox with lots of toys and lots of potential. As he told me more about the show, I started to see how logistically, and even creatively, it wasn't that different than movies. The approach seemed similar, but at a different speed and with fewer people. This is why Y was surprised by my question. He thought I would be slumming to work in TV. But to me, I was slumming creatively in film. I wanted to play in TV's sandbox.

Produce Yourself

I told him I honestly didn't know how I could help him. I didn't know a thing about TV. The titles, the roles, the staff, the crew; some seemed similar, but most of it was foreign to me. I'm sure I could figure it out, but his production didn't seem like it was in a safe enough place for me to learn.

He needed someone who was a pro to take charge and make it happen. Of course, that was his role. It was his first production company. It was his first show. But he admitted he, too, was sort of figuring it out (fake-it-til-you-make-it). A documentary this was not. This was a full-fledged network show with a lot of moving pieces.

I kind of laughed it off, reassuringly commented I was sure he'd figure it out, and left. I had gotten the bug, being at his offices, and knew this was an industry I wanted to pursue.

After returning to my nearby house, I climbed a tall ladder and continued to pull the drywall off a wall I was knocking out in a kitchen. I was only about 10 minutes in when Y called.

"The money sucks, but would you consider being my 2nd chair?" I didn't even have to think. Without knowing what "2nd chair" was, I took off my dust mask and slid around the hardwood floors, giddy with joy.

While I was used to being the boss, I'd never done TV. I was ecstatic not to be the main responsible Guy. Yet I entered what felt like an entirely new industry, and at a very high level, just one step below the top guy. I would effectively be the vice president to Y's president of this show.

It's highly unusual. But I also had produced 20 movies, run two production companies by now, and gained credibility by optioning Y's book. So I was legitimate and seasoned enough in a nearby industry. Proximity potential.

First time disclosing this: I went online and searched "How to produce television" because I was starting the next day. I would run the room of writers, deal with the 3 sets of field producers who were running around with their crews to shoot the comedy bits and pranks, and help Y overall with the set pieces, pro skateboarders, and post-production. There was also a live audience component to this show so we had sets to get built, hosts to cast, scripts to write, etc. It was a lot. But I was enjoying every minute. I couldn't get enough. I loved all of it.

I also started to bring over other allies from the film world to this adjacent one. Colleagues from my film world were just as enamored and fascinated as I. They couldn't believe the speed and creativity of the bits and sketches we were shooting. I'm sure to TV people we seemed like aliens. But coming from a world of molasses, this was hyperdrive.

I learned so much in this one production. Unlike film, once we were done, we had an airdate and millions of people watched it. There's no guarantee of that in independent film. I also got my hands dirty, learning specifically about cameras, equipment, lighting, etc. But that was fine. I'd renovated old houses and was used to dirty hands.

In film, I was so far removed from the technical stuff, I craved more creativity. In TV you can be right there in the action, you have a smaller footprint, and need to be more focused. The biggest surprise was that I was actually directing segments, something I would never do in film. But this being TV, and I second in command, I could basically do anything.

I'm beyond grateful for the opportunity. My approach was different. My process was a bit foreign. But production is production and I figured it out very quickly.

I know if Y ever were to come to film, he would figure it out his first day, too.

That was the start of my TV career, which would go on to span at least the next decade during my Road Back stage.

Produce Yourself

Drawing upon my adjacent experience from film in the Special World, and continuing to remind myself of my Ordinary World tools, I formed a new production company, 100 Percent Terry Cloth, and began developing and selling shows immediately.

Unlike film, the approach and process from concept to production for TV was efficient, deliberate, and no-nonsense. Development was short, and I never had to search for funding. I sourced concepts, created quick little sizzles and write-ups, and pitched them to the networks.

But unlike the studios with film projects, the networks maneuvered quickly. "Yes" or "No," and then let's go. That was it. Within a very short window, my company sold shows to Showtime, VH1, MTV, TruTV, Fox Sports, etc.

Because my entire Why of this TV pit stop was to find a deeper and more personal level of creativity, I hired myself as the showrunner for most of these shows. This, in turn, opened up additional neighboring streams of income for me as a "loan-out."

Networks would already have a show in development, or even on the air with prior seasons, and contract with me to take it over. So I would "loan" myself out to them. It was their show, but I would be the captain navigating the ship. This led to that nirvana of inspiration and creativity I was always seeking. TV offered it without the heavy weight of administration.

As showrunner, I would be in the thick of every scene, every story beat, every crew and staff member, sometimes picking up a camera myself, often directing the majority of scenes, writing storylines, sitting next to editors in the bays. Whereas in film that's the function of a dozen different people, television's smaller footprint and quicker speed-to-air allow a more singular absorption. Quality does occasionally suffer as a result, but as a lighter, digestible platform, it meets audience demand.

TV was the ultimate sandbox for me. BR was right. I'm glad I finally took his advice; or rather, I'm fortunate his advice finally found me. It clobbered me over the head for not heeding it the first time around decades prior.

I sometimes wish I had discovered TV during the first part of my journey, and not during my Road Back. But it was a reminder that the journey is never really complete; new travels appear all the time in unexpected places.

Proximity potential is powerful. And sometimes we just need to take a moment to think about the obvious, especially when it's within arm's length.

In the summer of 2016, I agreed to executive produce and show run a show for a smaller network I had never worked with. It was one of the best experiences of my life, combining the dynamics and complexities of everything I had learned to help shape and get a show into production. It required a ton of creativity from scratch, which is why I salivated and pinched myself for the opportunity, and was grateful for the skill set I'd acquired.

But it was also the most lamentable and heartbreaking experience of my TV career, one that had a profound effect.

I was to complete the Road Back sooner than I'd anticipated.

-

CHAPTER 24

The Resurrection: Authenticity · Happiness
(Stage 11)

"You're awesome. Enjoy being who you are."

- Miles Teller in *The Spectacular Now*

F OR THE FIRST TIME IN MY CAREER, I exited a project prematurely, but only as a last resort. It was the most heartbreaking and painful experience I've ever been through, career-wise, in a decade of television. But it also turned out to be the rebirth that fueled my Crossing of the Threshold... in reverse.

Never had this happened. Never had "quitting" been an option in my production lexicon. I was always "dad" driving the family to the Grand Canyon. I couldn't just leap out of the moving car and leave everyone to hope for the best.

But that's effectively what happened.

In this case, the network was a big 18-wheeler semi truck driving in front of us, back doors open with someone holding a shotgun pointed in our direction. I could remain driving the car and they'd blow us all up — the family, me, the car. Or I could jump-and-roll to create a diversion, allowing the car and family to continue on safely without me. They might not reach the Grand Canyon, but they would at least be safe if I sacrificed myself.

So I jumped and rolled in an act of self-immolation for the good of my crew and staff, enabling them to keep their jobs and stay on the show. It was a shame because it had less to do with constructive, supportive strategy for the show and more to do with political, corporate optics mixed with insecurity on the network's part.

The original show that the network wanted to develop didn't fit with their programming brand. It was an outlier from the start that belonged on a different platform. But I welcomed that. I was excited to help bring them more attention and stretch beyond their small scene. They wanted to innovate. I wanted to be a part of that.

But what appeared to be their courageous move in green-lighting something outside their convenient vicinity later segued into meddling and back peddling. They didn't go all in. They effectively tried to reverse engineer our unique, dynamic approach.

Their initial fortitude turned to fear, which resulted in an immediate mayday and evacuation to mediocrity and homogenization.

Our team's approach was contagious and had already infiltrated the entire process. It wasn't as simple to turn off. When you shoot episodes and scenes (sometimes out of order due to logistics), continuity becomes an issue.

Produce Yourself

Disillusionment conflicted with my Why for being in the TV space in the first place. This otherwise sandbox of infinite fancy was governed by and overrun with petrified executives, not necessarily on this show, but industry-wide. I was starting to see this attitude emerge across the board as networks imploded, merged, and redesigned their brands, always trying to chase and replicate what was currently successful.

Spike TV, where I've produced hundreds of hours of programming, became Paramount TV. A complete re-brand. And by the way, it was TNN, the Nashville Network, before it was Spike.

The Esquire network, an awesome upscale men's network where I produced a terrific little boxing show, got canned by its NBC parent. Gone. This network became the merger of what used to be G4, a gamers network combined with The Style Network, a women's fashion network.

The list goes on.

History Channel barely shows any history. TLC no longer stands for The Learning Channel. Seriously, they dropped it, just like KFC (apparently their chicken is no longer fried). When's the last time you saw a music video on MTV? What about Video Hits One network? VH1?

Even billionaire Mark Cuban's network HD Net, where I sold a show, is completely off the air now. By the time this book is published, I suspect a few more major networks will fall by the wayside or assimilate with others. Oxygen, a women's network has done a complete 180. They are now a crime network. Yet they're still called Oxygen.

Imagination is risky. Average is safe.

This is why we see so much of the same programming on TV. If something works, the other networks salivate and clone it. It's the most secure and fast route to guarantee an audience. But it brings down their average of 5. By continuing to replicate and duplicate, they end up copying the copy. And then the next network copies the copy of the copy.

It's like Michael Keaton in "Multiplicity." Thinking he could outsmart his relationship and family life, he magically copies himself to be in more places and accomplish more tasks simultaneously. But then the copy of himself makes a copy of the copied self, and so on, to where down the line there are degraded duplicates of Michael Keaton that have defective liabilities (mentally slow), defeating the entire exercise. This happens with corporate television. And I was in the midst of it.

In private, executives spoke like Jerry Maguire with a mission statement to change what's wrong with cookie-cutter TV. Many of them are close friends of mine. Individually, they're extremely bright, smart, intuitive and decisive. Collectively, not so much. They're often restricted to uninspired artificial intelligence, trying to cover their ass and keep their job.

They want creativity insofar as creativity will shower ratings and accolades. But taking chances and risks are only rewarded when it works. Since there's no guarantee of that output, they try to control or mirror familiar, proven input. So they are predisposed to seek the mean rather than deviate from it.

When the scene is boardrooms, shareholders, and ladder-climbing, a network executive puts his neck on the line by coloring outside the lines. I don't fault them for this. That's their job. It's partially why they're executives rather than producers. They seek a more structured, safe environment with rules, procedures, and systems — many put in place to protect stock price. They need that equanimity and security in their lives to balance out the uncertainty of babies, mortgages, and ego.

Advancement is often rewarded for not making a mistake rather than taking a chance. So their feet hover over the brakes, not the accelerator. If they don't venture near the fire, no one will be able to hold their feet to it.

Produce Yourself

I know that game. I can play that game well. I believe in being a team player. Loyalty is important to me. I genuinely care about my cast and crew. I wholeheartedly want them to succeed. And equally, I want the network executives to flourish. Again, many of these executives are my friends.

But sometimes executives need to be saved from themselves. They need to be shown alternatives, compromises, and plans that will set them up for success. I challenge their system, approach, or group of people when the journey veers too far from the course we've mapped. Sometimes I need to be saved from myself too. I don't want 'Yes' people to leave me unchecked and unchallenged. Executives can be good reality checks for what's really working, and what's not.

After a dozen conversations, reshoots, style changes, stop downs, deep-dives, new approaches, and system overhauls, the problem with the show became the actual changes themselves. This is where I raised my hand and reminded everyone that we had set out to build a pyramid, with pyramid blocks and pyramid artisans. But now, suddenly, without seeing a preliminary pyramid, our mandate was to turn it into a dome.

I know the executives were aware of this. They are not stupid people or specifically the problem. Not even close. They were doing their job. And they all make their bosses and bosses' bosses happy by not losing. Winning is great. But not losing is safer.

In the end, my theory was proven when, halfway through broadcasting, the network "sold" the show to another network to air the last few episodes. This is very rare. But sometimes it's done when a show isn't aligning with programming schedule.

I commend and praise the network's ambition for taking the chance in the first place. I have no idea what other internal battles they had to contend with.

But sometimes, if you want to expand your scene, grow your brand, or increase your worth; you can't just dip your toe in the water. You have to take the full plunge. The network, as an entity, never fully committed to the show's identity.

Full engagement is obviously no guarantee. But you can't ride a bike standing still. If the bike isn't moving, you fall over. The faster the bike is pedaled, the less balance is required.

So the responsible thing for me, as leader, to do was fall on my sword. It was my responsibility to get out of the way. That was the path of least resistance and the one big political move that could be made to temporarily "solve" an insoluble issue.

This was suddenly an eye-opening rebirth for my inner hero.

I would not be finishing the show. And it was no longer my show. There's a first for everything.

I said "Goodbye" to my cast, crew, staff, and left them in the best hands possible. My second-in-command was more than willing to be a forklift operator in a warehouse and simply follow instructions — good or bad, right or wrong. She was willing to perform. That's what the network needed. She was smart to recognize that.

There are dreamers and doers. There are creators and consumers. Similarly, there are producers and performers — every company or endeavor needs both. Both are essential to success. They both have their place.

Producers (not in the entertainment sense, but people who produce) think long-term strategy, growth, innovation, and take big swings. The most important advancements and the biggest profit centers for any company have always come from the producers.

Produce Yourself

This is what the network wanted from me — someone to take a chance and go big, grow ratings, widen their scene. I was a producer, not just a "Producer." But as the directive pivoted and reigned in my approach, they needed a performer. So as a producer, I had to get out of the way and let performers bring it home.

I felt cleansed from the ordeal. Because it happened so quickly, I didn't know what was next. I didn't care and wanted to live in the Now.

I stared at the endless blacktop and desert landscapes as I drove through the monotonous yet peaceful miles of dirt toward home. I entered a state of meditative flow where I counted my blessings and was immensely grateful to be alive, have love in my life, and be healthy.

I could have selfishly romanticized this tragedy and felt victimized, but I am but a blip in the matrix of life. We are those ants on the ground and those stars in the sky. Losing a TV show has zero impact on anything of significance not only in my zip code but in the world.

My scene, my tribe, my family don't care and aren't affected in any way that substantially matters. None of this moves the needle. It's just ego, and you can't let ego get in the way.

Less evolved, or at an earlier stage in my Hero's Journey, I might have let my ego turn to anger and get me into trouble. But ego is the enemy. I do my best to keep it at bay. I'm not always successful, but being cognizant of how toxic it can be aids my attempt.

Half the battle of the hero is having self-control and self-discipline. Everything — health, exercise, relationships, friendships, career, finance — can go terribly wrong when ego takes the driver's seat.

It's that same primal instinct that triggers aspects of our ego to pound our chest, huff-and-puff, get angry, lash out, protect and scare away. That instinct is important to have (survival requires it), but equally important to manage.

There's a level of awareness we can all attain with good habits to fight this primal instinct. This is the level at which we are at peace and happy with whom we are.

My inner hero had now come full circle, fully transformed and resurrected to the point I was giving up lucrative positions and opportunities to protect others and live fully within my true character.

I placed a value on happiness and authenticity over money and credits. I chose to suppress ego in favor of clarity and perspective. Hollywood didn't change. It isn't going to change. My perception changed.

In "Back To The Future," Michael J. Fox wakes up toward the end of the film, resurrected from the journey. It's his same Ordinary World where he started, back in his house with his parents, but everyone is improved. With the knowledge and insight he gained on the trip, he now sees everyone in their best possible form. Did he alter the future — or was it only his perception?

Similarly, in "The Wizard of Oz," Dorothy wakes up where she started, from colorful Oz to the black and white tones of Kansas. She reunites with her boring family, which is no longer so boring, no longer so embarrassing or bad. She has gained insight and now appreciates what she had all along. Her inner hero has transformed.

In both of those films, it's possible the entire journey was a dream and nothing more. If these movies were documentaries, they would further prove the power of dreams and how transformative they can be if we listen to our inner hero.

Intuition is there, underneath the ego, attempting to give us the tools we often need, but we have to get beyond the noise and distraction to hear it. It doesn't usually shout.

In "The Breakfast Club," the journey of detention has ended. Our group of heroes has died and their stereotypical selves — the athlete, the princess, the basket case, the brain, and the criminal — resurrect as their authentic selves. They've shed their stigmas and egos and come back to life anew.

This Resurrection stage represents that one last sacrifice we make in order to revive and rejuvenate our weary hero. It's been a long, tedious and imperfect journey, and we need the stamina to make it home.

This reawakening is Crossing the Threshold in reverse, that spot where you last left your Ordinary World. Some have a fast Delorean with a Flux Capacitor. Others have magical ruby red shoes.

As for you and me, we have our upgraded set of habits, approaches, and systems. And we have our mindset — the one that has grown and found clarity during this journey. This Resurrection helps our hero shed the final polarities that were unresolved or in conflict with each other when we first entered new domains, gathered new accomplices, fended off invaders, and challenged our identity.

The hero doesn't always know at the time this death is often for a higher cause. It's painful. No one wants involuntary change. But there's a fulfilling meaning behind it all. It may take retrospect to acknowledge it, depending on how evolved your inner hero is. That's okay.

It took distance and space for me to understand this. I now see, as much as I wouldn't wish the experience on anyone, that it was indeed a gift. We often say to a friend, when something doesn't go so well: "It's a blessing in disguise." I am thankful it happened to me, as it was definitely a blessing.

My Resurrection showered me with greater insight and objectivity of my entire campaign. I saw that the gratification and contentment I received from TV production was increasingly diminishing now that I was a decade into it. I told myself I loved TV. I told others I loved TV. I said it passionately. I defended it.

I'm an optimist by nature. I believe happiness is a choice, and I choose to focus on what I am fortunate to have, whom I am lucky enough to love, and what I am healthy enough to create. I'm not always successful with those thoughts. But that's the goal. I try every day.

I know time is finite. So with the available time I have, I don't want to outsource my happiness to other people, products, or a process. I don't want someone else to have control of my happiness app on their phone. It's for me to choose and engage. I choose it for myself rather than seek or buy validation.

In best-selling author Jodi Picoult's 2007 book "Nineteen Minutes," she writes that there's "A mathematical formula for happiness: Reality divided by Expectations." So to be happy, "Improve your reality or lower your expectations." I say, do both.

I produced a TV movie, "The Pact," based on Jodi's book, which my dad had recommended to me. So I've remained one of Jodi's biggest fans. I loved reading this formula, as I find it to be true.

But little did I know this is actually a somewhat widely accepted psychological concept. Of course, there are layers of complex details within the formula, but superficially, as a habit-reminder, it has validity.

I think we should also go big. Have big ambitions, hope for the best, and strive for excellence. No question. But if we lower our expectations, we will indeed be happier.

- Don't expect to sell that idea. Hope you pitch it well and properly tell the story. If they buy it, then great. But don't expect it.
- Don't expect to jump on the freeway and there not be traffic. Plan for it. If it's vacant, then wonderful. But don't expect it.
- Don't expect to win the lottery.
- Don't expect to have your email/phone call returned
- Don't expect to get a raise.
- Don't expect that person to love you back.
- Don't expect everyone to recognize your hard work.
- Don't expect to get that job title.
- Don't expect your hair to grow back
- Don't expect to get that apartment you want.
- Don't expect to lose all that weight in 3 months.
- Don't expect to get the house you just put an offer on.
- Don't expect to get that invitation
- Don't expect your computer to not crash
- Don't expect to run a mile in 6 minutes.

I hope all good things happen for you. You can hope they happen. Chances are they will. But don't expect them to.

Equally, part of this Happiness Formula is your Reality. Most unhappiness arises from the place where expectations and reality differ. You're expecting a 10. But reality is a 4. And 4 divided by 10 is less than 1. An "unhappy" number at just a fraction.

Your reality is your Now. It's your current state of everything. So when that state isn't constantly dwelling on the past, anxious about the future, or needing things, there's a state of simply being. There's a pristine default in your reality of just existing without the barrage of having to have, needing to compete, worrying and stressing. That is the reality we strive for.

This is why I believe the Hero needs to shed these elements that take her out of, and away from, the default reality that she had as a child. When she was young, living in the present moment and shunning noise and distraction, her reality was in a state of quiet existence.

She was able to turn off her ego (if she had one) and her mind in order to accept and be grateful for her Now.

It's not an easy state to achieve as we grow up. The experiences and imprints we collect help feed our judgments and decisions. So we are constantly fighting the pull from homeostasis. But the more we can limit the gravitational pull toward possessions and desires, the more we can find peace in our reality.

The more we can suppress the ego, the more we can minimize and simplify our lives, the more we live in the Now.

If you believe in this Happiness Formula, these habits will help your hero.

We should be authentic. We should feel. We should react. But just as we choose to brush our teeth in part because we want to have fresh breath around others, we can equally choose to be happy around others, which in turn makes us happy.

Bad things happen. Misfortune befalls us. This doesn't mean we should falsely skip around with joy like some clueless Pollyanna who is hiding her emotions. But for the same reason, you don't want to befoul a room with bad breath, you don't want to pollute your relationships, your family, your co-workers, your neighbors with a noxious attitude.

It doesn't help your situation. And it doesn't help you. If anything, it does the opposite.

We have the ability to accept a circumstance, process it, and make the best of it. We can't change the past. We can't alter the future. We only have now. So what happens, happens. But grumbling and complaining not only spreads that stench onto others, it engenders a further decline in your own mood that proves ineffective in solving or accepting the problem.

We have all been depressed or bummed out or disappointed. And again, often when we have expectations. Our reality is sometimes shaken to the core. It's terrible.

But we pick ourselves up. We shake off the dirt and move on. We want to live. We want to optimize our situation and be as happy as possible. That's the goal in life.

Good things, bad things, unexpected things will happen. Learn from them, accept them, and then move on. It's now the past. You have today. And today choose to be happy.

Everything that you want to fix and make better is still in your pile of "things to improve." But you can choose to be happy while doing that. Happiness isn't an end result. It's an attitude choice, just like curiosity or confidence. You choose it.

The alternative is to dwell in a pool of sadness or anger. But that doesn't solve the problem. It doesn't alter the events of the past. It only allows ego to rear its ugly head and often make you regret saying or acting on the wrong impulse.

Smile that you are alive and let that revelation of greater gratitude for what you have right now carry you forward with the right mindset to continue on with your purpose.

Choosing to be happy has immensely helped my hero make tough choices, knowing that I can be happy regardless of a situation. I have bad situations all the time. It's never fun. Sometimes it's scary. But I choose as best I can to be happy while working on my situation.

My approach and process were incrementally changing to accommodate the changes in network TV. It was never a big deal, as it was gradual. But 10 years later I had not realized how much my system for producing had shifted. I had not realized just how much time was spent watering down creativity from the corporate can of timidity.

It's akin to the frog in boiling water. If you throw a frog in a pot of boiling water, it will jump right out. But if you place the frog in a pot of room temperature water and slowly bring it to a boil, it will remain until it's fallen asleep and cooked. Tiny, gradual changes go unnoticed (forgive the analogy; I believe it's actually a myth).

But, unlike the frog, I suddenly had boiling water thrown in my face, which made me realize the temperature had been rising all along, unnoticed. In retrospect, I may not have assessed as carefully as I might have. Regardless the outcome, I chose happiness.

I will always choose happiness. But I have to be aware of and vigilant to weeds that grow in the cracks of any organization. Happiness to a fault can cloak these. But happiness with circumspection can encourage minor adjustments or preparations.

Without having a viable option acceptable to me, I chose death (and happily so). Not to be overly dramatic, but leaving a TV series where I was at the top of my game at the highest position possible as executive producer and showrunner is a fairly climactic move. There were repercussions beyond myself that included my family, my support team — managers, agents, lawyers. And all the crew and staff that depended on me to keep them employed.

But fortunately, I had evolved and transformed along the Hero's Journey to a place where I could have clarity and perspective on what's important in life. I greeted this event as a learning experience and opportunity to advance to the next stage. It meant having to say "No" for me, rather than "Yes" for others.

Produce Yourself

But I am living my life, not theirs. I am the hero of my own movie, not a supporting character in theirs. And by this point, I had learned the value in not outsourcing my happiness, destiny, or purpose to anyone else. I am in charge and have full choice in all of those. I am the producer of me. And everything that that embodies became abundantly clear during the Resurrection.

I was eager to get home, having now crossed the threshold back to my Ordinary World.

And I wanted to take advantage of the Elixir I had acquired on my journey.

CHAPTER 25

Return With The Elixir: Willpower · Creation Play · Ask · Time
(Stage 12)

"Some birds aren't meant to be caged. Their feathers are just too bright."

- Morgan Freeman in *The Shawshank Redemption*

OPPORTUNITY CAN, IRONICALLY, BE CRIPPLING — but need not be. It can be overwhelming when the prior act matured into structure with a time line, predictable habits, and patterns. The next act hasn't been written yet. It can be whatever you want it to be. You get to produce it. This can be both daunting and liberating.

Your hero has taken the journey back and is now rewarded with the spoils. This is your hero's mulligan to fight another day. Take advantage of and amplify this circumstance.

This good fortune is your new Now. You can now pursue, build, cultivate, curate, and increase your proximity to a new ambition, passion or undiscovered purpose.

All those things you wanted to do but were distracted from — you can do them Now.

- Systems you want to improve
- Projects you want to start
- Ideas you want to combine
- Friends you want to reconnect and collaborate with
- Businesses you want to launch
- Family you want to confide in and bond with
- Muses you want to explore
- Diets you want to ritualize
- Books you want to learn from
- Habits you want to adopt
- Influencers you want to connect with
- Licenses you want to obtain
- Skills you want to acquire
- Mindsets you want to reach

Now is the time. This is it.

As this main journey comes to a close, it spawns baby journeys of opportunity. Investigate those. Assess the Ordinary Worlds of those journeys. What can you glimpse in the Special Worlds just beyond the thresholds? Find the mentors for those journeys. Align with the allies.

Accept the tests and enemies that will come at you. They're experiments. They're building blocks to prepare you for the Special Worlds.

One of the secrets of the Hero's Journey is it never ends. The supposed ending is but a launching pad for more journeys to take, each time improving your approach. But it gets easier. It gets smoother. And it becomes more playful.

Play is key.

Take deep breaths. Imagine. Explore. This is when amazing things happen. And be playful. The opportunity and permission to play is part of your Elixir.

Studies have been done on pets wherein it was discovered why some dogs have social issues. The owners all took care of their dogs — fed and sheltered them, gave them water, nurtured and loved them. But owners who additionally played with their dogs had pets that didn't bark randomly at everyone, bite people, or have high anxiety. Owners who never played with their dogs (or didn't allow the dogs to be silly and curious) tended to have dogs that were more depressed, anxious, or socially inept. They also bit more.

The importance of play applies to so many products and services you consume and enjoy every day. The hero elected to explore, think, investigate, and play; as well as fizzle, flop and flounder. She wasn't forced or ordered to. It was organic. And that's when amazing things ensued, both for the inner and outer hero.

She also didn't waste this special moment by binge-watching 40 episodes of a TV show she wouldn't remember 2 years later, which would have robbed her of 40 hours of time to think and wonder. Consumption has bountiful benefits. But don't complain you have insufficient time to pursue a business, grow an idea, or upgrade an area of your life if you spend your disposable time mostly consuming.

In general, as a newly optimized hero, you will now seek creation, not consumption. Consumption will happen naturally anyway. You need it to survive. But you need creation to thrive. Like a grape that's been too long on the vine, you will shrivel and die if you don't allow your creativity to bring you to your purpose.

Play must be a conscious choice. It has to be the locomotive that drives your ambition train. Play will spur creation. And creation will spur play. They go hand in hand.

Warren Buffett went to Benjamin Graham, perhaps the greatest financial and economic genius of our time, and offered to work for him for free. Graham listened, then told Buffett that he was charging too much. "Free" put Buffett in the right environment to immerse and learn, but also be playful, which Graham clearly was. Unpaid, he wasn't confined to the rigid parameters of a paid factory employee.

Pay is often tied to a suppression of spontaneity and impulse. Most factory workers are paid to not think too much, to not be playful. But the ones who are making astounding sums of money are the ones who did think and were playful. And, because of that, they are running that company.

Offering services for free allows you to play. And play allows you to be creative and build value.

If a passion of yours is to own your own bar, find one within walking distance of your house or job and offer to work for free. Give the bar an hour every other day, Offer to help with the books, actually bartend, or even host to see how things are run. Like Benjamin Graham said, you're probably charging too much. But because of that, you'll be able to play and you just might invent a new product or process instead of just starting your own bar.

Produce Yourself

If your curiosity is to have a side hustle being a real estate stager, cold call half a dozen realtors right now (they will all pick up, I assure you) and offer your services for FREE. Every realtor has ugly homes and they only have two arms. Take pillows, frames, a chair, a lamp, whatever, from your own home and help someone's home come alive. Make it pop. Brand it. You will become invaluable to those realtors and will get the full-immersion education you need to succeed.

Many of the biggest tech companies today are successful because they made it part of their business plan to play, and offer their services for free. Their whole ethos is that you can't create or conduct deep work without being playful and periodically step away from the task at hand.

They know that sitting at a desk repetitively trying to figure out a problem or dream up a solution will only weaken your willpower and drain your ability. But carry that activity with you to the ping-pong table or arcade games and just maybe it will solve itself. Those ideas and issues continue to ruminate, multiply, and compound when you let your brain out of the barn to run free and do something else for awhile.

In addition, they offer that creativity they've farmed from play to their customers for free. Once they've built up an audience, they start charging. But not until they've provided value and proved their worth.

Your priorities will always dictate what you achieve. And within those priorities, you need to encourage creative immunity. No idea is necessarily a bad idea. There are only uncooked and unexpressed ideas.

Sadly, most ideas never leave our minds. We are afraid what others might think. We are afraid of failing. But be more afraid of not failing. Be afraid of not experimenting and learning. That's all failure is. Show me someone who isn't successful, and I'll show you someone who hasn't failed enough.

This is the time to indulge, unrestrained. Take the liberty to metaphorically (and literally):

- stretch
- be naked
- try things you would never do
- talk to a stranger, what's their story, hug them (amazing benefits)
- cold call a hero of yours (you'll be on cloud 9 afterwards)
- audit a class at the local college (knowledge is everywhere and free)
- intern in a completely different industry, just for a day (sometimes it takes an outsider to discover opportunity)

If you go to the same aisle and same shelf of the grocery store every time you shop, you'll find the same result. You have to go to that area and corner you always neglect because you're really not into mango chutney. But head over and see what else might be there. And don't forget mango chutney is an acquired taste.

Discovery is a tool that you, as the hero, should now be familiar with from this long journey. But you have to make it part of your daily process. It will be most effective when your willpower is strongest.

You know the real reason you always see Mark Zuckerberg in the same outfit? Ditto for the late Steve Jobs? Zuckerberg is notorious for his one gray short sleeve shirt, jeans and a hoodie. Steve was notorious for his black turtlenecks and jeans. Like rock stars, they seem to wear one outfit.

Willpower.

Both these titans and icons know the value of discovery and play, and how important it is to have the willpower to engage. By waking up in the morning and not having to contemplate what to wear every day, that's one less decision they have to make. Less really can be more.

Produce Yourself

Thinking of willpower as a currency, that's one daily ritual that cost them nothing, so they can spend their willpower on more impactful and deeper concerns.

It's a fact that we have only so much daily willpower. We start flush, overflowing with it at the top of the day, like a full tank of gas. But we can only make X number of decisions and face Y amount of distraction before we run out of willpower. Once we've run out, our decision making becomes poor.

Psychologists call this "decision fatigue." If we haven't budgeted our willpower properly, by the end of the day we're making poor eating choices, making rash decisions, not thinking clearly, neglecting exercise, being short with our temper, and lacking energy to play.

Christopher Nolan, director of "Dunkirk," "Batman Begins," and "Inception," is famous for his deep-thinking, mind-bending films. He mostly wears a blue shirt and blazer. Every day. He said, "I decided it was a waste of energy to choose anew what to wear each day."

Even Barak Obama, when President of the United States, stuck to only two choices of gray or blue suits. When referring to why, he said, "I'm trying to pare down decisions. I have too many other decisions to make."

Iconoclastic singer Henry Rollins is well-known for his simple black t-shirts and dark pants. He revealed, "The more time you spend worrying about clothes, the less time you have to grab life by the balls."

Willpower is relevant to work. It relates to deep or shallow work. It's important to shift more impactful and important activities to the top of your day when willpower is strongest. But equally, willpower needs to be budgeted so that you have it when you need it later in the day. If you know you're going to be devoid of willpower by 8 pm, don't make any important decisions, have important discussions, or attempt to create after 8 pm. Wait until the bank opens again tomorrow.

And to make it easier on your hero, eliminate as many perfunctory decisions as you can. You don't have to be as extreme as the founders of Facebook or Apple. But apply their lessons of simplicity to your daily process.

When every single decision you make throughout the day requires a unit of Willpower, keep as much as you can for when you need it. Save for the rainy moment that will surely surface at some point during the day.

On my drive back home from the desert, the clouds had cleared and I wanted to discover, play, and create. This gave me tons of willpower to make a smart decision rather than a rash one.

So I stopped in Palm Springs and bought a house.

A college buddy of mine had been prompting me with the idea of starting an Airbnb business by finding something in Palm Springs. I was skeptical, more from ignorance than insight. But I was intrigued. It sounded fun. I wanted to learn. I wanted to start something new. I wanted to create a new business. And Airbnb's brand had a whimsical and playful vibe. It was just what I needed.

Almost the minute I said goodbye to my cast and crew, I called my friend, V, to take him up on the idea. Passing through Palm Springs on my way home anyway, a rental house was low-hanging fruit and quite literally proximity potential.

Three hours later we were looking at houses, and shortly thereafter we made an offer.

I figured maybe I could transform something initially painful into something joyful by taking some of the money I made from the TV show and sinking it into a new adventure with promise. I could have bought a fancy car or splurged on any number of depreciating consumables. But I chose to create and build instead.

Produce Yourself

I wanted my Elixir from one journey that didn't end well to be the incubator for a new one with promise.

Real estate was obviously becoming an asylum for me. It seemed to be the time-out I gravitated to when I needed reliability and certainty in an uncertain industry. I suspect that's why I like both real estate and math. They're tangible, solid, easy to calculate and understand. And, unlike many other things in life, they don't disappoint. At least they've not disappointed me.

V and I made the only offer on a 1963 mid-century modern house (quintessential "Palm Springs") and got it. Although buyer's remorse is common (why did they accept our offer so fast?), we knew we got a good deal for how we planned to monetize it. We paid somewhat of a premium in exchange for having a turnkey situation. Every single spoon, fork, coffee filter, sofa, chair, bed, napkin, and pencil stayed with the house. Everything.

This would be our boutique "hotel." Having never been hoteliers, we needed to make as few decisions as possible (more willpower for us) so we could learn the more important needle-movers rather than get caught up with the distraction of needing extra light bulbs in a closet.

Cut to today. We've had positive cash flow from day one with almost back-to-back bookings. Aside from our initial deposit to purchase the house, everything (mortgage, taxes, insurance, numerous upgrades, cleaning, hosting, maintenance, landscaping, pool, utilities) has been completely covered by guest bookings.

We quickly automated everything to where both of us, dividing and conquering, can now run the entire operation from our phones (unlock/lock doors, thermostat, pool pump, heat, answer the doorbell) with minimal time commitment.

We spent the first several months with a deep dive of time, personally fixing up the house, hauling gravel around the backyard, painting walls, changing toilets, perfecting the system to work smart and let automation give our future selves the gift of time.

I wish I could say we were geniuses and cracked the code on how to run a successful hospitality and accommodations business, but we aren't and didn't. Far from it. We've made, and continue to make mistakes (who knew the wind was so strong it would knock over our grill or launch door mats up and over the fence into the neighbor's yard?). Neither of us had ever been in this space before. But we loved the business model and had each separately been guests on the platform. We had both been consumers, but knew the true spoils go to the creators — one thing V and I share in common.

V is someone who increases my average of 5 and helps me with proximity potential. His scene is music, marketing, social media, non-profits, and restaurants — areas I rarely play in. But our common intersecting interests overlap with real estate, entrepreneurship, and play.

We both lived through the real estate boom and bust from 2000-2008. And we've always kept in touch, even if it's only a couple times a year, to say: "Hey, what about that area over in East L.A.?" Two burritos later and we would have a fun afternoon exploring and discovering a new area of East L.A.

We're still learning every day. But by combining our skills — V with marketing, pricing and host communication, and I with infrastructure, financing, and administration — we figure it out. As the saying goes, it's not rocket science. And we love the process. We are enjoying being complete accommodation virgins — discovering, learning, and then monetizing as a by-product.

We also hold each other accountable. That's why partnerships — business, relationships, or just about any pursuit — are usually exponentially better than going solo. As you know by now, I've slowly gravitated toward partnerships along my journey, taking it with an ally.

With a partnership, you're the boss, but at the same time, you have the architecture of a system that demands responsibility, new ideas, updates, reviews, suggestions, and critique just like a normal hierarchy. It takes good habits, like any relationship.

One thing we discovered during the deep dive of ingesting podcasts, blogs, and other online sites, is that you want to find 5 adjectives that describe your place's brand. And then stick to that.

Chip Conley, global head of Airbnb for 4 years prophesies everything that you can see, touch or even hear — dishes, furniture, pool towels, music, pictures on the wall — needs to fit those 5 adjectives. If not, toss it. It doesn't belong there, and will, in fact, detract from the tone and vibe.

This creates the focused brand experience that guests desires, even if they don't know they want it. Their own home is usually a mishmash of probably 20 adjectives and that's why the Virgin hotel or the Hard Rock hotel looks appealing to them. It's a brand experience (fun exercise: figure out your home's 5 adjectives and get rid of anything that doesn't match those 5. You'll think you're perpetually on vacation and be inspired to create).

Strip the brand away and the guest could stay anywhere that just has a bed and a bathroom. That's all an accommodation really is. But the successful boutique hotels stick to their brands. Guests want a piece of that. They want to buy the emotion they feel when they are in that environment.

We picked mid-century, atomic, chill, white, and modern. Those adjectives naturally matched our architecture and the furniture that came with the house. So everything we added, from painting walls to pillows to even a frame on the wall, had to match that definition. A cool rock 'n roll guitar would have been fun to hang on the wall, but that's not our brand. Had we picked Coachella as one of our adjectives, it might have fit.

This is applicable to other areas of life. People want to know what they're getting from you. They want an emotional attachment, to you, to your products, to your pursuits. That's the prime value they receive. How can someone find or delineate you if the brand of you, your product or business isn't clear? Help them help you. Help customers find you so you can build a tribe of megaphones to consume and, in turn, broadcast your brand.

What are your 5 adjectives as they relate to your career, or your relationship, or your purpose, or that business you want to start? Each of them has a set of adjectives. But maybe they're too many or the wrong combination. Try to define those and stick to them. It will help rein in your focus and make you, your goals, or your pursuits more obvious to others. This is what I learned, and I believe the lesson is universal.

This is why that pair of jeans looks amazing in the store, and sometimes not so much when you get home. People say it's the lighting. It's not. In the store, those jeans are supported by the 5 adjectives that make up the look and display of the store. So it's the music you hear, the mural on the wall, the hardwood floors, the accessories you see on the mannequin. Even the employee helping you. You can turn the lights off and those adjectives won't disappear.

Ditto for anything and everything you purchase or consume. It's why almost 100,000 people flock to Burning Man. It's the middle of the desert. There's literally nothing. But I bet you can easily find the 5 adjectives that define that place and experience (my take: Mad Max meets Venice Beach meets EDM meets Woodstock meets Steampunk).

You already do this somewhat with your fashion. You have a "look." Everything else in your life needs a brand too. It should be authentic and honest. It should be you, of course. But by identifying those core adjectives, it will simplify the process, eliminate waste and indecisiveness, and begin to automate your life.

Here was my formula:

Proximity potential (real estate) + increasing my average of 5 with an ally (V) + turning obstacles into opportunities (leaving the TV show) + seeking creation over consumption (start a business rather than wallow in self-pity with a bowl of ice cream on a couch) = a fun muse (Airbnb business) that seeds a potential crop someday (other Airbnb businesses? Seminars? Books? An actual hotel?).

Maybe we'll launch another Airbnb property somewhere. Maybe we will double-down. We might fail, or we might succeed. We potentially will do both, as heroes often fail before they succeed.

The safety net is that I chose to enjoy the process and be playful with it. I chose to accept the approach for what it was, whether it worked or not, whether it made money or not. This would be a completely new enterprise and a new scene for me from top to bottom. So I appreciated the freedom I had to pursue and learn.

And because V was an ally, he chose the same attitude. We chose (and choose) to be happy and enjoy the process, even though there can be distractions (e.g. clogged toilet, broken chair, dirty pool, etc.)

Things are unimportant. This Palm Springs house? Unimportant. What money really buys is freedom. I had the freedom to leave a bad experience for a good one, all in a day's time. I bought liberation from a disheartening situation. I bought opportunity. I bought discovery and exploration. I bought play.

- If it wasn't this house, my creative play could have been deciding to go hiking and make a photography book.

- It could have been making a set of online videos on how to sell and pitch TV ideas.
- It could have been launching a creative consulting business.
- Or I could have driven north and bought land to lease out to timber companies.
- I could have driven east and revisited and recreated with my Duck Dynasty team.
- I could have driven south into Mexico to paint or blog while eating fish tacos.
- Instead, I drove west, toward home where I collaborated with a friend.

It doesn't matter what the creation is. It's the ability to do that is freeing. On one hand, sure, this ability is the culmination of prior seeds planted that are now dropping fruit into my basket of possibility.

Start planting those seeds (have I hammered this home enough yet? I hope so). Every day. You will have more than one stream of income, more than one sandbox to play in, and more than one member of your tribe to support you. Those seeds will be the oxygen and brain-fuel you need to survive.

And you can't truly live and feed your hero's purpose without play, regardless how easy it is to access — or not. Find play.

A year earlier, I exercised this same proclivity for real estate while on another show. We were filming our last episode of "Duck Dynasty" in Nashville. It was a special one-hour episode, our 100th, and there was much love in the air with the entire family, cast and crew. Maybe it was already on my mind. Maybe the entrepreneur in me would have done this anyway, but I like to think those heartfelt emotions and familial connections I had with my production bled over into my buying a house there. I was brimming with optimism and elation from having completed such a successful run with a successful franchise.

Produce Yourself

I wanted to celebrate. And I prefer to memorialize moments with creation rather than consumption. Maybe that's another reason why drugs don't interest me. Aside from choosing to be happy and to enjoy my reality, drugs simply outsource my creativity and control to chemicals. I don't want to delegate my Now to the unpredictable and addictive nature of processed chemicals.

V, the same friend I would later purchase the Palm Springs house with, saw on Facebook that I was in Nashville. He messaged me, writing: "We should buy a rental in Nashville while you're there." I laughed and told him I was already one step ahead of him, but that I welcomed a partner if he was serious. So he agreed to reimburse me 50 percent when the deal closed.

He did exactly as promised, and we formed a company. That company would later buy the current Palm Springs house.

Almost a decade prior, it happened once before, before both Palm Springs and Nashville. There was a time where I attended the SXSW film festival in Austin, TX every year with my movies. I fell in love with the city, the filmmakers, and the creative community. Just as, years later, in Nashville, I felt a strong connection to the scene and brand. So I bought a new loft, all glass and steel, in downtown Austin.

Another filmmaker friend of mine, K, whom I was casually advising about her investments, happened to call me when I was getting on a plane to come home from Austin. She learned I was buying a place and asked if she could partner with me. I had already purchased. The deal was done. But it was a new construction building, so there were plenty of others available.

Sight unseen, she purchased a unit right next to mine, one floor up. For close to a decade, we stayed in touch and managed our lofts together, having positive cash flow from day one from solid student renters. Another no-brainer, passive income generator.

I recently sold that Austin loft (K decided to keep hers) and with the profits purchased a couple of real estate trusts in other states. I now collect passive income without the toilets, trash, or tenants. These trusts are completely automated and will yield consistent fixed income for the next 7 years, at which point I'll sell, then buy into additional trusts or physical property to continue converting the taxes into more real estate assets (Google "1031 Exchanges and Delaware Statutory Trusts").

I asked to be Eric's producer for his films after seeing "My Life's In Turnaround" in the theater. He said "Yes" and it changed my life. It launched my film career wherein I produced major studio movies and TV shows with him.

R asked if he could learn to be a producer and partner with me. I said "Yes." That spawned a collaboration responsible for my most prolific and satisfying period of filmmaking.

I asked my buddy Y if he needed help back when I visited him that fateful day in his first TV office. He said "Yes." That launched my TV career from a silly little hidden camera prank show to "Duck Dynasty."

V asked if I needed help in Nashville. I said "Yes." We launched a real estate investment company. K asked what I was investing in, when I was in Austin, and now owns a cash-generating machine worth twice what she paid.

Be careful what you ask for. Sometimes you get it. You have to let the universe know what you want, or at least your universe.

It's safe to keep your desires and pursuits to yourself. No one has to know what you're trying to do, that you need help, or that you dislike your current situation. But by putting yourself out there and increasing the awareness of your brand and proclaiming what you want, you can align with an ally, gain a mentor, increase your scene's resources, cohabitate ideas, and accomplish amazing things.

Produce Yourself

The hero has to be an ambassador for herself. She learned back in Stage 6 of the journey that when she encounters her enemies, she herself is often her most formidable one. This may stem from keeping her ideas, desires, and playfulness to herself. There is exponential power and benefit in an announcement, collaboration, as well as basic inquiry.

I had recorded close to 50 podcasts with a comedian and TV colleague of mine called "Sorry To Bother You With My Stupidity." As the title implies, it was an experiment for us to fail. Neither of us — my friend or I — had ever podcasted before. But we loved the idea of giving ourselves permission to create on our own terms. We mostly talked about our TV profession, narrowcasting to just the people who were working on our TV shows. We never posted online or officially published the broadcast. We would just record and then the next day send emails out to a few of our friends.

We had a blast learning, failing, and being able to talk about whatever we wanted. But we were scared to push that "Publish" button. We were scared to be vulnerable to the point anyone in the world could hear us babble about the entertainment industry. We were scared to ask the world to listen. But asking is what creates opportunity.

After a few months now being home, it became clear to me that we had to click that "Publish" button. People could hate us. People could unsubscribe. But we'd never know until we asked. By not publishing, we weren't allowing ourselves the creative outlet we sought, because we were censoring ourselves.

So one night we talked about it, and the next morning we finally pushed that "Publish" button. Now we're on iTunes, Google Play Music, and iHeart Radio. We don't have a massive audience, and that's okay. We're building, slowly, until we figure out what it's all for. It's a recess for us. It's playing. It's a respite from everything else so we can explore and create without borders. And we have a small tribe of a few thousand fans who seem to tune in regularly.

Maybe this will go nowhere. Maybe the two of us will shut it down and rebrand it as something else. Or maybe we'll continue to grow it as the little engine that could. We don't monetize it at all. But we provide value to our listeners and I know there will be proximity potential or commingling of ideas around the corner. But we won't find out without playful experimentation.

My friend, P, the one from 7th grade who used to sit in my bedroom with me and contemplate movies (Chapter 13), is now my co-host on a new film podcast, "The Best of All Possible Worst Case Scenarios." In many ways, this podcast is the one I always wanted. But I might never have discovered that or had the courage to build it if I didn't first toy with "Sorry To Bother You With My Stupidity."

Obviously, not everything works out. As the hero with the Elixir, you will have failures; hopefully many of them, as it reveals you're trying new things, pushing boundaries, and leaving your comfort zone.

Close to 6 months now since I returned home, I started an e-commerce business with Y, the same friend who gave me my first start in TV. We have since shuttered its doors. Even though there is incredible monetary upside in the online product space, the approach was too far off our core compass.

It was a business that succeeded by sourcing cheap products we didn't care about or enjoy having to learn about. They didn't align with our values because we didn't believe the products themselves provided much value to the consumer.

Quite honestly, they were cheap, and there is a lot of money to be made because of that fact. But the process for this felt like a soulless numbers game. There was no inspiration involved. I need play and some modicum of imagination and design in just about anything I do. Y is the same. So the idea wasn't sustainable for us.

Y and I both know we could make substantial money from this business. But to scale to that level would take years, at a minimum, in the trenches with a system and process that is more costly than beneficial to our heroes. We still have the LLC and are contemplating how to reinvent and reinvigorate it into something else that sells products we care about or have a connection with.

But for now, let's call this venture a failure. As the hero, I call this a lesson and steppingstone to something greater.

One can always make more money in life. There are too many ways to list. But one will never have more time. Time is finite. Time is the most valuable commodity.

I have an app on my computer, and I can see it right at this moment while I'm writing. It's a death clock. There are many versions of it, and although gimmicky, it's impactful. After answering half-a-dozen elementary questions, including: do you smoke, your current age, etc. a skull and bones clock appears on your desktop.

It counts down backward how much time you have left before you die. As an artifice, it's probably far from accurate. But even if it calculated you would live to be 130, it makes no difference. Whenever I look over at that clock and see the minutes and seconds counting down, like the battery on your phone or a cooking timer, it puts idle time into perspective — it's precious. And it's going way too fast.

I want my remaining time to count. I won't live my life unhappily, unfulfilled, unloved or unexplored. I won't waste time doing things that don't inspire me or inspire others. Time is too limited. I can spend it doing whatever I want. But, unlike money, I will never have it back. I can't make more time.

So, in everything I do, I seek enjoyment and avoid tedium. Things I don't enjoy that are unavoidable, I will either outsource, delete, say "No" to or hack a way to make it so effectual the benefit far outweighs the cost in time consumption.

The Elixir that I had acquired taught me this: Life is about the journey. Life is about the input. The output may never come. I only have today. And today I have time. I need to make the most of it. For me, that means storytelling, building, collaborating, playing, thinking, loving, learning, educating, consulting, producing, and, above all, creating in everything I do.

I am not built to be a consumer. I don't know if that's really a core value, which is why I left it off my list (Chapter 5). But it's something that I find difficult to compromise on, outside of necessity and survival.

As the hero of my own life, I will not sit on the couch and absorb. But I'll go out and construct that couch. And I'll produce that movie or TV show for someone else to absorb. I'm the hero of my own life, and my hero creates.

This is what led me to convert some of my real estate properties into passive investments (selling physical properties and investing online with YieldStreet, PeerStreet, PatchofLand, and RealtyMogul to name a few). It's not as sexy. But by not letting others write my narrative, I can have more free time and less hassle with more passive investments. The upside financially is smaller. But the upside in time is greater. For me, that's a fair trade and a better return on my investment.

This has given me time to find a new love: the OneWheel. Picture snowboarding, but on concrete, dirt, grass, and sand. It's active, Zen, and lets me create literally new journeys, new groups of friends (over 20 of us carve the beach areas together monthly).

The Elixir represents change, success, and proof of the journey for the hero. She has upgraded her mindset to know what's important and what's not. She knows when she is genuinely fulfilled, or when she is distracted by envy, money, titles, noise, superficiality, and other petty inhibitors.

Now that she's cleared away the cobwebs, said "No," eliminated and delegated as many empty activities as possible in exchange for impactful ones, her mind is a fine-tuned apparatus for prospect, formulation, insight, and approach.

In "Mad Max: Fury Road," the Elixir is water. It was always there in Charlize Theron's "Ordinary World." But it took her traveling out into the Special World to acquire and harness her mindset and perspective. With this ability she could return and release the aquifer from the Citadel, showering the people with life-saving water. She always had the capability. But she needed the journey to show her the way.

In 2017's Oscar winner, "Moonlight," the Elixir is our hero finally accepting his true identity and living authentically. Growing up in an unaccepting and unhealthy environment, where drug dealing, cars, girls, and muscles engendered a masculine façade, he left for the Special World. Upon returning to his ordinary world, the hero takes off his fake teeth grills and reveals the true gay man he is. He recalls his mentor inspiring him thusly: "At some point you gotta ask yourself who you gonna be. Can't let nobody make that decision for you." It has taken a long journey of reticence and refusal, obstacles and pivots, enemies and allies, to finally accept who he is. This is his special Elixir.

In some movies, we never see the actual Elixir the hero brings home. But it's implied that there will be one in the future. This is true for all heroes. This final stage has ripple and ghosting effects that will last our hero a lifetime.

In "The Breakfast Club," we assume that the 5 heroes, having shed their stereotypes in front of each other, will be friends when school starts back up on Monday. They've evolved beyond their clichés and false identities to respect and love each other as real people.

Perhaps more profoundly, the Elixir is sometimes so strong, that the pursuit itself takes a backseat.

Case in point: Who do you think won the boxing match in "Rocky"?

Everyone knows the theme song: "Eye of the Tiger." Everyone uses "Rocky" as a metaphor for the underdog who trains and overcomes adversity. The "Rocky" training montage alone has become the classic format for copycats when needing to express improvement over a passage of time.

So who won? Say it out loud right now before reading further.

But guess what? Rocky lost. Almost no one remembers that. The Elixir that the Hero brings home is so pervasive and impactful that you forget and sideline who actually won the big boxing match. And this is what the entire journey was leading up to. But it's the journey that brings you the Elixir, not the destination. This was true for Rocky.

All Rocky wanted to do was "go the distance." He wanted to prove that he wasn't "just another bum from the neighborhood." He transformed himself with effective, compounding improvement that enabled him to go all 15 rounds of the fight. So the moment the fight ends, he calls out for Adrian, his love. Because winning the match was never the goal. It was never the destination. The prize was always gaining Adrian's respect.

Apollo Creed won by technical points because he couldn't knock out Rocky. Rocky gained his proof of the journey. He brought the respect he always sought back to his Ordinary World — his friends and family in the neighborhood. And for that, Rocky "won." That's why many people answer this question incorrectly.

Sometimes the Elixir that you return home with is nothing but a placebo. It's the MacGuffin that on its own isn't important. Did it matter what was in that FedEx box in "Castaway"? Tom Hanks never opens the box he stares at day in and day out, alone on that island. He even delivers it at the end of the movie. But what was inside? It's unimportant. It's a MacGuffin. It can be anything you want it to be, because it pales in comparison to the transformation — the Elixir he brought home from the experience.

J.J. Abrams gives a great TED talk about a "mystery box" that he purchased at a magic shop decades ago when he was a little boy. For $15 he bought what was advertised as having $50 worth of magic inside. It's just a simple shoebox sized cardboard box with a big emblazoned question mark logo on the outside. But it's a mystery as to what's inside. It's a gamble.

To this day, that cardboard box sits in his office, unopened. He has never opened it to see what his $15 bought him. Because for him, it's just his own personal MacGuffin. What's in it doesn't matter and never will. But unopened, it represents hope, possibility, and potential. For him, "Mystery is the catalyst for creativity." So he leaves it in his office where he can stare at it while creating some of our best films and TV shows.

And now you know why he never explains so many mysteries in his projects from the rabbit's foot in "Mission Impossible 3" to the numerous ones in the TV series "Lost." They're unimportant and subordinate to the Hero's transformation.

Even if the Elixir you return home with is money, fame, or whatever your dreams and desires are, those tangible items are MacGuffins. They don't matter. Don't cloud your new mindset with the physical. If those assets are a proxy measurement for your success, then great for you. But return home with the newfound powers you now have. That's your Elixir.

I was enlightened. I reached a point where I suddenly felt complete. I was able to observe my journey as a whole and reflect on whom I had become, what I had accomplished, and whom I had in my life. No longer just a label — movie producer, TV showrunner, mortgage broker, real estate renovator, investor, or podcaster — I saw me as me.

I realized I was a hyphenate. I am a hyphenate. So are you. Most heroes are. I don't have to fit anyone's bucket or pigeonhole, especially my own. Passions can ebb and flow. Identities can change, broaden or redefine. My purpose for creativity doesn't have to live only in the entertainment industry. It doesn't have to be just producing. It can be in anything I do, small or large, daily or over time.

Exploring and playing was always part of my purpose but earlier on I had viewed it as input rather than output. I mistakenly defined these activities as a means to an end.

I thought exploration was the initial research I had to do and get out of the way so that I could be a storyteller or create. And playing was just a break or procrastination.

But exploration and playing are both the meaningful means and the end all at once. Exploration never ends. And if it's just something to get out of the way to get somewhere, then that's a lot of tolerance and endurance for a result that may never transpire.

I now explore more. I now play more. Similar to being mindful and living in the Now, discovery itself should be a satisfying and fulfilling pursuit. I attempt to consciously be hyperaware of what I'm doing and how it makes me feel while taking those initial steps in anything I do. Because sometimes those initial steps are also the final steps. I have to make those steps my Now.

Superficially I succeeded, and some might say excelled, in the Special World. But the times I explored for exploration's sake were few. It was always about the output and the end game, so playfulness got in the way.

Produce Yourself

The irony is that the secret is in the input regardless of the output. I learned this during my journey, but still never fully gave it the same commitment as output.

This is why I pivoted from one approach to another, sliding laterally from one area of the business to another. Had I let my input be the output, had I let my discovery be the goal, had I let my exploration be the end game, I would have gained more fulfillment, and perhaps even other opportunities. The end game is going to happen despite the journey.

As I embark on new journeys with the Elixir I have now brought home, I know I will fail — a lot. I hope I continue to fail. I want to learn. And I want to succeed from what I learned. There will always be roadblocks. But I have to focus on and love the approach and the input. Because that may end up the only "-put" for that endeavor.

I will live in a world of relentless frustration if I view the journey as only a means to a destination. This is why I have hammered home how important approach, process, and systems are to everything. They may be all you get.

If tomorrow never comes, you only have today. Today is the approach you take, the process you engage, and the system you employ. So these should be optimized to the hilt, as they are both the means and the end.

I am the producer of my own movie. I am the producer of my own life. So I want to own that. I want to show up, every day excited and energized to own my life. I get to cast, write, and produce my hero to take any direction I please. That's an awesome power. And as all super-heroes know, with great power comes great responsibility.

The responsibility I now embrace is to cultivate and curate the best opportunities for my hero. I can only do that by optimizing my time, impacting my deep work, welcoming risk and failure, aligning with allies, shutting out distraction, finding flow, and listening to my inner hero.

I don't know what's next; a new TV series, a slate of films, a business, another book, more podcasting. Or perhaps my next adventure will be a combination of the above. I want to do it all, but with my newfound approach and mindset.

Everything is up to you. No one else is going to produce your life for you. It's not something you can contract out.

People try to do this every day. Every day, people delegate and assign their feelings, ego, identity, and self-worth to materialism, popularity, fashion, and optics.

If you produce your hero to have those things, then fine. Just don't let anyone besides you produce that for you. Own the process. Own the approach. Own the input. If you want something, want it for you, not for someone else.

Stop competing. Stop comparing. Stop doing things so you can meet someone else's characterization of whom you are supposed to be in their eyes. Don't be the supporting player in their movie. Be the hero of your own movie.

Henry David Thoreau wrote, "Be yourself — not your idea of what you think somebody else's idea of yourself should be."

The world is but a box of tools for you to use as you see fit.

Today, having experienced the Special World, I brought back all those acquired special tools to my ordinary one, officially making my Ordinary World special.

Make your world special. Because you are special.

Be the hero of your own life.

Produce Yourself

Produce Yourself.

Thank you for taking the time to read about my journey. I would love to learn about yours.

Please follow me on Instagram @ProduceYourself. You can also find me at TerenceMichael.com where I offer tailored consulting and financial strategy.

Finally, I have on request that would help me out a lot: if you can spare two minutes and rate this book on Amazon, it would help others find it. This link will take you there: https://tinyurl.com/produceyourselfbook

ABOUT THE AUTHOR

Emmy-nominated producer Terence Michael has produced over 20 movies and 30 TV shows. He invests in real estate, owns a mortgage business, strategizes investments for clients, and consults entrepreneurs on how to cultivate their passions.

He has been featured in The Los Angeles Times, Newsweek, Details, Business.com, The Penny Hoarder, Magnify Money, FitSmallBusiness, MyCorporation Blog, UpJourney and The Christian Science Monitor.

Additionally, he has guest lectured and consulted on development, financing, story, packaging and nuts-and-bolts producing panels for the Cannes Film Festival, the Los Angeles Film Festival, Independent Film Project (IFP), the SXSW Film Festival, AFI, and UCLA Film Extension.

He can often be found riding his Onewheel by the beach, playing with his dog, working on the house, or spending time with his girlfriend. Not in that order.

Terence Michael has collaborated with many artists and brands in film and TV, including:

Terence Michael

Actors: Scarlett Johansson, Alycia Debnam-Carey, Ben Stiller, Sarah Jessica Parker, Vera Farmiga, Jeffrey Tambor, Téa Leoni, Tom Sizemore, Katherine Heigl, Peter Dinklage, Giovanni Ribisi, Cuba Gooding, Jr., Patrick Dempsey, Jaime Pressly, Mia Kirshner, Michael McKean, Britt Robertson, Oliver Hudson, Emmanuelle Chriqui, Jonathan Tucker, Nora Dunn, Skeet Ulrich, Cheryl Ladd, Elizabeth Reaser, Megan Mullaly, Jennifer Morrison, Erin Bartlett, Jesse Bradford, Adam Goldberg, David Krumholtz, James Tupper, Eric Szmanda, Eric Mabius, Eric Schaeffer, Sam Lerner, and lates Alan King, Jill Clayburgh, and John Heard

Comedians: Jim Norton, Adam Carolla, Tom Green, Chris Hardwick, Flula Borg, Ken Marino, Alonzo Bodden

Athletes: Vince Papale, Rick Barry, James Stewart, Ryan Dungey, Todd Potter, and the Metal Mulisha team, Tony Hawk, Buckey Lasek, Jason Ellis, Shawn White, Wendy Ingraham and Chris Legh

Musicians: Aimee, Mann, The Verve Pipe, Jill Sobule, Blink 182, Amanda Kravat, Foxy Brown, Usher, Vanessa Carlton

Hosts/Authors: Catt Sadler, Amanda De Cadenet, Karla Cavalli, Allen Haff, Paul McKenna, Lisa Williams, Grant Imahara, Leeann Tweeden

Brands: Sony, Universal, MGM, Lionsgate, and HBO; NBC, Fox, MTV, VH1, Bravo, Showtime, Lifetime, TLC, TNT/TBS, Spike, Esquire, Syfy, Travel Channel, and A&E.,RedBull, Degree, Monster, Playboy, Jabbawockeez, The Golden Nugget, Joe's Crab Shack, Oakley, the Duck Dynasty family

www.ingramcontent.com/pod-product-compliance
Lightning Source LLC
LaVergne TN
LVHW041618060526
838200LV00040B/1327